MW00459166

Read Write Own

Read Write Own
Building the Next Era of the Internet
Chris Dixon

Random House New York

Copyright © 2024 by Chris Dixon

All rights reserved.

Published in the United States by Random House,
an imprint and division of
Penguin Random House LLC, New York.

RANDOM HOUSE and the HOUSE colophon are
registered trademarks of Penguin Random House LLC.

Image on page 151: Gartner, Hype Cycle. Gartner and Hype Cycle
are registered trademarks of Gartner, Inc. and/or its affiliates and
internationally and are used herein with permission. All rights reserved.

Library of Congress Cataloging-in-Publication Data
Names: Dixon, Chris.
Title: Read write own: building the next era of the Internet / Chris Dixon.
Description: First edition. | New York: Random House, 2024. |
Includes bibliographical references and index.
Identifiers: LCCN 2023041266 (print) | LCCN 2023041267 (ebook) |
ISBN 9780593731383 (hardback; acid-free paper) |
ISBN 9780593731406 (Ebook)
Subjects: LCSH: Internet industry—Popular works. |
Internet—Forecasting—Popular works. |
Blockchains (Databases)—Popular works. |
Internet—Economic aspects—Popular works.
Classification: LCC HD9696.8.A2 D59 2024 (print) |
LCC HD9696.8.A2 (ebook) | DDC 338.4/7004678—dc23/eng/20231127
LC record available at lccn.loc.gov/2023041266
LC ebook record available at lccn.loc.gov/2023041267

Printed in the United States of America on acid-free paper

randomhousebooks.com

9 8 7 6 5 4 3 2 1

FIRST EDITION

Book design by Rodrigo Corral Studio

To Elena

When the great innovation appears, it will almost certainly be in a muddled, incomplete and confusing form.
To the discoverer himself it will be only half understood; to everybody else it will be a mystery. For any speculation which does not at first glance look crazy, there is no hope.

—Freeman Dyson

Contents

Introduction   xiii

    Three Eras of Networks   xxi

    A New Movement   xxii

    Seeing the Truth   xxiv

    Determining the Internet's Future   xxvi

Part One: Read. Write.

1 Why Networks Matter   3

2 Protocol Networks   8

    A Brief History of Protocol Networks   8

    The Benefits of Protocol Networks   17

    The Fall of RSS   21

3 Corporate Networks   27

    Skeuomorphic and Native Technologies   27

    The Rise of Corporate Networks   30

    The Problem with Corporate Networks:
    The Attract-Extract Cycle   34

Part Two: Own.

4 Blockchains   49

    Why Computers Are Special:
    The Platform-App Feedback Loop   49

    Two Paths to Adoption: "Inside Out" versus "Outside In"   52

    Blockchains Are a New Kind of Computer   55

    How Blockchains Work   56

    Why Blockchains Matter   66

5 Tokens   70

    Single-Player and Multiplayer Technologies   70

    Tokens Represent Ownership   72

    The Uses of Tokens   74

    The Importance of Digital Ownership   79

    The Next Big Thing Starts Out Looking Like a Toy   81

6 Blockchain Networks   86

Part Three: A New Era

7 Community-Created Software   101

    Modding, Remixing, and Open Source   104

    Composability: Software as Lego Bricks   106

    The Cathedral and the Bazaar   110

8 Take Rates   112

    Network Effects Drive Take Rates   113

    Your Take Rate Is My Opportunity   118

    Squeezing the Balloon   122

9 Building Networks with Token Incentives   128

    Incentivizing Software Development   128

    Overcoming the Bootstrap Problem   131

    Tokens Are Self-Marketing   135

    Making Users Owners   137

10 Tokenomics   141

    Faucets and Token Supply   143

    Sinks and Token Demand   144

    Tokens Can Be Valued Using Traditional Financial Methods   147

    Financial Cycles   150

11 Network Governance   154

    The Nonprofit Model   157

    Federated Networks   158

    Protocol Coups   161

    Blockchains as Network Constitutions   164

    Blockchain Governance   164

Part Four: Here and Now

12 The Computer versus the Casino   171

    Regulating Tokens   173

    Ownership and Markets Are Inextricable   177

    Limited Liability Corporations: A Regulatory Success Story   179

Part Five: What's Next

13 The iPhone Moment: From Incubation to Growth   185

14 Some Promising Applications   189

   Social Networks: Millions of Profitable Niches   189

   Games and the Metaverse:
   Who Will Own the Virtual World?   194

   NFTs: Scarce Value in an Era of Abundance   198

   Collaborative Storytelling:
   Unleashing Fantasy Hollywood   207

   Making Financial Infrastructure a Public Good   210

   Artificial Intelligence:
   A New Economic Covenant for Creators   216

   Deepfakes: Moving Beyond the Turing Test   222

Conclusion   226

   Reinventing the Internet   227

   Cause for Optimism   228

   Acknowledgments   231

   Notes   233

   Index   271

Introduction

The internet is probably the most important invention of the twentieth century. It transformed the world much as earlier technological revolutions—the printing press, the steam engine, electricity—did before.

Unlike many other inventions, the internet wasn't immediately monetized. Its early architects created the network not as a centralized organization but as an open platform that anyone—artists, users, developers, companies, and others—could access equally. At a relatively low cost and without needing approval, anyone anywhere could create and share code, art, writing, music, games, websites, startups, or whatever else could be dreamed up.

And whatever you created, you owned. As long as you obeyed the law, no one could change the rules on you, extract more money from you, or take away what you built. The internet was designed to be permissionless and democratically governed, as were its original networks, email and the web. No participants would be privileged over others. Anyone could build on top of these networks and control their creative and economic destinies.

This freedom and sense of ownership led to a golden period of creativity and innovation that drove the growth of the internet through the 1990s and 2000s, leading to countless applications that have transformed our world and the way we live, work, and play.

And then everything changed.

Starting in the mid-2000s, a small group of big companies wrenched control away. Today the top 1 percent of social networks account for 95 percent of social web traffic and 86 percent of social mobile app use. The top 1 percent of search engines account for 97 percent of search traffic, and the top 1 percent of e-commerce sites account for 57 percent of e-commerce traffic. Outside of China, Apple and Google account for more than 95 percent of the mobile app store market. In the past decade, the five biggest tech companies grew from about 25 percent to nearly 50 percent of the market capitalization of the Nasdaq-100. Startups and creative people increasingly depend on networks run by megacorporations like Alphabet (parent of Google and YouTube), Amazon, Apple, Meta (parent of Facebook and Instagram), and Twitter (rebranded as X) to find customers, build audiences, and connect with peers.

The internet got intermediated, in other words. The network went from permissionless to permissioned.

The good news is that billions of people got access to amazing technologies, many of which were free to use. The bad news is that for those same billions, a centralized internet run by a handful of mostly ad-based services meant fewer software choices, weakened data privacy, and diminished control over their online lives. And it became much harder for startups, creators, and other groups to grow their internet presences without worrying about centralized platforms changing the rules on them and taking away their audiences, profits, and power.

Even though Big Tech companies deliver significant value, their services come with considerable negative externalities. Widespread user surveillance is one issue. Meta, Google, and other ad-based companies run elaborate tracking systems that monitor every click, search, and social interaction. This has made the internet adversarial: an estimated 40 percent of internet users use ad blockers that protect against tracking. Apple has made privacy a centerpiece of its marketing—a thinly veiled dig at Meta and Google—while simultaneously expanding its own advertising network. In order to use online services, users need to agree to complicated privacy policies—which almost no one reads and even fewer can understand—that allow their personal data to be used in almost any way the services please.

Big Tech also controls what we see and watch. The most visible example of this is deplatforming: when services eject people, usually without transparent due process. Alternatively, people may get silenced and not even know it, a practice called shadowbanning. Search and social ranking algorithms can change lives, make or break businesses, and even influence elections, yet the code that powers them is controlled by unaccountable corporate management teams and hidden from public scrutiny.

A subtler and equally troubling point is how these power brokers architect their networks to restrict and constrain startups, impose high rents on creators, and disenfranchise users. The negative effects of these design choices are threefold: (1) they stifle innovation; (2) they tax creativity; and (3) they concentrate power and money in the hands of a few.

This is especially dangerous when you consider that the killer app of the internet *is* networks. Most of what people do online involves networks: The web and email are networks. Social apps like Instagram, TikTok, and Twitter are networks. Payment apps like PayPal and Venmo are networks. Marketplaces like Airbnb and Uber are networks. Almost every useful online service is a network.

Networks—computing networks, of course, but also developer platforms, marketplaces, financial networks, social networks, and all variety of communities coming together online—have always been a powerful part of the promise of the internet. Developers, entrepreneurs, and everyday internet users have nurtured and nourished tens of thousands of networks, unleashing an unprecedented wave of creation and coordination. Yet the networks that have lasted are mostly owned and controlled by private companies.

The problem stems from permission. Today creators and start-ups need to ask for permission from centralized gatekeepers and incumbents to launch and grow new products. In business, permission seeking is not like asking your parents or teachers for permission, where you get a simple yes or no answer. Nor is it like traffic lights setting the rules of the road. In business, permission becomes a pretense for tyranny. Dominant tech businesses leverage the power of permission to thwart competition, desolate markets, and extract rents.

And those rents are exorbitant. The combined revenue of the five largest social networks—Facebook, Instagram, YouTube, TikTok, and Twitter—is about $150 billion per year. Nearly all major social networks have "take rates"—the percentage of revenue network owners take from network users—of 100 percent, or near to it. (YouTube is the one outlier with a take rate of 45 percent, for reasons we'll get into later.) This means the vast majority of that $150 billion goes to those companies instead of the users, creators, and entrepreneurs who contribute, build on top, and create value for all.

Mobile phones—which dominate computing today, especially internationally—underscore the imbalance. People spend about seven hours per day on internet-connected devices. About half that time they spend using phones, where apps occupy 90 percent of their time. That means people spend about three hours per day in the thrall of an app store duopoly: Apple and Google. These companies charge up to 30 percent for payments. That's more than ten times the payment industry norm. Such steep take rates are unheard of in other markets, and they reflect how powerful these companies have become.

This is what I mean when I say corporate networks tax creativity. The taxation is literal.

Big Tech companies also wield their power to squelch competitors, reducing options for consumers. Facebook and Twitter famously took antisocial turns in the early 2010s, cutting off third-party companies that were building apps for users on top of their platforms. These abrupt crackdowns punished many developers and, therefore, punished users by offering fewer products, fewer choices, and less freedom. Most other large social platforms have executed the same playbook. Today almost no new startup activity takes place on top of social networks. Developers know better than to lay foundations on quicksand.

Pause for a moment: Social networks, whether in person or online, are the essence of human connection and coordination. They are one of the most widely used applications by people of all ages, and yet no new startups have survived, let alone thrived, on top of these platforms for many years. And all for a simple reason: Big Tech says so.

Facebook isn't the only capricious gatekeeper. Other platforms are just as ruthless, as Facebook itself pointed out in response to antitrust lawsuits brought by the Federal Trade Commission and state attorneys general at the end of 2020. "This restriction is standard in the industry," a Facebook spokesperson said of the platform's third-party-neutering practices, citing similar policies at LinkedIn, Pinterest, and Uber, among others.

The biggest platforms are anticompetitive. Amazon learns which products in its marketplaces are top sellers and then undercuts their makers with its own cheap basic versions. While physical retailers like Target and Walmart do this all the time with their own version of generic brands alongside name brands, the difference here is that Amazon is not just the store but the infrastructure. It would be as if Target controlled not just its store shelves but also the roads that all stores build on. This is too much control for one corporation to wield.

Google abuses its power too. In addition to charging high mobile payment fees, Google faces scrutiny over using its popular search engine to boost the prominence of its own products over those of its competitors. Many searches today show only sponsored ads, including Google products, above the fold, crowding out smaller rivals. Google also aggressively collects and tracks user data to improve its ad targeting. Amazon plays a similar game, ranking its own products above others and harvesting people's data to enlarge its fast-growing, $38 billion ad business, which trails only Google's ($225 billion) and Meta's ($114 billion).

Apple commits similar sins. While many people love using Apple's devices, the company routinely rejects competitors from its App Store and squeezes the ones it lets in—to the point that it is now embroiled in multiple high-profile lawsuits. Epic, the developer of the ultra-popular game *Fortnite,* is one plaintiff, taking Apple to court after the company shut down Epic's game developers' ability to access the App Store. Spotify, Tinder, the location tag maker Tile, and others have filed similar complaints over Apple's high fees and anticompetitive rules.

Big Tech platforms have more than just a home field advantage. They get to rewrite the rules of the entire game for their sole benefit.

Is that so bad? Many people don't see a problem with the way things are, or they don't think much about it. They are satisfied with the comforts afforded by Big Tech. We live in an age of abundance, after all. You can connect to anyone you want (assuming the corporate network owners are okay with it). You can read, watch, and share as much as you like. There are plenty of "free" services to satiate us—the price of entry being just our data. (As they say, "If it's free, then you're the product.")

Lots of people are happy with the status quo. Maybe you too think the trade-off is worth it, or perhaps you see no other viable alternative for life online. Either way, whatever your stance, one trend is undeniable: centralizing forces are drawing the internet inward, collecting power into the center of what was supposed to be a decentralized network. This inward turn is stifling innovation, making the internet less interesting, less dynamic, and less fair.

To the extent that anyone recognizes a problem, they usually assume the only thing that might rein in existing giants is government regulation. That may be part of the solution. But regulation often has the unintended side effect of cementing existing giants' power. Larger companies can deal with compliance costs and regulatory complexity that overwhelm smaller upstarts. Red tape restrains newcomers. We need a level playing field. And in service of that, we need thoughtful regulation that respects this fundamental truth: startups and technologies offer a more effective way to check incumbents' power.

Moreover, knee-jerk regulatory responses ignore what sets the internet apart from other technologies. Many of the usual calls for regulation assume that the internet is similar to past communications networks, like telephone and cable TV networks. But these older, hardware-based networks are different from the internet, a software-based network.

The internet depends, of course, on physical infrastructure owned by telecom providers, such as cabling, routers, cell towers, and satellites. Historically, this infrastructure has been a strictly neutral transport layer, treating all internet traffic without bias. Today, regulation over "net neutrality" is in flux, but so far the industry has mostly upheld its policies of nondiscrimination. In this model, software takes priority. It is the code running at the network edges—on PCs, phones, and servers—that drives the behavior of internet services.

This code can be upgraded. With the right set of features and incentives, new software can propagate across the internet. Thanks to its malleable nature, the internet can be reshaped through innovation and market forces.

Software is special because it has a nearly unbounded range of expressiveness. Almost anything you can imagine can be encoded in software; software is the encoding of human thought, just like writing or painting or cave drawings. Computers take those encoded thoughts and run them at lightning speeds. This is why Steve Jobs once described the computer as "a bicycle for the mind." It accelerates our abilities.

Software is so expressive that it is better thought of not as engineering but as an art form. The plasticity and flexibility of code offer an immensely rich design space, far closer in the breadth of possibilities to creative activities like sculpting and fiction writing than engineering activities like bridge building. As with other art forms, practitioners regularly develop new genres and movements that fundamentally shift what's possible.

That's what's happening today. Just as the internet seemed to be consolidating beyond repair, a new software movement emerged that can reimagine the internet. The movement has the potential to bring back the spirit of the early internet, secure property rights for creators, reclaim user ownership and control, and break the stranglehold Big Tech has on our lives.

That's why I believe there's a better way and that these are still the early days. The internet can still fulfill the promise of its original vision. Entrepreneurs, technologists, creators, and users can make it happen.

The dream of an open network that fosters creativity and entrepreneurship doesn't have to die.

Three Eras of Networks

To understand how we got here, it helps to be familiar with the broad strokes of internet history. Below I'll provide a brief overview, which I'll unpack in greater detail in the chapters ahead.

The first thing to know is that power on the internet derives from how networks are designed. Network design—the way nodes connect, interact, and form an overarching structure—might seem like an arcane technical topic, but it is the single most relevant factor in determining how rights and money are distributed across the internet. Even small initial design decisions can have profound downstream consequences on the control and economics of internet services.

Simply put, network design determines outcomes.

Until recently, networks came in two competing types. The first, "protocol networks," like email and the web, are open systems controlled by communities of software developers and other network stakeholders. These networks are egalitarian, democratic, and permissionless: open to anyone and free to access. In these systems, money and power tend to flow to the network edges, incentivizing systems to grow around them.

"Corporate networks" are the second type: networks that companies, instead of communities, own and control. These are like walled gardens with one groundskeeper; they're theme parks controlled by a single megacorp. Corporate networks run centralized, permissioned services that allow them to quickly develop advanced features, attract investment, and accrue profits to reinvest in growth. In these systems, money and power flow to the network center, to companies that own the networks, and away from users and developers at the network edges.

I see the history of the internet as unfolding in three acts. Each act is marked by a predominating network architecture. In the first act, called the "read era," circa 1990 to 2005, early internet protocol networks *democratized information.* Anyone could type a few words into a web browser and read about almost any topic through websites. In the second act, the "read-write era," roughly 2006 to 2020, corporate networks *democratized publishing.* Anyone could write and publish to mass audiences through posts on social networks and other services. Now a new type of architecture is enabling the internet's third act.

This architecture represents a natural synthesis of the two prior types, and it is *democratizing ownership.* In the dawning "read-write-own era," anyone can become a network stakeholder, gaining power and economic upside previously enjoyed by only a small number of corporate affiliates, like stockholders and employees. This new era promises to counteract Big Tech consolidation and return the internet to its dynamic roots.

People can read and write on the internet, but they can also now *own.*

A New Movement

This new movement goes by a few names.

Some people call it "crypto," since the foundation of its technology is cryptography. Others call it "web3," implying that it is leading to a third era of the internet. I sometimes use these names, but I generally try to stick to well-defined terms like "blockchains" and "blockchain networks," which are the technologies driving the movement. (Many industry practitioners refer to blockchain networks as protocols, but I avoid this label to better distinguish these networks from protocol networks, two very different concepts in this book.)

Whichever name you prefer, the core technology of blockchains presents unique advantages, if you know where and how to look.

Some people will tell you that blockchains are a new type of database, one that multiple parties can edit, share, and trust. That's a start. A better description is that blockchains are a new class of computer, one you can't put in your pocket or on your desk, as you might with a smartphone or laptop. Nevertheless, blockchains fit the classic definition of computers. They store information and run rules encoded in software that can manipulate that information.

The significance of blockchains lies in the unique way that they, and the networks built on top of them, are controlled. With traditional computers, the hardware controls the software. Hardware exists in the physical world, where an individual or organization owns and controls it. That means that, ultimately, a person or group of people is in charge of both the hardware and the software. People can change their minds and therefore the software they control at any time.

Blockchains invert the hardware-software power relationship, like the internet before them. With blockchains, the software governs a network of hardware devices. The software—in all its expressive glory—is in charge.

Why does this matter? Because blockchains are computers that can, for the first time ever, establish inviolable rules in software. This allows blockchains to make strong, software-enforced commitments to users. A pivotal commitment involves digital ownership, which places economic and governance power in the hands of users.

You may still be wondering, *So what? What problems do blockchains solve?*

The ability for blockchains to make strong commitments about how they will behave in the future allows *new networks* to be created. Blockchain networks solve problems that plague earlier network architectures. They can connect people in social networks while empowering users over corporate interests. They can underpin marketplaces and payment networks that facilitate commerce, but with persistently lower take rates. They can enable new forms of monetizable media, interoperable and immersive digital worlds, and artificial intelligence products that compensate—rather than cannibalize—creators.

So yes, blockchains create networks, but unlike other network architectures—and here's the key point—they have more desirable outcomes. They can incentivize innovation, reduce taxes on creators, and let the people who contribute to the networks share in decision making and upside.

Asking "What problems do blockchains solve?" is like asking "What problems does steel solve over, say, wood?" You can make a building or railway out of either. But steel gave us taller buildings, stronger railways, and more ambitious public works at the outset of the Industrial Revolution. With blockchains we can create networks that are fairer, more durable, and more resilient than the networks of today.

Blockchain networks combine the societal benefits of protocol networks with the competitive advantages of corporate networks. Software developers get open access, creators get direct relationships with their audiences, fees are guaranteed to stay low, and users get valuable economic and governance rights. At the same time, blockchain networks have the technical and financial capabilities to compete with corporate networks.

Blockchain networks are a new construction material for building a better internet.

Seeing the Truth

New technologies are often controversial. Blockchains are no exception.

Many people associate blockchains with scams and get-rich-quick schemes. There is some truth to these claims, as there was truth to similar claims about tech-driven financial manias of the past, from the railroad boom of the 1830s to the dot-com bubble of the 1990s. The 1990s were full of spectacular failures, such as Pets.com and Webvan. The public discussion mostly focused on IPOs and stock prices, but there were also entrepreneurs and technologists who looked beyond the ups and downs, rolled up their sleeves, and built products and services that eventually delivered on the hype. There were speculators, but there were also builders.

Today, the same cultural divide exists around blockchains. One group, which I call the casino, is often the much louder of the two, and it is primarily interested in trading and speculation. At its worst, this culture of gambling has led to catastrophes like the bankruptcy of the crypto exchange FTX. This group gets most of the media attention, which influences the public image for the entire category.

The other group, which I call the computer, is the far more serious of the two, and it is motivated by a long-term vision. This group's practitioners understand that the financial aspects of blockchains are only a means to an end, a way to align incentives toward a larger goal. They realize the real potential in using blockchains is to build better networks, and therefore a better internet. These people are quieter and don't get as much attention, but they are the ones who will have lasting effects.

This isn't to say the computer culture isn't interested in making money. I work in venture capital. Most of the tech industry is profit-driven. The difference is that real innovation takes time to generate financial returns. That's why most venture capital funds (ours included) are structured as ten-year funds, with purposefully long hold periods. Producing valuable new technologies can take up to a decade and sometimes longer. Computer culture is long term. Casino culture is not.

So, it's the computer versus the casino battling it out to define the narrative for this software movement. Of course, optimism and cynicism can both be taken too far. The dot-com bubble, followed by bust, reminded many people of that.

The way to see the truth is to separate the essence of a technology from specific uses and misuses of it. A hammer can build a home, or it can demolish one. Nitrogen-based fertilizers help grow crops that feed billions of people, but they can also be used in explosives. Stock markets help societies allocate capital and resources where they can be most productive, but they also enable destructive speculative bubbles. All technologies have the capacity to help or harm; blockchains are no different. The question is, how can we maximize the good while minimizing the bad?

Determining the Internet's Future

This book aims to give you an appreciation for the essence of blockchains, the technology—that is, the computer—and all the exciting new things it can do. My hope is that you will, along the way, come to understand exactly what problems blockchains solve and why the solutions they present are so urgently needed.

The thinking, firsthand observations, and mental models I share here are the result of my experiences over the course of a twenty-five-year career in the internet industry. I started as a software developer, then became an entrepreneur in the 2000s. I sold two companies, one to McAfee and the other to eBay. Along the way, I took up investing, placing early bets on companies such as Kickstarter, Pinterest, Stack Overflow, Stripe, Oculus, and Coinbase, all of which have products in wide use today. I have been a longtime advocate for community-owned software and networks, and I have been blogging on the topic, as well as technology and startups, since 2009.

My own path into blockchain networks began in the early 2010s after reflecting on the failure of protocol networks like RSS, an open-source publishing protocol, against corporate-owned rivals like Facebook and Twitter. These experiences turned me toward a new model of investing, one that guides my philosophy today.

I believe to understand the internet's future, you must understand its past. To that end, in part 1 of the book, I chart the history of the internet, focusing on the two most recent eras from the early 1990s through today.

In part 2, I dive deeper into blockchains, explaining how they work and why they matter. I show how blockchains and tokens can be used to construct blockchain networks, and explain the technical and economic mechanisms by which they work.

In part 3, I show how blockchain networks empower users and other network participants, answering the "why blockchains?" question people often ask.

In part 4, I address controversial questions head-on, including policy and regulatory topics and the harmful casino culture that has developed around blockchains that hurts their public perception and undermines their potential.

Finally, in part 5, building on the history and concepts presented earlier, I go deeper into intersecting areas like social networks, video games, virtual worlds, media businesses, collaborative creation, finance, and artificial intelligence. I hope to give a flavor for the power of blockchain networks, and how they can underpin better versions of existing applications along with new applications that weren't possible before.

This book encapsulates what I've learned throughout my internet career. I've had the privilege to work with many outstanding entrepreneurs and technologists. Much of what I discuss here, I learned from them. I hope that whether you're a builder, founder, corporate leader, policymaker, analyst, journalist, or someone who just wants to understand what is happening and where we're all headed, this book can help you build, navigate, and participate in the future.

Blockchain networks are, I argue, the most credible and civic-minded force to counterbalance internet consolidation. I believe this is the beginning, not the end, of internet innovation. There's an urgency to that conviction, though: the United States is already losing its lead in this new movement, with the share of global software developers here going from 40 percent to 29 percent in the past five years. The rapid rise of artificial intelligence will also likely accelerate the trend toward Big Tech consolidation. Artificial intelligence holds incredible promise but tends to favor well-capitalized companies with large accumulations of data.

The decisions we make now will determine the internet's future: who builds, owns, and uses it; where innovation happens; and what the experience will be for everyone. Blockchains, and the networks they enable, unlock the extraordinary power of software as an art form, with the internet as its canvas. The movement has an opportunity to change the course of history, to remake humanity's relationship to the digital, to reimagine what's possible. Anyone can participate—whether you're a developer, creator, entrepreneur, or user.

This is a chance to create the internet you want, not the internet you inherited.

Part One
Read. Write.

1. Why Networks Matter

I am thinking about something much more important than bombs. I am thinking about computers.

—John von Neumann

Network design is destiny.

Networks are the organizing framework that enables billions of people to intelligibly interact. They decide the world's winners and losers. Their algorithms decide where money and attention will flow. The structure of a network guides how that network will evolve and where wealth and power accumulate. Given the scale of the internet today, software design decisions up front, regardless of how seemingly small, can have cascading downstream consequences. Who controls a given network is the central question when analyzing power on the internet.

This is why critics who knock the tech startup industry for placing more emphasis on the digital world than the physical world—on "bits" versus "atoms"—miss the mark. The internet's influence extends far beyond the digital realm. It intersects, permeates, and shapes large-scale social and economic landscapes.

Even pro-tech investors play up the idea. As Peter Thiel, the venture capitalist and PayPal co-founder, once mused, "We wanted flying cars, instead we got 140 characters." The dig takes aim at Twitter, which originally limited tweets to 140 characters, but it's intended to pan the perceived frivolity of the software-obsessed tech industry at large.

Tweets may seem frivolous, but they affect everything from personal thoughts and opinions to the outcomes of elections and pandemics. People who claim technologists aren't focusing enough on problems like energy, food, transportation, and housing overlook that the digital and the physical worlds are interconnected and entwined. Internet networks mediate most people's interactions with the "real world."

The merging of the physical and the digital happens discreetly. Science fiction sometimes portrays automation as a visible process, where one physical thing gets replaced, one for one, by another as a direct substitution. In reality, most automation happens indirectly, where physical objects transmute into digital networks. Robo–travel agents didn't replace human travel agents. Rather, search engines and travel websites absorbed their tasks. Mail rooms and postboxes still exist, but they handle far lower volumes of correspondence since the rise of email. Personal aircraft haven't upended physical transportation, but internet services like videoconferencing have, in many cases, obviated the need for travel.

We wanted flying cars, instead we got Zoom.

People tend to underestimate the digital world due to the internet's newness. Consider the language people use. Subordinating prefixes like "e-" in "email" and "e-commerce" diminish digital activities' value as compared with their "real world" counterparts of "mail" and "commerce." Yet, increasingly, mail is email and commerce is e-commerce. When people refer to the physical world as the real world, they fail to appreciate where they spend more and more of their time. Innovations like social media that were initially dismissed as nonserious can now shape everything from global politics, business, and culture to the worldview of any one person.

New technologies will further fuse the digital and the physical worlds. Artificial intelligence will make computers vastly smarter. Virtual and augmented reality headsets will enhance digital experiences, making them more immersive. Internet-connected computers embedded in objects and places—also called Internet of Things devices—will permeate our environments. Everything around us will have sensors to understand the world as well as actuators to alter it. All of this will be mediated through internet networks.

So yes, networks matter.

At their most basic level, networks are lists of connections between people or things. Online, they often catalog what people might direct their attention toward. They also inform algorithms that further curate attention. If you visit your social media feeds, algorithms churn up all manner of content and advertisements based on your presumed interests. "Likes" on media networks and ratings on marketplaces direct the flow of ideas, interests, and impulses. Without this curation the internet would be a deluge—unstructured, overwhelming, unusable.

The internet economy turbocharges networks. In an industrial economy, corporations accrue power mainly through economies of scope and scale; that is, ways of decreasing production costs. The diminishing marginal cost of producing more steel, cars, pharmaceutical drugs, fizzy sugar water, or whatever other widget lends an advantage to whoever owns and invests in the means of production. On the internet, the marginal costs of distribution are negligible, so power primarily accrues another way: through network effects.

Network effects dictate that the value of a network grows with the addition of each new node, or connection point. Nodes can be telephone lines, transportation hubs like airports, connection-oriented technologies like computers, or even people. Metcalfe's law, one well-known formulation of the network effect, stipulates that the value of a network grows quadratically, meaning proportional to the number of nodes squared (that is, raising by an exponent of 2). For the mathematically minded, a network with ten nodes would be twenty-five times as valuable as a network with two nodes, while a network with a hundred nodes would be a hundred times as valuable as one with ten nodes, and so on. The law takes its name from Robert Metcalfe, a co-creator of Ethernet and the electronics maker 3Com who popularized the idea in the 1980s.

Because not all network connections may be equally useful, some argue for variations to the law. In 1999, David Reed, another computer scientist, put forward his own self-named spin: Reed's law, which states that the value of large networks can scale exponentially with the size of the network. The formula best applies to social networks, where people are the nodes. Facebook has nearly 3 billion monthly active users. According to Reed's law, that means Facebook's network value is 2 to the 3 billionth power—a number so eye-blisteringly large that it would take 3 million pages just to print it.

Whichever approximation of network value you prefer, one thing is clear: the numbers get big, fast.

It makes sense that network effects would dominate the internet, the ultimate network of networks. People cluster around other people. Services such as Twitter, Instagram, and TikTok are valuable because hundreds of millions of people use them. The same is true of many networks that make up the internet. The more people exchange ideas on the web, the richer that information network. The more people message over email and WhatsApp, the more relevant these communication networks. The more people conduct business across Venmo, Square, Uber, and Amazon, the more valuable these marketplaces. As a rule: more people, more value.

Network effects take small advantages and snowball them into avalanches. When corporations are in control, they tend to guard their advantages jealously, making it difficult for anyone to leave. If you build an audience on a corporate network, leaving means forfeiting your audience, so you're discouraged from doing so. This partly explains why power has consolidated into the hands of a few large tech companies. If this trend continues, the internet could end up even more centralized, commandeered by powerful intermediaries that use their might to crowd out innovation and creativity. Left unchecked, this will lead to economic stasis, homogeneity, unproductivity, and inequality.

Some policymakers seek to defang the largest internet companies with regulation. Their remedies include blocking acquisition attempts and proposing to split companies into parts. Other regulatory proposals require companies to interoperate, allowing easy integrations between networks. Users could then bring their connections wherever they like, and they could read and post content across networks according to their preferences. Some of these proposals could rein in incumbents and make room for competitors, but the best long-term solution is to build new networks from the ground up that won't lead to concentrations of power for the simple reason that they *can't*.

Many well-funded startups are trying to build new corporate networks. If they succeed, they'll inevitably re-create the same problems with today's large corporate networks. What we need are new challengers that can win in the market against corporate networks but provide greater societal benefits. Specifically, we need networks that provide benefits like those afforded by the open and permissionless protocol networks that characterized the early internet.

2. Protocol Networks

What was often difficult for people to understand about the design was that there was nothing else beyond URLs, HTTP and HTML. There was no central computer "controlling" the Web, no single network on which these protocols worked, not even an organisation anywhere that "ran" the Web.
The Web was not a physical "thing" that existed in a certain "place." It was a "space" in which information could exist.
—Tim Berners-Lee

A Brief History of Protocol Networks

In the fall of 1969, the U.S. military bootstrapped the earliest version of the internet: ARPANET, named after the Department of Defense's Advanced Research Projects Agency (ARPA).

A broad community of researchers and developers spearheaded the internet's development through the next couple decades. These academics and tinkerers brought with them a tradition of open access. They believed in the free exchange of ideas, equal opportunity, and meritocracy. In their view, the people who used internet services—the users—should have control. The structure and governance of their research communities, advisory groups, and task forces embodied their democratic ideals.

The internet carried this culture forward when it crossed from government and academia to mainstream users in the early 1990s. As more people joined the network, they inherited the egalitarian ethos. Cyberspace was radically open. As John Perry Barlow, the poet-activist and sometime lyricist for the Grateful Dead, would write in 1996 in his "Declaration of the Independence of Cyberspace," "We are creating a world that all may enter without privilege or prejudice accorded by race, economic power, military force, or station of birth." The internet represented freedom, a fresh start.

That same spirit infused the technology itself. The internet was underpinned by permissionless protocols, sets of rules for computers to participate in networks. In ancient times, "protocol," from the Greek *prōtokollon,* meant "first sheet of a volume," often referring to a table of contents. Over time, the word evolved to mean "diplomatic conventions" and, later, in the twentieth century, "technical standards for software." The computing context became widespread with the advent of ARPANET because protocols—accessible by and open to all—were foundational to the development of the internet.

Think of protocols as analogous to natural languages, like English or Swahili. They enable computers to communicate with one another. If you change how you speak, there's a risk other people won't understand you. You cease to interoperate, in tech vernacular. If you're influential enough, you might get others to change how they speak too because dialects can splinter into new languages, but only if other people join in. Protocols and languages both require consensus.

Protocols layer on top of one another, and ultimately on computing devices, in what is called the internet "stack." For a computer scientist, knowing all layers of the stack and the nuances between them may be useful. (A popular model, called the Open Systems Interconnection model, or OSI for short, identifies seven layers.) For this discussion, just picture three layers where the lowest one consists of hardware: servers, PCs, smartphones, internet-connected devices like TVs and cameras, along with the networking hardware that connects them all. Other layers build on top of this foundation.

Above the physical layer is the networking layer, known simply as internet protocol, or IP. This protocol defines how to format, address, and route packets of information between the first layer's machines. Vint Cerf and Robert Kahn, researchers at the same lab responsible for ARPANET, developed this standard in the 1970s. (That lab, ARPA, later renamed DARPA, also helped invent futuristic technologies like stealth vehicles and GPS.) The network officially completed implementing internet protocol on January 1, 1983, a date most people regard as the birthday of the internet.

Networks

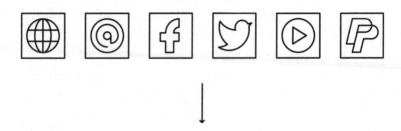

Internet

Devices

On top of the internet layer is the application layer, so called because it's where user-facing applications plug in. Two protocols chiefly define this layer, the first of which is email. The protocol behind email is called Simple Mail Transfer Protocol, abbreviated SMTP. Jon Postel, a researcher at the University of Southern California, created the protocol to standardize email communication in 1981, and his contribution primed email for widespread uptake. As Katie Hafner and Matthew Lyon recount in their history of the internet, *Where Wizards Stay Up Late*, "Just as the LP was invented for connoisseurs and audiophiles but spawned an entire industry, electronic mail grew first among the elite community of computer scientists on the ARPANET, then later bloomed like plankton across the Internet."

The second protocol from which many applications have bloomed is the web, also known as Hypertext Transfer Protocol, or HTTP. Tim Berners-Lee, a British scientist, invented the protocol, along with Hypertext Markup Language, or HTML, for formatting and rendering websites, while working at the Swiss physics lab CERN in 1989. (Though people often use "internet" and "web" interchangeably, these are different networks: the internet connects devices; the web links web pages.)

Email and the web succeeded because of their simplicity, generality, and openness. After these protocols were created, programmers codified them into email clients and web browsers, many of which were open source. Anyone could download a client (what most people would call an app today) to join a network. Clients build on top of protocols and enable people to access and participate in underlying networks. Clients are like portals, or gateways, to protocol networks.

People interact with protocols through clients. For instance, the web started going mainstream only after the 1993 debut of the consumer-friendly Mosaic web browser, one such client. Today, the most popular web clients are proprietary browsers like Google

Chrome, Apple Safari, and Microsoft Edge, while the most popular email clients are Gmail (proprietary, hosted on Google servers) and Microsoft Outlook (proprietary, downloadable to local machines). A wide range of software, both proprietary and open source, also remains available for running web and email servers.

The communications system that underpins the internet was designed to be decentralized and, therefore, resilient enough to survive nuclear attack. The system treated all nodes equally, so it could continue functioning even if sections were destroyed. Email and the web inherited this design philosophy. All nodes are "peers," none privileged above any other.

Protocol Network

One component of the internet was, however, designed differently, and it controlled a special function: naming.

Naming is a requirement in every network. Names are the most basic kinds of avatars, essential components for building communities. I am @cdixon on Twitter, and my website is cdixon.org. These human-friendly names make it easy for other people to identify and reach me. If people want to follow me, friend me, or send me something, they do so by referencing one of my names.

Machines have names too. On the internet, computers identify one another by what are called internet protocol addresses, sets of numbers that are difficult for humans to remember but easy for machines. Imagine having to summon up numbers for every web page you want to visit. Browsing Wikipedia? Try 198.35.26.96. Searching for a YouTube video? Hit up 208.65.153.238. People need directories, like contact lists on phones, to aid memory.

Through the 1970s and 1980s, one organization maintained the official internet directory. The Stanford Research Institute's Network Information Center compiled all addresses into a single file, HOSTS.TXT, which it updated continuously and distributed to everyone on the network. Every time an address changed or another node joined the network (which happened often), everyone had to update their hosts file. As the network grew, record-keeping became a hassle. People needed a less clunky system to serve as a single source of truth.

Enter domain name system, or DNS. Paul Mockapetris, an American computer scientist, invented this solution to the network naming conundrum in 1983. Under the hood, DNS was complex, but the main idea was simple: mapping human-friendly names to physical-computer IP addresses. The system was hierarchical but also distributed. At the topmost level, a collection of international organizations—government-affiliated agencies, universities, companies, nonprofit groups, and more—managed thirteen sets of root servers that to this day remain the system's ultimate authorities.

From the 1980s through the rise of the commercial internet in the 1990s, a team directed by Postel administered DNS at the University of Southern California. In 1997, *The Economist* summed up the significance of his role: "If the Net does have a god, he is probably Jon Postel." As the internet took off, a longer-term solution to DNS governance became necessary. In the fall of 1998, the U.S. government began transitioning oversight of the internet's name space to a new organization, the nonprofit Internet Corporation for Assigned Names and Numbers, or ICANN. (In October 2016, ICANN became independent and moved to a global multi-stakeholder governance model that continues to supervise the system we use to this day.)

DNS is crucial to a working internet. When you search on a browser for a website, like google.com or wikipedia.org, your internet service provider routes the request through a special server called a DNS resolver that asks the top-level domain servers, responsible for domain suffixes like .com or .org, for further directions. These top-level servers then point to lower-level servers that provide the appropriate IP addresses to your browser to get you where you're going. This whole process is called a DNS lookup, and it happens in a flash every time you try to connect to a website. (To make lookups faster, DNS providers also store, or cache, IP addresses on servers nearer to users.)

The protocols underlying email and the web are free to use except for DNS, which charges modest fees that go to ICANN and internet registrars. As long as users pay the fees, typically around $10 per year, and as long as they obey the law, they can do what they please with their domain names. Users can buy, sell, or hold on to them indefinitely. The fees behave more like property taxes than leasing fees.

Names are an important leverage point in the control of networks. In networks like Twitter and Facebook, corporate owners control the names. I am @cdixon on Twitter, but Twitter owns this name. Twitter can revoke it, charge me more money, or take away my audience. By controlling my name, Twitter also controls my relationships with other people. It can modify algorithms that show my posts more or less frequently, for example. I have no power except to quit the network.

The key design decision in DNS is that users, not a company or other higher authority, own and control their names. Specifically, users control the mapping between their names and IP addresses. They can therefore move their names from one computer to another, at any time for any reason, and run whatever software they want, without losing their network connections or anything else they've built.

Let's say I host cdixon.org at Amazon's web hosting services. Imagine that Amazon decides to charge me more money, throttle my website, censor my content, or do something else I don't like. I can simply transfer my files to another provider and redirect the cdixon.org DNS record. I could even choose to self-host, the digital equivalent of living off the grid. When I redirect my name, all my network connections remain intact. People can still send me emails and the inbound web links that search engines use to rank my site still work. The switch to a new hosting provider happens behind the scenes. It is invisible to other participants on the network. Amazon knows this and knows it must therefore act within the guardrails of network norms and market forces, or risk losing customers.

This simple design decision—giving users full control of their names—keeps businesses honest. It restrains Amazon and other companies, forcing them to offer competitive services at competitive prices. Companies can still avail themselves of traditional business moats like economies of scale (the more servers they run, the lower their costs, the higher their margins), but they can't rely on network effects to trap users the way centralized networks do.

Contrast how DNS works with what happens when you try to leave a service like Twitter or Facebook. Most corporate networks have a "download your data and delete your account" feature. You get records of your posts and maybe of your followers and friends. But you lose your network connections and your audience because those people followed your Twitter or Facebook account, and you can't redirect that account to a new service. You don't control the mapping. You can get the data, but you lose your network. These "data download" features are feints. They gesture toward openness and freedom, but they do nothing to increase user choices. The company has total control. Your only choice is to stay, or leave and start from scratch somewhere else.

Corporate services like Facebook and Twitter operate networks that interoperate with the web, using components like HTTP, but they are not part of the web in any meaningful sense. They do not adhere to the web's entrenched customs and norms. Indeed, they break the web's many technical, economic, and cultural tenets— like openness, permissionless innovation, and democratic governance. These centralized networks are essentially separate networks that sit adjacent to the web. They have their own rules, economics, and network effects.

The genius of DNS is that users own their names in the same way they own things in the physical world, providing the online equivalent of property rights. When you own something, you have an incentive to invest in it. That's why, starting in the 1990s and continuing today, there has been so much investment in businesses related to email and the web, networks built around DNS.

Giving users control of their names might seem like a small design choice. But it has had cascading downstream consequences, ultimately enabling new industries to grow and flourish, from search engines and social networks to media and e-commerce sites.

As a side effect, digital ownership can spawn speculative markets. Buying and selling domains is a multibillion-dollar industry. Short English-word .com domains routinely sell for millions of dollars. (A recent example is voice.com, which sold for $30 million.) The market for domain names goes up and down, alternately creating and losing fortunes. In this way, the domain market is similar to real estate, which also suffers from bouts of speculation and, every so often, bubbles. Blockchain tokens, which enable a newer form of digital ownership, as we'll discuss later, have also spawned speculative markets. In all these cases, speculation is a side effect. Yet the positives of ownership far outweigh the negatives.

Today, content moderation is a hot topic, especially with respect to social networks. Email and the web, however, don't moderate content. They have just one job: deliver information reliably. The philosophy is if the protocols were to do the policing, they would become fragmented and dysfunctional. Different regions have different laws and customs where what's illegal in one country may be permissible in another. To be universal, protocols must be unopinionated.

Content moderation still happens, but it's done by users, clients, and services built at the network edges. This might seem risky: Can you trust the decentralized masses to successfully police themselves? Yet, in practice, the system does work well. Clients and servers enforce laws, regulations, and moderation. If you operate an illegal website, domain name registrars and web hosting companies will take it down. Search engines will de-index it. The sprawling community of software developers, app and website makers, tech companies, and international bodies that governs the web will exile it. The same is true for email. Clients and servers at the network edges filter spam, phishing, and other malicious content. Laws and incentives make the system work.

Email and the web, supported by DNS, have brought powerful general-purpose networks to the internet. The design lets users own what matters most: their names and, therefore, their connections and whatever else they decide to build on top of the network.

The Benefits of Protocol Networks

Protocol networks endow users with ownership, which benefits all network participants, including creators, entrepreneurs, developers, and others.

Like all networks, protocols have network effects: they get more valuable as more people use them. Email is useful because it is ubiquitous—because so many other people have email addresses.

The difference between a protocol network like email and a corporate network like Twitter is that email's network effect accrues to a community instead of a company. No company owns or controls email and anyone can access it through software created by independent developers that supports the underlying protocol. It's up to developers and consumers to decide what to build and use. Decisions that affect the community are made by the community.

Because protocol networks have no central intermediary, they don't charge "take rates," or fees on money that flows through the network. (I'll discuss take rates and their effects in depth in the chapter "Take Rates.") Moreover, the structure of protocol networks provides strong assurances they'll never charge take rates. This encourages innovation on top. If you are building something on top of email or the web, you know you can invest time and money, because you know that whatever you build, you will own and control. Larry Page and Sergey Brin, Jeff Bezos, Mark Zuckerberg, and countless other internet entrepreneurs were inspired by this promise.

Users also benefit from protocol networks. A vibrant software market and low switching costs mean users can shop around. If users don't like how an algorithm works, or how a service tracks their data, they can switch. If users pay subscription fees or watch ads, the money earned goes directly to creators, instead of network intermediaries, incentivizing further investment in their preferred content.

The more predictable the incentives, the better, just as in the physical world, where predictable laws like property rights encourage investment. The interaction between private businesses and highway systems is a helpful analogy. Because highway systems are predictably open and mostly free, people and businesses are willing to build on top of them—meaning they're willing to invest in resources such as buildings, vehicles, and communities whose ongoing value depends on the highways. This, in turn, stimulates more highway use, which encourages more private investment. In a well-designed network, growth begets growth, creating a healthy and dynamic system.

Corporate networks, like Facebook and Twitter, have unpredictable incentives and therefore limited investment by third parties. Corporate networks usually have high take rates, allowing them to claim a larger share of the revenue that flows through the network and eat into the profits that might otherwise flow to the edges. Today, the incumbent corporate networks—including Facebook, Instagram, PayPal, TikTok, Twitter, and YouTube—are owned by companies with aggregate market capitalizations in the trillions of dollars. It's reasonable to assume that if these networks were protocols, a significant portion of that value would instead be distributed to developers and creators at the edges.

These dynamics explain why email, namely newsletter writing, is having a renaissance among so many content creators. Email gives creators a direct relationship with their audiences, unmediated by central network operators who can change the economics, access rules, or content rankings on a whim. If newsletter services like Substack, which layer on top of email, were to change the rules or the rates, users could simply leave and take their subscribers with them. (Many of these services currently let users export email subscriber lists.) The ability to exit lowers switching costs and, therefore, take rates. That's the power of decoupling names from services in protocol networks. Users may not understand all the nuances of network design, but they do intuit their own economic risks, especially after many years of well-documented issues between content creators and corporate networks.

Software developers are further along in their disillusionment. In the early 2010s, companies like Facebook and Twitter, despite originally presenting themselves as open and inviting, slammed their networks shut and revoked developers' access. In January 2013, when Vine, a short-form video app (acquired by Twitter a few months earlier), made its debut, Mark Zuckerberg personally approved its neutering. According to court documents unsealed years later, Zuckerberg gave the nod to shut down Vine's access to Facebook's application programming interface, or API, a software connection that applications use to interoperate. "Yup, go for it," he told another exec. The move crippled Vine's growth, and Twitter discontinued the service in 2017 after years of neglect. Vine's demise is well-known. Fewer people remember Facebook's crackdowns on apps like BranchOut (job hunting), MessageMe (messaging), Path (social networking), Phhhoto (GIF making), and Voxer (voice chat).

The promise of ownership motivates builders and investors alike. Because protocol networks don't have network fees—and are guaranteed never to have them—startups are strongly incentivized to build on top of them. For example, the early web was hard to navigate and search. Dozens of technical teams started companies to solve this problem, including well-known companies like Yahoo and Google. When spam became a serious issue in the late 1990s, venture capitalists funded dozens of companies to address the problem, an effort that mostly succeeded. There's still spam of course, but we've gotten a lot better at handling it.

Contrast this with how corporate networks like Twitter approach spam, bots, and similar problems today. Outside companies have no incentive to solve the problems. Only the company itself tries to solve them, reducing the pool of talent and resources that could be helping. That's why some of these networks are drowning in bots and spam today.

I credit the opportunities I had as an entrepreneur to the design of protocol networks. In the early 2000s, issues like phishing and spyware were rampant. Today it's hard to picture how bad the situation was. At the time, most people were using a notoriously insecure version of Microsoft's web browser that made it easy for malicious software to install itself on their PCs. In 2004, I co-founded a web security startup called SiteAdvisor that built a tool to protect users from these threats. Because the web is a protocol network, we were able to crawl and analyze websites and build software that worked inside browsers and search engines. We didn't need to ask for permission. No company owns the web or email.

Developers don't need permission to build clients and apps on protocol networks. These networks are open, allowing the independent developer community to solve problems and develop new features. Even better, builders and creators can capture whatever economic value they create. These conditions and incentives allow markets to solve problems that protocols don't.

It would have been impossible for my startup to have been built on a corporate network. Corporate networks are inhospitable to founders, and most venture capitalists know better than to fund people building on them. McAfee eventually acquired our company for a premium because it knew that we owned what we built. The web couldn't change the rules or the rent. No higher power could take away what we made. The web, as a community, of which we were a part, succeeded because of the protocol architecture and the incentives it created.

The Fall of RSS

Since the rise of email and the web, no protocol network has succeeded at scale. It's not for lack of trying. In the last thirty years, technologists created many credible new protocol networks. In the early 2000s, Jabber, an open-source instant messaging protocol (since renamed XMPP), tried to take on AOL Instant Messenger and MSN Messenger. Later in the decade, OpenSocial, a cross-platform social networking protocol, tried to challenge Facebook and Twitter. Diaspora, a decentralized social network that made its debut in 2010, tried to do this too. These protocols were technically innovative and built passionate communities, but none went mainstream.

Email and the web succeeded in part because of their special historical conditions. In the 1970s and 1980s, the internet consisted of a small number of collaborative researchers. Protocol networks grew in the absence of centralized competition. In more recent years, upstart protocol networks have had to compete with corporate alternatives with far more features and resources.

The competitive disadvantages of protocol networks are perhaps best illustrated by the fate of RSS, or "really simple syndication," the protocol that came closest to challenging corporate social networks. RSS is a protocol with functionality similar to a social network. It lets you make lists of users you want to follow, and it allows those users to send you content. Web administrators can embed code on their sites to output updates in a format called XML, short for "extensible markup language," whenever a new post is published. The updates get pushed to the customized feeds of subscribers, who follow the sites and blogs of their choice using their preferred RSS "reader" software. The system is elegant and decentralized. But it's bare bones.

In the 2000s, RSS was a credible competitor to corporate networks like Twitter and Facebook. But by 2009, Twitter started supplanting RSS. People were relying on Twitter instead of RSS to subscribe to bloggers and other creators. Some members of the RSS community thought this was fine, because Twitter had an open API and a stated commitment to continuing to interoperate with RSS. To them, Twitter was simply a popular node in the RSS network. I continued to worry about where things were headed, as I blogged at the time:

> The problem is Twitter isn't really open. For Twitter to be truly open, it would have to be possible to use "Twitter" without in any way involving Twitter the institution. In-

stead, all data goes through Twitter's centralized service. Today's dominant core internet services—the web (HTTP), email (SMTP), and subscription messaging (RSS)—are open protocols that are distributed across millions of institutions. If Twitter supplants RSS, it will be the first core internet service that has a single, for-profit gatekeeper. . . . At some point Twitter will need to make lots of money to justify their valuation. Then we can really assess the impact of having a single company control a core internet service.

Unfortunately, my worries were justified. As Twitter's network grew more popular than RSS, only social norms—nothing firmer— kept the company from pulling the plug. In 2013, as soon as doing so suited its corporate interests, Twitter stopped supporting RSS. Google shut down its main RSS product, Google Reader, that same year, highlighting how far the protocol had fallen.

RSS was once a credible protocol-based approach to social networking. While niche communities continued to use RSS in the 2010s, it was no longer a serious rival to corporate social networks. RSS's decline directly correlated with the consolidation of network power among a few internet giants. As one blogger put it, "That little tangerine bubble"—a reference to RSS's orange logo— "has become a wistful symbol of defiance against a centralized web increasingly controlled by a handful of corporations."

There are two main reasons why RSS lost. First: features. RSS couldn't match the ease of use and advanced functionality of corporate networks. On Twitter, a user could sign up, choose a name and accounts to follow, and be up and running all in a few clicks. RSS was, by contrast, simply a set of standards. No company was behind it, and therefore no one ran a centralized database to store things like people's names and lists of followers. The products built around RSS had more limited features, lacking user-friendly mechanisms for content discovery, curation, and analytics.

RSS expected too much from users. Like email and the web, the protocol used DNS for naming, but that meant content creators had to pay to register domains and then transfer those domains to their own web servers or RSS hosting providers. This onboarding experience was fine for email and the web back in the early days of the internet, when there were no alternatives and when many users were technologists who were accustomed to putting in the effort. But as people with less willingness and know-how came online, RSS couldn't compete. Free, streamlined services like Twitter and Facebook offered easier ways for people to publish, connect, and consume, enabling them to amass tens, then hundreds of millions—and in Facebook's case, billions—of users.

Other attempts by protocols to match the capabilities of corporate services foundered too. In 2007, *Wired* magazine documented its bid to build a social network of its own using open tools like RSS. The demo hit a dead end just before the finish line when the developers realized they were missing a key piece of infrastructure: a decentralized database. (In retrospect, the developers were missing exactly the technology that blockchains would later provide.) As the team wrote,

> For the last couple of weeks, Wired News tried to roll its own Facebook using free web tools and widgets. We came close, but we ultimately failed. We were able to recreate maybe 90 percent of Facebook's functionality, but not the most important part—a way to link people and declare the nature of the relationship.

Some developers, like Brad Fitzpatrick, who started the blog network LiveJournal in 1999, suggested solving this problem by creating a database of social graphs run by nonprofit organizations. In a 2007 post called "Thoughts on the Social Graph," he proposed,

Establish a non-profit and open source software (with copyrights held by the non-profit) which collects, merges, and redistributes the graphs from all other social network sites into one global aggregated graph. This is then made available to other sites (or users) via both public APIs (for small/casual users) and downloadable data dumps, with an update stream / APIs, to get iterative updates to the graph (for larger users).

The idea was that a conventional database containing social graphs could help RSS match the streamlined onboarding of corporate social networks. Giving control of the database to a nonprofit would keep it credibly neutral. Implementing this, however, required widespread coordination between software developers and nonprofit groups. The effort never gained traction, and people have struggled to get nonprofits to work in other tech startup contexts too (which I cover later in "The Nonprofit Model").

Meanwhile, corporate networks didn't need to coordinate. They could simply move fast, even if it meant breaking some things.

This gets at the second reason RSS lost: funding. For-profit companies can raise venture capital to hire more developers, build advanced functionality, subsidize hosting costs, and so forth. As they grow, more capital becomes available. Companies like Facebook and Twitter, and almost every other large corporate network, have raised billions of dollars from private and public investors. RSS was just a loosely connected group of developers with no access to capital beyond voluntary donations. It was never a fair fight.

To this day, open-source software funding is subject to market forces that sometimes, but not always, correspond to what's good for the internet. In 2012, a software update introduced a critical vulnerability into OpenSSL, an open-source project that powers a large portion of the internet's encryption software. The bug, dubbed Heartbleed, endangered the security of broad swaths of internet communications. Security engineers only discovered it two years after its introduction. When people looked into why no one found the bug sooner, they learned that the nonprofit responsible for maintaining the internet protocol, the OpenSSL Software Foundation, consisted of just a few overworked volunteers and that it subsisted on paltry funding, including about $2,000 in direct donations per year.

Some open-source projects are well funded because their success aligns with the interests of big companies. The most widely used operating system in the world, Linux, falls into this category. Companies that benefit from the proliferation of open-source operating systems, like IBM, Intel, and Google, support Linux development. But building new protocol networks generally doesn't align with corporate interests. Indeed, the strategy of most tech companies is to capture, control, and monopolize networks. The last thing they would want to do is fund a potential competitor. Protocol networks are in the collective interest of the internet, but the internet hasn't had a significant source of direct funding since the government bankrolled it in the early days.

Protocol networks like email and the web succeeded because they arrived before serious alternatives. The incentives they created led to a golden period of creativity and innovation that persists to this day, despite the encroachment of Big Tech. But later attempts to build protocol networks have failed to go mainstream. The decline of RSS epitomizes the challenges protocol networks face. RSS's cautionary tale also shows how protocol networks planted the seeds for a newer, more competitive network design, one that would define the next era of the internet.

3. Corporate Networks

When I was in college, I remember thinking to myself,
this internet thing is awesome because you can look up
anything you want, you can read news, you can download
music, you can watch movies, you can find information on
Google, you can get reference material on Wikipedia,
except the thing that is most important to humans,
which is other people, was not there.

—Mark Zuckerberg

Skeuomorphic and Native Technologies

People use new technologies in one of two ways: (1) to do something they could already do but can now do faster, cheaper, easier,
or higher quality; or (2) to do something brand-new that they
simply couldn't do before. Early in the development of new technologies, the first category of activities tends to be more popular,
but it's the second set that has more lasting effects on the world.

Improving existing activities happens first because it's more
straightforward. Discovering the real powers of a new medium
takes time. When Johannes Gutenberg, inventor of the movable-
type printing press, published his namesake Bible in the fifteenth
century, he made it look like a handmade manuscript copy. Who
could imagine a book as anything else? And yet, as Alan Kay, the
computer scientist and Turing Award winner, once observed, "the
real message of printing was not to imitate hand-written Bibles,

but 150 years later to argue in new ways about science and political governance"—a catalyst for revolution.

Doing new things requires leaps of imagination. Early film directors shot films like plays. Effectively, they were making theatrical productions with better distribution models. Filmmaking changed only after true innovators realized the potential for a visual grammar native to the new form. The development of electricity followed a similar path. People originally switched from gas and candles to electric light for the convenience. Only decades later did they tap the electric grid to power all manner of appliances, from toasters to Teslas.

Technology that borrows from what came before is sometimes called skeuomorphic. The term originally referred to design elements in art that are intentional, albeit unnecessary, holdovers. During the Steve Jobs era, Apple popularized the idea as a description of digital graphics that look like familiar objects, like a wood-grained bookshelf as decoration in a reading app or a trash can icon to represent deleted files. Skeuomorphic design made it easier for people to adapt to interactions with computer screens. Now people in the tech industry use the term to describe technologies that mimic existing activities or experiences. Copying things that already exist makes new things feel familiar and helps people get comfortable with them.

The internet was skeuomorphic in the 1990s. At the time, it mostly consisted of digital adaptations of pre-internet things: websites imitating brochures and catalogs, email as an extension of letter writing, and shopping reminiscent of mail-order commerce. People called this the read era because, although people could send emails, submit data, and buy things, information typically flowed one way: from website to user. The analogy is to a read-only digital file, which can be opened and viewed but not edited. Website making was a specialized skill back then, and most activities didn't involve publishing to wider audiences.

It's hard to picture this now, but the internet of the 1990s and early 2000s was nothing like the always-on, high-speed mobile internet of today. People would sit in front of a bulky desktop PC and "log on" only intermittently, usually to check email, plan travel, or browse the web. Images loaded slowly, and video streaming, when it worked at all, was janky. Most people logged on via dial-up modems—slow landline connections that plunked and plodded along at speeds people today would regard as excruciating.

Even at the height of dot-com mania, enthusiasm for the internet went only so far. Just before the excitement peaked in March 2000, the National Academy of Engineering placed the internet thirteenth on its list of greatest engineering achievements of the twentieth century. The invention ranked below radio and telephones (sixth), air-conditioning and refrigeration (tenth), and space exploration (twelfth).

Then—pop!—the bubble burst. Stocks tanked across the board. In 2001, Amazon's share price hit an all-time low. The retailer's market cap reached a nadir of $2.2 billion (less than half a percent of what it is today). When the Pew Research Center, a prominent polling firm, asked Americans in October 2002 if they would adopt broadband, the majority said no. People mostly used the internet for email and web "surfing." Did it really need to be faster? The mainstream consensus was that the internet was cool, sure, but it had limited uses and probably wasn't a good place to build a livelihood. The market crash proved that.

Yet the internet was on the cusp of a renaissance—even as the industry smoldered, a small but growing movement was coalescing.

By the mid-2000s, technologists were beginning to explore internet-native product designs. If "skeuomorphic" means more of the same, then "native" indicates *novelty*. New services were cropping up that would take advantage of the internet's unique capabilities, rather than merely retreading paths beaten by offline analogs. Key trends included blogging, social networking, online dating, public résumé building, and photo sharing. Technical innovations like APIs allowed seamless integrations between internet services. Websites became interoperable. They also became dynamic, able to refresh automatically. "Mash-ups" of applications and data were suddenly everywhere. The web had become fluid.

Richard MacManus put it best in the first post on his early, influential tech blog, *ReadWriteWeb*, in April 2003. "The web was never just supposed to be a one-way publishing system, but the first decade of the web has been dominated by a tool which has been read-only—the web browser," he wrote. "The goal now is to convert the web into a two-way system. Ordinary people should be able to write to the web, just as easily as they can browse and read it."

That the internet could be more than a read-only medium inspired and invigorated a new generation of builders and users. That this reimagination of the internet could allow anyone to easily create content and put it in front of large audiences—not only to *take in* information, but to *broadcast* it—opened whole new fields of possibilities. And so the web would begin its next phase, enabling people to consume *and publish*, freely, and at unprecedented scale: activities that had no precursor in the pre-internet world.

The read-write era, also known as Web 2.0, had arrived.

The Rise of Corporate Networks

The read-write era also marked a shift in network design. Some technologists stuck to the open protocol network architecture, building new protocols and, on top of that, apps. But the developers who would be most successful pursued a different tack: the corporate network model.

Corporate networks have a simple structure. In the middle, a company controls centralized services that power the network. This company has complete control. It can rewrite its terms of service, determine who has access, and redirect how money flows, at any time, for any reason. Corporate networks are centralized because there is ultimately one person, usually the chief executive officer, who makes all the rules.

Corporate Network

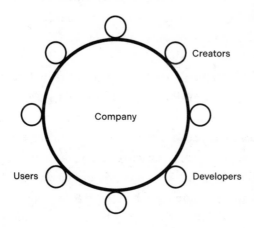

Users, software developers, and other participants are pushed to the network's edges, where they are subject to the central corporation's whims.

The corporate network model allowed a new generation of builders to move faster. Developers could quickly ship features and iterate, instead of waiting to coordinate with standards groups and other stakeholders. They could create advanced, interactive experiences by centralizing services inside data centers. And crucially, because the prize of owning a network was irresistible to venture capital investors, they could raise capital to invest in growth.

In the 1990s, internet startups ran many experiments, but by the 2000s it became clear that the best business models involved owning a network. eBay showed the way. Founded in 1995 as AuctionWeb, the company quickly became a stock market darling, and people considered it a case study for how valuable networks could be. The company was more profitable than Amazon, its main competitor, and most people believed it had a better business model. eBay had a strong network effect and didn't hold inventory, reducing its costs. Amazon had a weaker network effect and held inventory, resulting in higher costs. The success of eBay, along with other network-effect-harnessing businesses, like PayPal (which eBay bought in 2002 and would spin out thirteen years later), kicked off a wave of venture capital funding for startups trying to create networks.

YouTube's story illustrates the rise of corporate networks. In the mid-2000s, broadband home internet started going mainstream as infrastructure improved and costs fell. High-quality video streaming became practical for ordinary users. Entrepreneurs took notice and started building internet video startups. Some of these startups enabled existing video providers, like TV networks, to stream online. Others supported open protocols, like Media RSS and RSS-TV, which were multimedia extensions of RSS. Still others built their own corporate networks around "social video," making it easy for anyone with an internet connection to publish videos.

YouTube championed this last approach. The service started as a video-dating site before expanding its focus to video broadly. YouTube's first hit feature enabled users to embed videos in their own websites. At the time, YouTube's website had a small audience. To the extent video creators had followings, it was usually on their own websites. Hosting video was expensive and complex, and YouTube made it free and easy.

YouTube's video-embedding product is an example of a tactic I call "come for the tool, stay for the network." The idea is to attract users with a tool that piggybacks on existing networks, like the websites of video creators, and then to entice those users to participate in another network, like YouTube's website and app. The tool helps a service reach a critical mass, at which point network effects can kick in. Over time, the alternative network becomes more valuable than the preexisting networks—and harder for competitors to replicate. The tool might get better as the company adds features, but the value of the network increases much more rapidly, at a compounding rate. Today, many services host videos for free, but YouTube stays ahead because the service has such a large audience—which is to say, a large network. The tool is the hook, but the network is what creates long-term value for users and the company.

Fledgling corporate networks regularly employ this tactic. Instagram's initial hook was a free photo-filtering tool. Other apps offered photo filters at the time, but most of them cost money. Instagram made it easy to share touched-up photos on existing networks, like Facebook and Twitter, while simultaneously sharing them on Instagram's network. Eventually, people stopped bothering to share photos anywhere but on Instagram.

YouTube demonstrated the power of this strategy. The service drew in content creators by subsidizing the storage and bandwidth costs of streaming video. Any videos could be uploaded to YouTube and played on any other website for free. The company reasoned that the upside to controlling the network for internet video distribution would exceed the cost of providing a video-embedding tool.

Still, YouTube needed someone to foot the bills. Running a business hosting so many videos was an expensive proposition, and raising outside funding wasn't a surefire solution. Venture capital was a much smaller industry in the mid-2000s, and it was suffering from the aftereffects of the dot-com crash. As users uploaded copyright-infringing material, YouTube also faced existential legal challenges. So, in 2006, YouTube sold to Google, a business flush with ad money whose visionary founders recognized the network's potential as well as its synergy with their existing business. The bet paid off. Today, YouTube contributes more than $160 billion to Google's market cap, according to various Wall Street analyst estimates.

Subsidization helps explain why protocol networks have so much difficulty competing with corporate networks. Services tied to a community-supported network, like RSS, have no source of financing that can subsidize hosting costs to the extent that company-supported networks can. The treasuries of donation-based projects pale in comparison to the war chests of Big Tech giants. Giving away the tool makes financial sense only when the company doing the subsidizing—not the community—will own the ultimate prize: the network.

The Problem with Corporate Networks: The Attract-Extract Cycle

If you ask people to name a specific example of corporate competition, they will likely cite a rivalry between makers of similar products: Coke versus Pepsi. Nike versus Adidas. Mac versus PC. Products that are essentially interchangeable are, in business lingo, called substitutes.

Competition between substitutes is straightforward. A meal at either McDonald's or Burger King will (probably) satisfy a person's appetite, and you wouldn't expect a typical customer to visit both restaurants during a lunchtime rush. Similarly, someone might buy a pickup truck from Ford or GM, but that same person probably won't splurge on both at once. If a customer is going to buy a single product, businesses fight to make sure it's their own.

Products that are bundled or used together are, in contrast, called complements. Coffee and cream are complements. So are spaghetti and meatballs, cars and gasoline, and computers and software. Social networks and content creators, like YouTube and MrBeast, the host of one of YouTube's most popular channels, are complements too. The pairings reinforce the value of the parts: what's a hot dog without its bun, or an iPhone without apps?

One might expect such couplings to be the best of friends, but complements are, in fact, the greatest of frenemies. If customers are willing to pay no more than a fixed amount for a given bundle, complements will fight to claim the greatest share of sales from that bundle. The battles between complements can be brutal, zero-sum affairs. Indeed, some of the most ferocious competition in business occurs between bedfellows.

Imagine a hypothetical clash between food truck suppliers, for instance. If a customer is willing to pay $5 for a hot dog, savvy sausage makers will maneuver to capture more of the $5 that might otherwise go to the bun baker next door. Perhaps the butchers will buy bread wholesale and underprice the competition by pairing cheaper buns, gratis, with wieners. Or maybe they'll market trendy ways of eating hot dogs sans buns, as in organic, gluten-free wurst. Irate bakers might, in retaliation, raise livestock and flood the market with meat to lower the price of a sausage relative to bread. Or maybe they will introduce vegan franks to cut the butchers out entirely.

These examples are silly, but the point is more value for one complement means less value for the other. Both sides will jockey to get ahead as they seek to grow the market for hot dogs in what can be described only as a, yes, dog-eat-dog world.

Network effects complicate the competition between corporate network complements by setting up incentives that are in conflict. On the one hand, a corporate network's complements help grow the network and strengthen its network effect. On the other hand, a corporate network's complements can siphon away revenue that might otherwise have gone to the network owner. The tension between these goals almost always causes the relationship between corporate networks and their complements to snap.

In the 1990s, Microsoft provided a high-profile demonstration of this when it made strategic moves against complements of its operating system, Windows. Microsoft wanted third-party application developers to build on Windows, but it didn't want individual applications to get too popular. When an app started doing well, Microsoft would bundle a free version with Windows, as it did with its Microsoft-branded media player, email client, or, most famously, internet browser. Most of the third-party apps that survived these attacks were too small for Microsoft to care about. From a profit maximization perspective, the best outcome for a platform like Windows would be to have lots of smaller complements with weak, fragmented power, but for the sum of those complements to make the platform more valuable as a whole. (Microsoft's complement-crushing strategy was a major reason why the U.S. Department of Justice accused the company of antitrust violations in 1998.)

Social networks also have a history of conflict with their primary complements, content creators. Consider modern ad-based social networks that seek to maximize profits. Most social networks have high fixed costs covering software development and infrastructure. The marginal costs are low: adding more servers and bandwidth generates more revenue than it costs. For the most part, raising profits boils down to raising revenue. Simple as that.

Social networks can maximize revenue in one of two ways. The first is to grow the network. The most effective way to do this is to create a positive feedback loop where more content leads to more users, and more users leads to more content. It's a virtuous cycle. If people spend more time on the network, the company can make more advertising revenue.

The second way for a social network to maximize revenue is through promoted content. Social feeds generally consist of two kinds of content: organic and promoted. Organic content shows up in users' feeds through the usual algorithmic processes. Promoted content appears because creators have paid to feature it. Social networks can juice revenues by getting more content creators to pay up. The networks can charge more per promotion, and they can also pad users' feeds with more sponsored content. The risk is that at some point the strategy could degrade the user experience and exceed people's tolerance for ads.

A common tactic social networks use to get content creators to promote more content is to let creators achieve a certain scale of audience, and then to adjust the algorithm so the creators no longer receive the same levels of attention organically. In other words, once creators are generating meaningful revenue and have become economically dependent on the network, the network owners dampen the creators' reach so they are forced to buy sponsored posts to maintain or grow their audience. This makes growing one's audience increasingly expensive over time. Content creators call the move a bait and switch, and if you talk to them, you'll hear the complaint regularly.

Companies face the same problem. If you read the regulatory filings of public companies that advertise on social networks, you'll see that the marketing costs for most are rising. Social networks are very good at extracting maximum profits from their most important complements: content creators (including advertisers). This doesn't mean the bait and switch is a nefarious conspiracy by corporate management. It just means that corporate networks will end up behaving this way if they are smart about profit optimization. Why is the pattern so consistent and enduring? Because only the networks that are smart about profit optimization survive.

Independent or third-party software developers are the other important category of social network complements. Developers are valuable to networks because they outsource the production of new software. Social networks often encourage the growth of third-party apps at first. Later the networks identify the apps as a competitive risk and cut them off, just as Facebook once did to Vine and others.

Corporate networks that don't crush complements will often copy or, sometimes, acquire them. When Twitter released its first iPhone app in 2010, it put out a rebranded version of Tweetie, a third-party app it had acquired that year. Soon after, Twitter deprecated features available to other third-party apps, including a variety of feed readers, dashboards, and filters. Developers felt betrayed. Andrew Stone, the founder of one affected app, Twittelator, told *The Verge* in 2012, "Whatever perceived gains that might be achieved by eliminating the third parties should be weighed against the lingering public perception that Twitter got greedy."

Twitter was acting, Stone added, like "the mythological Greek Titan Cronos, [who] began eating each of his children as they were born."

Building startups on top of social networks was widespread in the second half of the 2000s, before the reversal. Conventional wisdom among startups held that besides mobile phones social networks were the next big platform for entrepreneurs. Many of the hottest startups at the time, such as RockYou (ad network), Slide (social app maker), StockTwits (stock market tracker), and UberMedia (another social app maker), were built on top of social networks. Many founder friends of mine were building startups and applications on top of Facebook, Twitter, and other social networks back then. Even Netflix introduced an API in 2008 to encourage third-party development, until shutting it down six years later.

Building on Twitter was particularly popular. People considered it the most open of the corporate networks—that is, until the company changed its policies and killed its developer ecosystem. I worried at the time about startups depending too much on Twitter, a concern I expressed in a 2009 blog post, "The Inevitable Showdown Between Twitter and Twitter Apps."

I should have heeded my own advice. My second startup, Hunch, an artificial intelligence company I co-founded in 2008, depended on Twitter's API. Hunch learned users' interests and offered product recommendations based on Twitter data. My co-founders and I sold the company to eBay in 2011, partly because so much of the open data we depended on was becoming unavailable. (eBay had its own data it could feed into our machine learning tech.)

The transition from open social networks to the closed versions people are familiar with today dates to 2010. One tell, as I noted at the time: Google started warning users who attempted to export their Google Contacts to Facebook, "Hold on a second. Are you super sure you want to import your contact information for your friends into a service that won't let you get it out?" At the time Facebook let users download their personal information—photos, profile info, and so on—but only as an unwieldy .zip file. Facebook made no easy-to-use, interoperable API available. The company was clamping down on its social graph, preventing anyone from easily downloading friend lists. Google blasted Facebook's policy as "data protectionism."

As corporate networks clenched their fists, venture capital funding for applications built on top of social platforms dried up. If these networks wouldn't let anyone building on top get too big, then why invest there? It was very different from the era of protocol networks, like the web and email, when everyone trusted the networks to remain accessible and rent-free in perpetuity and understood that they could get as big as a market allowed. The arrival of corporate networks ended those implicit promises. Building on a corporate network was like building on a broken foundation. The term of art to describe this hazard of the new era: platform risk.

Without third-party developers, corporate networks must rely solely on their own employees for new product development. Look no further than Twitter to see the consequences of misaligned network incentives in action. More than seventeen years after its founding, Twitter is still wrestling with nasty spam problems. Bill Joy, the co-founder of Sun Microsystems, once famously observed that no matter who you are, most of the smartest people work for someone else. When email had a spam problem, smart people who worked for someone else (or often for themselves) came to the rescue. No cavalry would come for Twitter. Platform risk scared everyone away.

Almost all new technologies follow an "S-curve," a growth-over-time chart that resembles the letter S. The curve starts out flat in the first phase, as a technology's developers search for a market and find early adopters. As the builders find product-market fit, the curve begins to tilt up quickly, reflecting mainstream uptake. The curve then flattens again as the product saturates the market.

Network adoption tends to follow an S-curve. As networks climb the curve, the relationship between corporate networks and their complements unfolds in a predictable pattern. The engagement starts out friendly. Networks do everything they can to recruit complements like software developers and content creators to make their services more compelling. The network effects are weak at this early stage. Users and complements have many choices, and they're not locked in yet. The perks are flowing, people are happy, everything's kumbaya.

Then the relationship sours. As the network moves up the S-curve, the platform begins to wield more power over users and third parties. Network effects strengthen, but growth slows. The relationship between the platform and its complements turns hostile. Positive sum becomes zero-sum. To keep profits coming, platforms start capturing more of the money that flows through the network. This is what happened when Facebook strangled Vine and other apps, and when Twitter swallowed its third party

**Life cycle of a network's relationship
to users, developers, and creators**

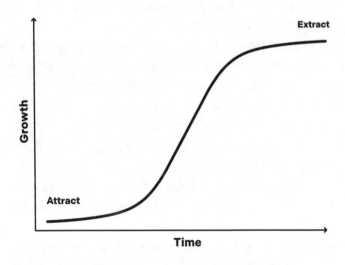

offspring whole. Platforms eventually cannibalize their complements.

An example helps explain why bigger networks often stop interoperating. Suppose you have two networks, a smaller one with
ten nodes, A, and a larger one with twenty nodes, B. If the two
networks interoperate, they will both have thirty nodes. There are
different ways to approximate the value of a network. Let's use
Metcalfe's law, which you may recall states that the value of a network varies with the square of the number of nodes. When interoperating, A's value vaults to nine hundred (thirty nodes squared)
from one hundred (ten nodes squared). B gains less. It also reaches
a value of nine hundred (thirty nodes squared) but from a base of
four hundred (twenty nodes squared). So A becomes 9 times as
valuable, while B becomes only 2.25 times as valuable. A gets a
much better deal.

This is a simple example, but it shows why, as a network grows, adding complements and interoperating with other networks become less attractive. The moment a platform has maximum leverage is the same moment it makes sense to do an about-face. Bigger networks have less to gain and more to lose by interoperating. Why boost potential competitors?

Facebook's fraught relationship with a once-close partner, the game maker Zynga, demonstrates these concerns. For years after its founding in 2007, Zynga was the social network's biggest sensation. Hits like *Zynga Poker, Mafia Wars,* and *Words with Friends* attracted tens of millions of players. Alluding to Zynga's first major breakout game, *FarmVille,* in a 2011 post for *New York* magazine, one writer described the company's popularity thus: "Pretty much anybody who has been on Facebook long enough, which these days is almost everybody, has at some point received a request to adopt a cow."

For Zynga, virtual cows were a cash cow. By 2012, the company had grown to account for double-digit percentages of Facebook's revenue, including by selling users digital livestock. Wall Street analysts called out Zynga's outsized contribution to Facebook's top line as a significant risk. The game maker could lure people away to a gaming platform of its own, after all. So Facebook diversified its revenue and ripped up its partnership with Zynga, nearly killing the company. (Zynga later restarted its business after a years-long turnaround effort and, in 2022, another gaming company, Take-Two Interactive, bought it for $12.7 billion.)

The lesson: big networks can gain from interoperating under the right circumstances, but rivals may gain more. The trade-off favors cooperation early and competition later.

I call this the attract-extract cycle. Corporate networks obey its logic without fail. For complements, the transition from cooperation to competition feels like betrayal. Over time, the best entrepreneurs, developers, and investors become wary of building on top of corporate networks. Decades of evidence show that doing so will end in disappointment. It's impossible to quantify how much innovation this has cost the world. The closest window into the alternative universe where corporate networks remain community owned is to look at the entrepreneurial activity that continues to build on email and the web, which remains considerable even after all these decades. Every year, entrepreneurs create millions of websites and newsletters alongside new software companies, media enterprises, small business e-commerce sites, and more.

Some startup founders and investors, feeling burned, have turned away from the corporate network model—myself included. I know many well-intentioned people who work for corporate networks. The problem is not the people. It's the model. The interests of the company and network participants are simply misaligned, resulting in a worse experience for the user. A corporate network that doesn't run the bait-and-switch strategy will be squashed by competitors that do.

Opacity is another downside of corporate networks. People lose trust when functions like algorithmic rankings, spam filtering, deplatforming, and other decisions are managed inside a black box by for-profit entities. Not sure why your account got suspended? Or why your app was rejected from an app store? Or why you no longer seem to have as much social clout as you once did? Corporate networks have become critical tools affecting people's lives, and they are constant subjects of debate and frustration. Management might change, sometimes sharing your values and other times not. Again, the real problem is the model. Everyone is at the whim of corporate platforms.

Compare this with the transparency of protocol networks. Email and the web are governed by a coalition of entities that enforces laws, as well as communities of users and software developers that make technology decisions. Both processes are open and democratic. Client software is free to add moderation and filtering. If users don't like the way the software works, they can switch to new software without losing their connections. The power is in the hands of the community. Expanding stakeholdership builds trust.

On the bright side, corporate networks like Facebook, Twitter, LinkedIn, and YouTube played a significant role in helping to grow the internet over the last twenty years. The iPhone's introduction in 2007, and the App Store's debut a year later, led to a wave of useful networks that included WhatsApp, Snap, Tinder, Instagram, and Venmo. These corporate networks helped bring advanced services to five billion internet users. They enabled anyone with internet access to become a publisher, build an audience, and potentially make a living. Corporate networks drastically lowered the barrier to entry for people to reach broad audiences in ways that were less specialized and labor-intensive than website making and much more effective than using email alone. In this way, corporate networks improved upon protocol networks. The web's second era helped achieve the dream of the technologists in the early 2000s to upgrade the internet from "read-only" to "read-write."

Corporate networks beat protocol networks because of superior features and sustainable funding. Only email and the web, legacies of the early internet, have resisted the centralizing forces of corporate networks, thanks to their unique history, longevity, and entrenched customs—an instance of the "Lindy effect," where the longer something has been around, the likelier it is to stick around. (Although there is always the possibility that even these protocol networks could get subsumed by corporate networks, even if it's hard to imagine.)

More recent protocol networks enjoy no such resiliency. No credible protocol network, after thirty years of attempts, has succeeded beyond niche adoption. Newer protocol networks are a rarity, and those that technologists do create invariably struggle to gain traction. Corporate networks colonize and overtake new protocol networks like kudzu. Successful networks succumb to the inescapable, profit-driven logic of the attract-extract cycle—just as happened in the case of Twitter versus RSS and so many other examples. The corporate model has simply become too effective.

But software is a creative medium with boundless room for exploration, and the internet is still early in its development. New network architectures can address the problems created by corporate networks. Specifically, networks built on blockchains can combine the best features of prior networks, benefiting builders, creators, and consumers and ushering in a third era of the internet.

Part Two
Own.

4. Blockchains

Whereas most technologies tend to automate workers on the periphery doing menial tasks, blockchains automate away the center. Instead of putting the taxi driver out of a job, blockchain puts Uber out of a job and lets the taxi drivers work with the customer directly.

—Vitalik Buterin

Why Computers Are Special:
The Platform-App Feedback Loop

In the 1989 sequel to *Back to the Future*, the main character travels from 1989 to 2015. Flying cars zip across skyways, but people still use phone booths. Smartphones don't exist.

This is common in pre-internet science fiction: almost no stories foresee the fantastic success of computers and the internet. Why do storytellers so consistently get this wrong? Why do portable internet-connected supercomputers arrive, in reality, before flying cars? Why do computers and the internet improve so much faster than everything else?

The explanation is partly technological. The laws of physics allow us to shrink transistors, the smallest unit of computing machinery, and therefore pack more computing power into smaller volumes. The rate that describes this process is known as Moore's law, named after Gordon Moore, a founder of the chip company

Intel. Moore's law states that the number of transistors that can fit on chips roughly doubles every two years. History proves the rule: a modern iPhone has more than 15 billion transistors, compared with a 1993 desktop PC, which has only about 3.5 million. Very few technologies experience more than a thousand times improvements like this. The physical constraints in other engineering fields are harder to overcome.

The remainder of the explanation is that an economic phenomenon is also at work: a reciprocal relationship between applications, or apps, and the platforms that underpin them. The iPhone today contains many more transistors and other components than the original iPhone, but it also has many more apps. Those apps are far more useful and advanced than the earliest available apps. New apps help sell more phones, which leads to increased reinvestment in phones and, in turn, back into apps. This is the platform-app feedback loop. Platforms, like the iPhone, enable new applications. New apps make platforms more valuable. The back-and-forth creates a positive feedback loop of compounding improvements.

Technological advances and platform-app feedback loops make computers faster, smaller, cheaper, and more feature rich. These forces recur throughout the history of computing. Entrepreneurs created word processors, graphic design programs, and spreadsheets for PCs. Developers put search engines, e-commerce, and social networking on the internet. Builders brought messaging, photo sharing, and on-demand delivery services to mobile phones. In each case, investment alternated between platforms and apps, creating rapid, multiyear growth.

The platform-app feedback loop applies to both community-owned and corporate-owned platforms. Protocols like the web and email benefited from the feedback loop, as did the open-source operating system Linux. On the corporate side, Microsoft benefited from similar loops in the 1990s as developers built apps for Windows computers. App developers are doing the same for Apple's and Google's mobile operating systems today.

Sometimes multiple trends converge and amplify one another, like constructive interference between overlapping waves. Social networks were a killer app for mobile phones; they helped make the devices popular. Meanwhile, cloud computing offered flexible infrastructure that startups could use to quickly scale up their apps, such as social networks, so they could support billions of users. Mobile phones made everything accessible and affordable. Together these trends combined to bring us the magical handheld supercomputers that are ubiquitous today yet which most science fiction failed to imagine.

Major computing cycles typically come along every ten to fifteen years. Mainframes dominated in the 1950s and 1960s. Minicomputers reigned in the 1970s. Then came PCs in the 1980s. The internet took off in the 1990s. And, most recently, mobile phones became ubiquitous starting in 2007, when the iPhone launched. There is no rule that says this pattern needs to continue, but there is a logic to it: Moore's law suggests that it takes roughly ten to fifteen years to improve computing power by a hundred times, and it also takes about that long for many research projects to mature. If the ten-to-fifteen-year pattern continues, then we're in the midst of another cycle.

Multiple trends will drive the next cycle. Artificial intelligence is one of them. The sophistication of AI models appears to be growing at an exponential rate, a function of the number of parameters in their underlying neural networks. The pace of improvement suggests that future models will be much more powerful than already impressive ones out in the market. Another breakout will be new hardware devices like self-driving cars and virtual reality headsets. These devices are advancing rapidly thanks to improvements in sensors, processors, and other components. Big companies like Apple, Meta, and Google are making significant investments in these areas. These are the consensus bets—the conventional picks—for what's next in computing. Almost everyone agrees on their significance.

Blockchains are different. They're a non-consensus bet. While plenty of people recognize their potential—including me—much of the establishment disregards them. In fact, a prevailing view in the tech industry assumes that the only vectors of technological improvement that matter are the ones incumbents are already focused on: bigger databases, faster processors, larger neural networks, smaller devices. The view is myopic. It puts too much weight on technologies originating from established institutions while ignoring ones that come from elsewhere, from the long tail of outside developers.

Two Paths to Adoption: "Inside Out" versus "Outside In"

New technologies follow one of two paths: "inside out" or "outside in." Inside-out technologies start inside Big Tech. They are the more obvious of the two, coming out fully baked from inside established institutions and getting better at the rate at which corporate employees, staff researchers, and others on the payroll improve them. They tend to need significant capital and formal training, which raises barriers to entry.

Most people recognize the value of inside-out technologies even before they exist. It's easy to imagine that internet-connected pocket-sized supercomputers might be popular, as Apple proved with the iPhone. It's also easy to imagine that people might want machines that can learn to act intelligently and do all sorts of tasks, as university and corporate research labs showed with AI. Incumbents pursue these technologies because they see obvious potential.

Outside-in technologies arrive, in contrast, on the fringes. Hobbyists, enthusiasts, open-source developers, and startup founders hatch them outside the mainstream. The work usually involves less capital and formal training, which helps level the playing field with insiders. A lower bar also causes insiders to take these technologies and their proponents less seriously.

Outside-in technologies are much harder to see coming, and they're routinely underestimated. Their builders work out of garages, basements, dorm rooms, and other unconventional spaces, outside official hours. They tinker after work, during breaks, and on weekends. They're motivated by a distinct philosophy and culture that can look strange to the outside world. Other people don't get them. The outsiders launch products half-baked, without clear uses. Most onlookers dismiss their technologies as toylike, weird, unserious, expensive, or even dangerous.

Software is an art form, as you'll remember: just as you wouldn't expect all great novels or paintings to come from people at established institutions, so you shouldn't expect all great software to come from them either.

Who are the outsiders? Picture a counterculture-loving, twentysomething Steve Jobs attending the Homebrew Computer Club, a den of microcomputer-obsessed geeks that hosted monthly meetups in California in the 1970s. Picture Linus Torvalds as a student at the University of Helsinki in 1991, coding up a personal project that would become his namesake Linux operating system. Or picture Larry Page and Sergey Brin dropping out of Stanford and moving into a Menlo Park garage in 1998 to turn their web-link-cataloging project, BackRub, into Google.

The value of outside-in technologies is often unclear before their invention—and may remain so for many years afterward. The web started out half-baked when Tim Berners-Lee concocted it at a Swiss physics lab in 1989, but it grew exponentially as it attracted developers and entrepreneurs who saw its potential. As my technologist friend Sep Kamvar jokes, if you asked people at that time what they needed to make their life better, they likely wouldn't have said a decentralized network of information nodes that are linked using hypertext. And yet, in retrospect, that's exactly what they needed.

Hobbies fuel future industries. Open-source software started out as a niche anti-copyright movement before going mainstream. Social media began as a pastime among idealistic blogging enthusiasts before the world embraced the idea. That T-shirt- and flip-flop-wearing hobbyists spawn large industries may seem like an amusing eccentricity of the tech industry, but hobbies are important for a reason. Businesspeople vote with their dollars: they are mostly trying to create near-term financial returns. Engineers vote with their time: they are mostly trying to invent interesting new things.

Hobbies are what the smartest people spend time on when they aren't constrained by near-term financial goals. I like to say that what the smartest people do on the weekends is what everyone else will do during the week in ten years.

These two modes of tech development—inside out and outside in—are often mutually reinforcing, as you can see in the combination of trends that powered the growth of computing over the last decade. As mentioned earlier, mobile, an inside-out technology pioneered by Apple, Google, and others, brought computers to billions of people. Social, an outside-in technology cobbled together by hackers like the Harvard dropout Mark Zuckerberg, drove usage and monetization. Cloud, another inside-out technology, spearheaded by Amazon, allowed back-end web services to scale. The two modes can unleash powerful forces when they line up, like nuclei fusing.

Blockchains are a classic outside-in technology. Most incumbent technology companies are ignoring blockchains, and some of their employees even dismiss and ridicule them. Many people neglect blockchains because they don't even think of them as computers. Startup founders and independent groups of open-source developers are driving the technology's development. In this way, industry outsiders are leading this new computing movement, just as they did for the early protocol networks like the web and open-source software like Linux.

Blockchains Are a New Kind of Computer

In a 2008 paper, Satoshi Nakamoto, a pseudonymous inventor or team of inventors (the identity remains unknown), introduced the world's first blockchain. Although he didn't call his invention a blockchain at the time—he used the terms "block" and "chain" separately—the community that formed around his ideas would eventually stick the two words together. His paper described a new kind of digital money, Bitcoin, as "an electronic payment system based on cryptographic proof instead of trust, allowing any two willing parties to transact directly with each other without the need for a trusted third party." To remove the trusted third party, Nakamoto needed a way for the system to run computations inde-pendently. To this end, he described a new kind of computer, a blockchain.

Computers are an abstraction, defined by what they do rather than what they're made of. Originally, "computers" referred to peo-ple who perform calculations. In the nineteenth and twentieth centuries, the word started referring to machines that can calcu-late. Alan Turing, a British mathematician, set a more rigorous foundation in a famous 1936 paper on mathematical logic in which he investigated the nature and limits of algorithms. In it, Turing defined what computer scientists would today call a state machine, and what everyone else would simply call a computer.

A state machine consists of two parts: (1) a place to store infor-mation and (2) a means to modify that information. Information stored is called state, equivalent to computer memory. Sets of in-structions, called programs, specify how to take one state, an input, and produce a new state, an output. I like to describe computing through the lens of language, since more people can read and write than can program. Imagine *nouns* represent state or memory: things that can be manipulated. *Verbs* represent code or programs: actions that do the manipulating. As you'll hear me repeat, anything you can dream up, you can code, which is why I compare coding to creative activities like fiction writing. Computers are extremely versatile in this way.

A state machine is the purest way to think about a computer. Nakamoto's blockchain is not a physical computer, like a PC, laptop, phone, or server. It is a virtual computer—meaning it is a computer in function, not in conventional physical embodiment. Blockchains are a software abstraction that overlay on top of physical devices. They're state machines. Just as the meaning of "computers" once shifted from people to machines, so too has the term since encompassed not just hardware but software as well.

Software-based computers, or "virtual machines," have been around since IBM developed the first one in the late 1960s and released it in the early 1970s. The IT giant VMware later made the tech popular in the late 1990s. Today, anyone can run virtual machines by downloading so-called hypervisor software on a PC. Companies commonly use virtual machines to streamline the management of corporate data centers, and they're key to the operations of cloud service providers. Blockchains extend this model of software-based computing to a new context. Computers can be built in many different ways; they are defined by their functional properties, not by what they look like.

How Blockchains Work

Blockchains are by design resilient to manipulation. They are built on top of a network of physical computers that anyone can join but that is extremely difficult for any one entity to control. These physical computers maintain the state of the virtual computer and control its transitions to new states. In Bitcoin these physical computers are called miners, but the more common term today is "validators" since what they're really doing is validating state transitions.

If state transitions sound too abstract, an analogy may help. Think of Bitcoin as a fancy spreadsheet, or ledger, with two columns. (It's more complex than that, but bear with me.) Each row of the first column has a unique address. Each row of the second column contains the number of bitcoins held at that address. State transitions update the rows in the second column to reflect all the transfers of bitcoin executed in the latest batch. That's the gist, really.

If anyone can join the network, how does the virtual computer arrive at a single source of truth about its state? Phrased differently, if the spreadsheet is open to all, how can anyone trust the numbers that appear in its rows? The answer: through mathematical guarantees involving cryptography (the science of secure communication) and game theory (the study of strategic decision-making).

Here's how a proposed state becomes the next state of the computer. During each state transition, the validators run a process to reach a consensus on the next state. First, the validators do as their name says: they validate, making sure every transaction comes with an appropriate digital signature. The network then randomly selects one validator to bundle together qualifying transactions to create the next state. Other validators check to make sure the new state is valid, that all the bundled transactions are also still valid, and that the computer's core commitments have been upheld (for example, in the case of Bitcoin, that there will never be more than twenty-one million bitcoins). Validators effectively cast their vote for a new state by building on it as the transition to the next state starts.

The process is designed to ensure everyone is working off the same, valid version of history—to reach *consensus*. If a validator (or subset of validators) tries to cheat, the other validators have every opportunity to catch it lying and outvote it. The rules of the process are set up in such a way that you would generally need a majority of validators to collude for it not to work.

In our simplified example above, the new master copy spreadsheet is the one proposed by the winning validator. Of course, in reality, there is no spreadsheet. There are only state transitions—the essence of computation. Each state transition is called a block, and the blocks are chained together so that anyone can verify the complete history of the computer by examining the blocks. Hence the name blockchain.

State transitions can contain more than just numbers representing simple account balances. They can hold whole sets of nested computer programs. Bitcoin comes with a programming language, called Bitcoin Script, that software developers can use to create programs that modify the transitions between states. This programming language is, however, limited by design. It mostly enables people to send funds between accounts or to create accounts controlled by multiple users. Newer blockchains like Ethereum, the first general-purpose blockchain, which made its debut in 2015, allow developers to program in much more expressive programming languages.

The addition of advanced programming languages to blockchains is a major breakthrough. It's analogous to Apple's introducing an app store to the iPhone (except where mobile app stores are curated, blockchains are open and permissionless). Any developer in the world can write and run apps, ranging from marketplaces to metaverses, on blockchains like Ethereum. This is a very powerful property that makes blockchains far more expressive and versatile than an accountant's notebook. This is why it's wrong to think of blockchains as mere ledgers for tabulating numbers. Blockchains are not databases; they're full-fledged computers.

Running apps on computers takes resources, though. Both application-specific blockchains like Bitcoin and general-purpose ones like Ethereum need people to pay for the computing power that validates state transitions, and so they must give people a reason to invest in these networks. To that end, Nakamoto introduced a clever twist: the system's digital currency—in Bitcoin's case, bitcoin—would itself be the source of funding for the computers that power it. Other blockchains have since copied the design.

Every blockchain has its own set of internal incentives to get people to participate. In most systems, every new block, or state transition, gives away a small bounty to a lucky validator. ("Validator" can refer to computers that vote on state transitions or to the person or group operating those computers.) The validators that behave honestly—the ones that faithfully verify digital signatures and propose only valid changes to the blockchain—get rewarded. This financial incentive encourages the validators to continue supporting the network and behaving honestly. (Money also flows into blockchains through fees charged to users; more on how this works, and how tokens are valued, in the chapter "Tokenomics.")

Blockchains are permissionless, so anyone with an internet connection can participate. Nakamoto designed the original blockchain, Bitcoin, this way because he believed that existing financial systems were elitist, favoring privileged intermediaries, like banks. Instead, he wanted to put everyone on an equal footing. Requiring an application or screening process would introduce new privileged intermediaries, re-creating the problems he associated with the existing system. But this design had a complication: if any computer could vote, then spam and bad actors could easily overwhelm the network.

Nakamoto's solution was to charge a "fee" to participate. To vote on the next machine state, a miner would need to perform computational work, which costs energy, and submit proof that it did that work. This system—aptly called proof of work—enabled open, permissionless voting while also filtering out spam and other nefarious schemes. Other blockchains, like Ethereum, have adopted another system, called proof of stake (PoS). Instead of requiring validators to spend money on electricity, proof of stake requires them to "stake" collateral, meaning to put money at risk in escrow. If the validators behave honestly, they earn monetary rewards. If they get caught lying—by voting for contradictory state transitions or proposing multiple conflicting state transitions simultaneously, for example—their collateral gets "slashed," or confiscated.

One of the main criticisms of Bitcoin is its excessive energy consumption, which could harm the environment. While clean energy sources, such as excess renewable energy from dams and wind turbines, can mitigate the environmental effects of proof of work, a better approach can be to replace proof of work altogether with less energy-intensive systems, like proof of stake, which eliminate environmental objections to blockchains.

Proof of stake is as secure as proof of work, if not more so, while also being cheaper, faster, and far more energy efficient. Ethereum finished transitioning from proof of work to proof of stake in the fall of 2022, and the results have been dramatic. The next chart shows Ethereum proof-of-stake energy consumption compared with other popular systems.

Many blockchains mentioned in this book, with the notable exception of Bitcoin, use proof of stake. In the future, I expect proof of stake will power the most popular blockchains. Concerns over energy consumption shouldn't hold anyone back from using this powerful new technology.

Neither should the popular misconception that blockchains enable secrecy and anonymity. "Crypto," a word connoting statecraft and intrigue, literally means "encoded" or "hidden." Confusion over how the word is used to describe the industry leads people to believe, mistakenly, that blockchains hide information,

Annualized Energy Consumption (TWh) Comparison to PoS Ethereum

Banking System	239	92,000 x
Global Data Centers	190	73,000x
Bitcoin	136	52,000x
Gold Mining	131	50,000x
All Gaming in USA	34	13,000x
PoW Ethereum	21	8,100x
Google	19	7,300x
Netflix	0.457	176x
PayPal	0.26	100x
Airbnb	0.02	8x
PoS Ethereum	0.0026	1x

and therefore that they're perfectly suited for illegal conduct. This inaccuracy is common, for example, in TV and movies that depict criminals using cryptocurrency to secretly transfer money. It's also dead wrong.

In fact, everything that happens on popular blockchains like Bitcoin and Ethereum is public and traceable. As with email, you can sign up using a fake identity, but there are companies that specialize in de-anonymizing, and it's straightforward for law enforcement to do so. Blockchains are *so* public by default that their innate transparency could actually hinder adoption. This may seem counterintuitive, given the erroneous public perception of crypto as a black box, but it's true. People may be reluctant to use blockchains for certain activities if they fear doing so will expose sensitive information, such as salaries, medical bills, or invoices. Some projects are working to solve this problem by giving users the option to make transactions private. The most advanced projects employ cutting-edge cryptography—especially innovations like "zero knowledge proofs"—which enables auditing of encrypted data that can mitigate the risk of illegal activities and satisfy the needs of regulatory compliance.

Blockchains are "crypto" not because they enable anonymity (they don't) but because they're based on a mathematical breakthrough from the 1970s called public key cryptography. The main thing to know about public key cryptography is that it lets multiple parties who have never before communicated perform cryptographic operations with one another. The two most common operations are (1) *encryption,* which encodes information so it can only be decoded by the intended recipient, and (2) *authentication,* which lets a person or computer sign information, proving it's authentic and actually came from that source. When people describe blockchains as crypto, they mean it in the latter sense of "authenticated," not "encrypted."

Public and private cryptographic key pairs are the foundation of blockchain security. People use private keys, numbers they keep private, to create network transactions. Public keys, in contrast, identify public addresses where transactions come and go. A mathematical relationship ties the key pair together such that it is easy to derive the public key from the private key, but it takes vast amounts of computing power to derive the private key from the public key. This is what enables a blockchain user to send money to someone else by signing a transaction that basically says, "I give you this money." The signature is analogous to signing a check or legal document in the offline world, but it uses math to prevent forgery instead of handwriting.

Digital signatures are widely used behind the scenes in computing to verify the authenticity and integrity of data. Browsers make sure websites are legitimate by checking digital signatures. Email servers and clients use digital signatures to ensure messages aren't spoofed or manipulated in transit. Most computer systems will verify that software downloads are coming from the right source and haven't been tampered with by confirming digital signatures.

Blockchains use digital signatures too. They use them to operate trustless, decentralized networks. "Trustless" may sound confusingly ambiguous, but when people say this in blockchain contexts, they just mean that blockchains need no higher authority—no intermediary, no central corporation—to oversee transactions. Through their consensus processes, blockchains can securely verify the senders of transactions all by themselves, and no one computer has the power to alter the rules.

Well-designed blockchains use incentives to get validators to behave honestly. Sometimes they also punish misbehavior, as in Ethereum's case. Again, consensus systems are the basis of blockchains' security assurances. If the costs to attack a blockchain are high enough and if most of the validators act honestly in accordance with their financial self-interest (as is true for the most popular blockchains), then the system is secure. In the unlikely event of a successful attack, participants could split, or "hard fork," the network and roll back the blockchain to a previous checkpoint—another deterrent for attackers.

Even if some users are dishonest and would rather game a blockchain for profit, the system keeps everyone honest. This is the genius of the system: a set of incentive structures that makes it self-policing. Through well-calibrated economic rewards, blockchains get users to keep one another in check. And so, even though they may not trust one another, they can trust in the decentralized, virtual computer they are collectively helping to secure.

In practice, this trustlessness enables people to design networks that operate very differently from traditional online systems. Most internet services, like online banks or social networks, require you to log in to access your data and money. Companies keep your data and log-in credentials in their databases, which can be hacked or misused. Corporate networks use cryptography in some places but mostly rely on perimeter security, an approach involving a stack of technologies, like firewalls and intrusion detection systems, designed to keep outsiders and unauthorized parties away from internal data. The model is like putting a wall around a fort that's stocked with gold and then trying to protect only the wall. It doesn't work. Data breaches are so common they barely make the news anymore. The perimeter security model heavily favors attackers; it takes only a single gap for an attacker to break in.

In contrast, blockchains let you store data and money, but you can't log in, because *there's nothing to log in to.* Instead, if you want to do something like transfer money, you submit signed transactions to the blockchain. You keep your private data private; you don't have to share it with any service you don't want to. Unlike corporate networks, blockchains have no single point of failure. There are no internal servers to "break into," as there are in typical internet services. Blockchains are open, public networks. "Breaking into" one, if you can even call it that, would require taking over a majority of the nodes on the network—an extraordinarily expensive and entirely impractical proposition.

A key concept in security is the "attack surface," which refers to all the places an attacker might find vulnerabilities. The security philosophy of blockchains is to use cryptography to minimize the attack surface. In the blockchain model, there is no gold to be stolen from inside the fort. Data that needs to be private is encrypted. Only users (and anyone they authorize) have keys to decrypt the data. The keys need to be secured, of course, and users can choose to have third-party software custodians do this for them. The difference is that these custodians are solely focused on security. In the corporate model, all sorts of random businesses with little security expertise are tasked with storing and managing data. A hospital secures health records, an auto dealer secures financial records, and so on. Blockchains unbundle security from business functions and let specialists like custodians do what they do best.

When you hear about alleged blockchain hacks, these almost always refer to attacks on institutions that use crypto, or else they refer to old-fashioned phishing attacks on individuals. They don't usually refer to hacks of blockchains themselves. In the exceedingly rare instances in which blockchains actually do get hacked, they almost always involve small, obscure, insecure blockchains. A successful attack can disrupt transaction processing or enable attackers to "double spend" the same money in multiple places. These attacks are known as 51 percent attacks because their conspirators must gain control of more than half a system's validators to be successful. Feeble systems, like Ethereum Classic and Bitcoin SV, have succumbed to 51 percent attacks. Successfully attacking a major blockchain, like Bitcoin or Ethereum, would, in comparison, be so prohibitively costly as to be infeasible.

That hasn't stopped people from trying. There have been many attempts to attack popular blockchains like Bitcoin and Ethereum, but none have come close to succeeding. The tech is battle tested. These blockchains are, in effect, the world's biggest bug bounty programs. Hacking them could yield a massive financial prize, enabling attackers to transfer large sums of money, worth hundreds of billions of dollars, to themselves. But this has never happened. The security assurances of well-designed blockchains work not only in theory but also, so far, in practice.

Why Blockchains Matter

What would motivate someone to write software that runs on blockchains instead of traditional computers, like web servers or mobile phones? We'll cover the answer to this in greater detail throughout part 3, but let's quickly review blockchains' novel properties.

First, blockchains are democratic. They are accessible to everyone. Blockchains inherit the ethos of the early internet, providing an equal opportunity to participate. Anyone with an internet connection can upload and execute whatever code they want. No user is privileged above any other, and the network treats all code and data equally. It's a fairer framework than the gated status quo of today's tech industry.

Second, blockchains are transparent. The complete history of their code and data is publicly available for anyone to inspect. If the code and data were available only to some people, that would put other participants at a disadvantage, which would undermine the egalitarian promise of the technology. Anyone can check a blockchain's history and be assured that a valid process generated the system's current state. Even if you don't personally audit the code and data, you know others can and probably have. Transparency begets trust.

Third and most important, blockchains can make strong commitments about their future behavior—that any code they run will continue to operate as designed. Traditional computers can't make commitments like these. Traditional computers are controlled by individuals or groups of people, either directly, in the case of personal computers, or indirectly, in the case of corporate computers. Their commitments are weak. Blockchains invert this relationship, putting the code in charge. The consensus mechanism described earlier and the immutability of their software makes blockchains resistant to human intervention. You don't need to trust the promises of people or companies when using them.

Engineers at companies like Google, Meta, and Apple think about computers as machines they can set to do their bidding. Whoever controls the computer controls the software. The only assurances users receive about how the computers will operate are long "Terms of Service" legal agreements written by the software providers which mean little and almost no one bothers to read, let alone negotiate. (As the saying goes, "The cloud is just someone else's computer.")

Blockchains are different. They're remarkable for what they cannot do as much as for what they can do. A blockchain can resist manipulation, a feature that may contribute to the misconception that they're more like databases than computers. Blockchain software runs on other people's computers, but—and this is the key—the software is in charge. A person or company can try to manipulate the software, but it will resist tampering. The virtual computer will continue operating as intended, despite attempts to subvert it.

This resistance to tampering goes not just for blockchains but also for the software that runs on top of them. Applications built on programmable blockchains like Ethereum inherit the platform's security guarantees. This means apps—social networks, marketplaces, games, and more—can also make strong commitments about their future behavior. The entire tech stack, blockchains and anything built on top of them, can make these strong commitments too.

Critics who fail to appreciate the power of blockchains tend to have different priorities. Many people, including lots of workers within Big Tech companies, care about improving computers along familiar dimensions, such as memory and computing power. They see blockchains' abilities as constraints—as weaknesses rather than strengths. It's hard for people accustomed to free rein to appreciate that computers could improve on a dimension that is designed, in part, to undermine their authority.

Breakthroughs that fall outside the norm often get dismissed for the same reason that skeuomorphic thinking is more prevalent than native thinking in the early developmental stages of a new technology: preconceived notions hold innovation captive.

Still, you may wonder, why do computers and applications that can make strong commitments about future behavior matter? As Nakamoto showed, one reason is to create a digital currency. A requirement for successful financial systems is trust in their long-term commitments. Bitcoin commits that there will never be more than twenty-one million bitcoins, a commitment that makes bitcoins credibly scarce. Bitcoin also guarantees that people can't play tricks like "double spending," or using the same money in two places at once. These commitments are necessary but insufficient conditions for Bitcoin's currency to have value. (The currency also needs sustainable sources of demand, a topic I'll discuss in "Sinks and Token Demand.")

Commitments don't carry the same weight on traditional computers because the people or organizations who control them can simply change their minds. If, hypothetically, Google used the standard servers in its data centers to mint GoogleCoins and declared there will only ever be twenty-one million coins, nothing would bind the company to that commitment. Google management could change the rules, and the software, whenever it pleased, unilaterally.

Corporate commitments aren't reliable. Even if Google put a pledge in its service agreements, it could at any time break those terms by revising the agreements, working around them, or shutting down the service (as it has done to nearly three hundred products to date). Companies simply cannot be trusted to keep promises to users. Fiduciary duty trumps other concerns. Corporate commitments don't work, and haven't worked, in practice. This is why the first credible attempt to create digital money was built on a blockchain and not by a company. (In theory, a nonprofit organization might be able to make long-term commitments to its users, but this has had its own challenges, which I discuss in "The Nonprofit Model.")

Digital currencies are just the first of many novel applications that blockchains enable. Blockchains, like all computers, are canvases that technologists can use to invent and create. The unique properties of blockchains unlock a range of applications that simply can't be created on traditional computers. The full range will be discovered in time, but many will involve building new networks that improve on existing networks by offering new capabilities, lower fees, greater interoperability, fairer governance, and shared financial upside.

Some examples include financial networks that commit to borrowing, lending, and other activities on transparent and predictable terms; social networks that commit to better economics, data privacy, and transparency for users; gaming and virtual worlds that commit to open access and favorable economics for creators and developers; media networks that commit to new ways for creators to make money and collaborate; and collective bargaining networks that commit to paying writers and artists fairly when AI systems use their work. I'll discuss these and other networks, and how they lead to better outcomes, throughout the rest of the book (especially in part 5, "What's Next"), but first we'll cover the mechanism by which blockchains enable ownership.

5. Tokens

Technologies that change society are technologies
that change interactions between people.
—César A. Hidalgo

Single-Player and Multiplayer Technologies

If you were stuck on a desert island, alone in the world, money
wouldn't be very useful. Lacking connectivity, neither would computer networks. On the other hand, a hammer, box of matches, or
food supplies would come in handy. So might a stand-alone computer, if you had a power source.

Context matters. Some technologies are social, and some are
not. Money and computer networks are social technologies. They
help people interact with other people. Sometimes, borrowing
from video games, people call technologies that are useful alone
single player. Social technologies are, by analogy, multiplayer.

Blockchains are multiplayer. They let you write code that
makes strong commitments. Individuals and organizations don't
have much need to make commitments to themselves. That's why
attempts to create "enterprise blockchains," which function exclusively inside existing corporate organizations, haven't been suc-

cessful. Blockchains are useful for enabling coordination among people who don't have preexisting relationships. They are most useful when they are not just multiplayer but *massively* multiplayer—in broad use across the internet.

Any social technology that tries to scale to billions of people needs simplifying assumptions. Software, where every line in a code base is a logical statement, can be complicated. At the scale of the internet, which five billion people use today, it gets even more complicated. Each overlapping logical interdependency introduces a greater likelihood for mistakes. More code means more bugs.

A powerful way to address this complexity is through a software technique called encapsulation. Encapsulation reins in complexity by circumscribing units of code within well-defined interfaces, making the code easier to use. If that sounds unfamiliar, it might help to think about an example from the physical world, a device that's so simple people rarely give it much thought: the electrical outlet.

Anyone can plug into an outlet to access electricity and run any number of appliances: light fixtures and laptops, alarms and air conditioners, coffee makers and cameras, blenders and blow-dryers, Xboxes and Model Xs, and so on. Outlets unlock the electrical grid and give humans superpowers without anyone having to understand what's happening on either side of the socket. Outlets abstract away the details. The interface—the encapsulation—is all that matters.

Because software is so flexible, encapsulated code has another benefit: it can easily be reused. Encapsulated code is like Lego bricks. The bricks can be combined into sets of bricks that create much larger and more impressive structures. Encapsulation is especially helpful when large groups of people are developing software, as is the case for most modern software. One developer can create a few Lego bricks—basic pieces of programs that can, for example, store, retrieve, or manipulate data, or access various services, like email or payments. Other developers can then take those components and reuse them, without either party having to understand the details of what the other is doing. The bricks just snap into place.

When it comes to blockchains, a key simplifying concept is units of ownership called tokens. While people often think of tokens as digital assets or currencies, a more accurate technical definition would describe them as data structures that can track quantities, permissions, and other metadata for users on a blockchain. If that sounds abstract, that's because tokens are an *abstraction*. This abstraction makes them easy to use and simple to program. Tokens encapsulate complicated code into an uncomplicated wrapper, just like an electrical outlet.

Tokens Represent Ownership

What tokens *are* matters less than what they *do*.

Tokens can represent the ownership of anything digital, including money, art, photos, music, text, code, game items, voting power, access, or whatever people come up with next. Using some additional building blocks, they can also represent real-world things, like physical goods, real estate, or dollars in a bank account. Anything that can be represented in code can be wrapped inside a token to be bought, sold, used, stored, embedded, transferred, or whatever else a person might want to do with it. If that sounds so simple as to seem trivial, that's by design. Simplicity is a virtue.

Tokens enable ownership, and ownership means control. Tokens that run on traditional computers, like the hypothetical GoogleCoin example from earlier, can be taken away or changed at will, undermining user control. Tokens that run on computers that can make strong commitments about future behavior—namely, blockchains—unlock the technology's true potential.

Take games, for instance. Digital objects and virtual goods have existed for a long time in computer worlds. Popular games like *Fortnite* and *League of Legends* make billions of dollars per year selling virtual goods such as cosmetic items for players' avatars. These kinds of digital goods aren't bought; they're borrowed. Users are renters. The company behind a game can remove or change the terms at any time. Users can't transfer the goods outside the game or resell them or do any of the things people associate with ownership. The real owner—the platform—calls the shots. If the value of an item goes up, the user doesn't reap the reward. Almost invariably, games eventually fade away or shut down, and along with them their virtual goods blink out of existence.

The same is true of most popular social networks. As we've covered, users don't own their names and followers. Platforms do. Some recent examples of Big Tech's bigfooting: When Facebook rebranded itself as Meta in October 2021, the company a few days later revoked the Instagram handle of an artist, @metaverse. (After an outcry and a *New York Times* article, Meta reinstated her account.) Similarly, when Twitter rebranded itself X in 2023, it commandeered the @x handle from a longtime user. Oustings like this happen all the time. You don't have to look far for examples of political figures, activists, scientists, researchers, celebrities, community leaders, and other users getting suspended by corporate networks. Companies that control networks have complete control of accounts, ratings, social relationships, and more. User ownership in corporate networks is an illusion.

Blockchains shift control to software governed by immutable code, not people, and thereby make ownership real. Through the building block of tokens, they give the concept of ownership teeth.

In the early web, the concept of a website played a similar role as a building block. The web's founding idea was to have a sea of information, connected by links, controlled by many different people. It was a profound and ambitious vision, one that could have gotten mired in complexity. But websites were designed to be simple units that could provide a foundation for more complex constructions—building blocks that could, at scale, create the digital equivalent of city blocks.

The read era of the internet was defined by the website, which encapsulated information. The read-write era was defined by the post, which encapsulated publishing, making it easy for anyone, not just web developers, to reach broad audiences. The internet's latest phase—the read-write-own era—is defined by a new simplifying concept: tokens, which encapsulate ownership.

The Uses of Tokens

Tokens, while simple seeming, are not simplistic. They are an expansive technology that comes in two overarching types: fungible tokens, like bitcoin and ether, and non-fungible tokens, also known as NFTs.

Fungible tokens are interchangeable. One token in a set of fungible tokens can be swapped for any other token in the same set. It's apples to apples. Money is similarly fungible. If someone has $10, they don't care which $10 bill they have, just that they have $10.

With NFTs, each token is unique, in the same way many objects in the physical world are unique. I have a set of books—different titles, different authors—on my bookshelf that are distinct and, despite all being books, are not interchangeable with one another. These are non-fungible.

Fungible tokens have many uses, the most prominent being as a way for software to hold and control money. Traditional financial applications don't hold money. They hold references to money, but the money itself resides somewhere else, like a bank. Money that is held and controlled by software is a new idea that didn't exist before blockchains.

The best-known example of a fungible token is a cryptocurrency like Bitcoin. Many public discussions assume that cryptocurrencies are the main use for blockchains. Prominent voices who promote Bitcoin as an alternative to government-controlled money exacerbate the confusion. As a result, many people incorrectly associate blockchains and tokens with libertarian politics even though these technologies are, in fact, politically neutral.

Cryptocurrency, as in new systems of money, is only one of many uses of blockchains and tokens. Fungible tokens can also be used to represent national currencies. People call currency-pegged tokens stablecoins, since they tend to be less volatile than other tokens. One common misconception is that stablecoins pose a threat to the status of the U.S. dollar as the world's reserve currency. In fact, the opposite appears to be true. Demand for internet-native dollars is so strong that most stablecoin issuers have opted to peg their stablecoins to the U.S. dollar. U.S. congressman Ritchie Torres (D-N.Y.), a member of the House Financial Services Committee, which monitors stablecoin adoption, has argued that the technology "reinforces rather than challenges the supremacy of the U.S. dollar" and has "enabled the U.S. to outcompete countries like China in the realm of digital currencies even without a CBDC," an abbreviation for "central bank digital currency." (So far, the U.S. government has no CBDC, whereas the People's Bank of China mints a digital renminbi.)

In the absence of a U.S.-government-backed stablecoin, the private sector has produced a number of stablecoins that vary in the way they maintain their pegs. Some stablecoin issuers back their tokens, one for one, with fiat money held in a bank. USD Coin (USDC) is a popular fiat-backed stablecoin that's managed by a financial tech firm called Circle. The system is designed so that one token can be redeemed for one U.S. dollar. When people trust that the tokens can be redeemed for dollars, they value the tokens that way, even if they rarely redeem them. Many applications use USDC tokens for programmatic money transfers, including decentralized finance (DeFi) applications.

"Algorithmic" stablecoins are another model. These try to maintain their pegs through automated market-making processes. To stay solvent, they automatically sell collateral, such as tokens held in escrow, when market prices decline. Thanks to careful stewardship of reserves, some algorithmic stablecoins, most notably a system called Maker, have successfully maintained their pegs even during periods of extreme volatility. Other algorithmic stablecoins that played fast and loose with collateral have collapsed, including Terra, which infamously crashed in 2022.

Tokens are general-purpose software primitives. They can be designed well or poorly. It's worth noting, by the way, that some people differentiate between the terms "coins," "cryptocurrencies," and "tokens." As you might have noticed, I treat these mostly interchangeably, although I, and many others in the industry, do prefer "tokens" because the term communicates the abstract, generalizable nature of the technology. "Tokens" sounds neutral and so rings truest: it doesn't over-index on financial aspects, as "coins" does, and it doesn't have the political connotations of "cryptocurrency."

Another use for fungible tokens is as fuel for blockchain networks. Ethereum has a native fungible token, called ether, that serves a dual purpose. The first is as a means of payment within Ethereum-based networks, like NFT marketplaces, DeFi services, and other apps. The second is as payment for "gas," a measure of computational effort, which Ethereum requires to run software on its network. Many other blockchains use the same design, requiring token payments to purchase computing resources. The pay-as-you-go model, a throwback to computing in the 1960s and 1970s when time-sharing on mainframes was popular, has made a comeback.

Non-fungible tokens also have multiple uses. NFTs can represent ownership of physical items, like artwork, real estate, and concert tickets. Some people have bought and sold property, such as apartments, using NFTs (tied to LLCs) to transfer ownership and keep a record of transactions, similar to a deed. NFTs are best known, however, as a way to represent ownership of pieces of digital media. The media can be anything, including art, videos, music, GIFs, games, text, memes, and code. Some of these tokens have code attached that can do things like manage royalties or add interactive features.

Because NFTs are so new, it's not always clear what buying one means. In the physical world, when you buy a painting, you are buying the object and the right to use it. You are generally not buying the copyright to the art, or the right to prevent others from using its likeness. Similarly, when you buy an NFT representing an artistic image you are generally not buying the copyright (although buying this is possible—it just depends on the design of the token).

Most of today's NFTs act more like signed copies, analogous to autographed paintings or record albums. The value of an artwork depends on many things, including its scarcity and critical appraisal, but it also depends on some complex mix of social and cultural signals. People assign financial premiums beyond utility value to many things, including art, baseball cards, handbags, sports cars, and sneakers. Similarly, people can assign premiums to tokens that represent objects with cultural or artistic significance. Value is a function of many factors, some objective and some subjective.

NFTs can also have digital utility. One popular use of NFTs is to track transactions such that artists can receive royalties from secondary sales. In games, NFTs can represent objects, skills, and experiences that give players special items and abilities—a warrior's sword, a wizard's wand, a new dance. They can provide access to subscriptions, events, or discussions, as they do in some popular token-gated social clubs through which members convene both digitally and physically.

Another use for NFTs is connecting digital and physical objects. Tiffany & Co. and Louis Vuitton created NFTs that can be redeemed for jewelry, handbags, and other merchandise. The artist Damien Hirst created a collection where the NFTs represent digital artworks but can also be redeemed for physical versions. Other NFTs blur the line between the digital and physical worlds. Nike created NFTs that represent digital sneakers that owners can display and wear in the video game *Fortnite*. Owners also get access to new product drops and events like chats with pro athletes.

For users, the NFTs act as a digital twin of the physical object, breaking down the barrier between the on- and offline worlds. They get the usual benefits of owning the physical products plus online benefits like the ability to trade on marketplaces, showcase on social sites, or equip characters in games. The brands get an ongoing digital relationship with their customers, something most don't have today.

NFTs can also act as identifiers, analogous to DNS names. Recall that by giving users ownership of their names, DNS lowered switching costs in protocol networks. NFT identifiers can play a similar role in newer social networks, letting users switch applications with their names and connections intact.

Users hold and control tokens through software "wallets." Every wallet has a public address, derived from a public cryptographic key, that acts as an identifier. If someone knows your public address, that person can send you tokens. If you have the corresponding private key, you control the tokens in the corresponding wallet.

The term "wallet" originated back when tokens were used solely to represent currencies, but the label is somewhat misleading today. Wallets continue to serve as persistent inventories of tokens that can be carried across the internet, but they are also used for many other types of token, application, and software interactions. A better analogy is that wallets are to blockchains as web browsers are to the web; they're interfaces for users.

Like wallets, "treasuries" bundle tokens together and serve as an interface for users, but they do so at a greater scale. Whereas wallets are mostly used by individuals, treasuries make it easy for larger groups to coordinate. On Ethereum, you can write a treasury application that puts a community, often called a DAO, or decentralized autonomous organization, in control. The community can vote on how to administer the treasury's assets, such as by funding software development, security audits, operations, marketing, R&D, public goods, charitable donations, or educational initiatives. Both wallets and treasuries can also be set to autopilot, automatically investing or disbursing money, or engaging in other programmatic activities.

If tokens are like cells, then treasuries are like full-blown organisms. Treasuries are multiplayer reserves, controlled by software that ensures tokens move only according to prescribed rules. These capabilities give blockchains the ability to stand up to offline organizations like companies or nonprofits—they give blockchains muscle.

The Importance of Digital Ownership

Maybe all this sounds far-fetched or inconsequential. People like to joke that DAOs are just a "chat group with a bank account," that NFTs are just glorified JPEGs, and that tokens are no better than Monopoly money. Even the word "token" is reminiscent of games and arcades. But it would be a mistake to underestimate these technologies' significance.

Blockchains represent a radical departure from the status quo. Through tokens, they flip the script on digital ownership—making users, rather than internet services, owners.

People are mostly accustomed to the reverse. They're used to having all the things they acquire online remain attached to digital services. The same is true of many downloads. You don't really own that e-book you ordered from Amazon Kindle, or that movie you bought from Apple's iTunes store, for example. Companies can revoke these purchases at will. You can't resell them. You can't transfer them from one service to another. Every time you sign up for a new service, you have to start from scratch.

The only internet objects most people feel as if they own are their websites, and only when they own their own domain names. I own my website because I own the domain. As long as I stay within the law, no one can take it away from me. Similarly, companies own their corporate domains. That the one digital asset people feel as if they own is built on the web is no coincidence. Protocol networks, like blockchain networks, respect digital ownership. Corporate networks do not.

Most people are so habituated to the corporate network norm they don't even register its peculiarity. In the physical world, people would be upset if they had to start over whenever they visited a new place. We take for granted that we have a persistent identity and can take objects from place to place. The concept of ownership is so deeply embedded in our lives that it's difficult to imagine how the world would look if that were taken away. Imagine if the clothes you bought could be worn only in the venue you bought them in. What if you couldn't resell or reinvest in your house or car? Or what if you had to change your name wherever you went? This is the digital world of corporate networks.

Perhaps the closest offline analogue to corporate networks are theme parks, where a single company tightly controls the entire experience. Theme parks are fun to visit, but most of us wouldn't want our everyday lives to work that way. Once you pass through the turnstiles, you're subject to the business owner's unchallenged policies. In the real world, outside the park gates, people have agency. They have the freedom to do with their possessions as they please, such as to open shops and businesses that resell goods, and to bring their possessions wherever they wish. People get value and satisfaction from owning and investing in things.

Ownership has positive secondary effects too. Most people's wealth comes from appreciation of the assets they own, such as their houses. Homeowners are known to invest in and care for their places and, by extension, their neighborhoods far more than renters. Improving one's lot improves everyone's lot.

Ownership is also a prerequisite for many startup ideas, so innovation depends on it. A novel service like Airbnb can exist only in a world where people are free to do as they like with their homes, including renting them out. The process of making physical goods usually requires taking other goods as inputs and remixing them without asking for permission. Buy whatever inputs you want and do whatever you want with them because you own them. Many businesses take existing things and reuse them in ways their original creators never imagined—and sometimes might not like. Within limits, like patent law, ownership is a basic freedom that means you don't have to ask for permission to do something new.

The importance of ownership may seem obvious when laid out as I've done above, yet most of us don't really think about it in the context of the internet. We should. The digital world would be a better place if ownership were as widespread there as it is in the physical world.

The Next Big Thing Starts Out Looking Like a Toy

Today tokens are used by a small group of enthusiasts, a tiny proportion of total internet users, perhaps a few million people. It is easy to underestimate them, these early adopters of an odd-seeming, outside-in technology. But this would be a mistake. Big trends start small.

One of the amazing things about the technology industry is how often tech giants miss major new trends and allow startups to rise up as challengers. TikTok mastered short-form video before anyone else, catching tech giants like Meta and Twitter off guard.

It wasn't as if these incumbents were being complacent; most of them aggressively crushed, copied, acquired, and built products to avoid being displaced. Instagram and Twitter had video capabilities well before TikTok became popular, but they prioritized their legacy products instead. Twitter shuttered its short-form video app Vine in 2017. A year later, TikTok went viral in the United States.

The reason incumbents whiff is that the next big thing often starts out looking like a toy. This is one of the main insights of the late business academic Clayton Christensen, whose theory of disruptive technology starts with the observation that technologies tend to get better at a faster rate than users' needs increase. From this simple insight follow nonobvious conclusions about how markets and products change over time, including how startups are so often able to take incumbents by surprise.

Let's review Christensen's theory. As companies mature, they tend to cater to the high end of a market and improve products by increments. Eventually, they add capabilities that exceed what most customers want or need. By this time, the incumbents have developed myopia, focusing on profitable niches to the exclusion of the low end of a market. And so they overlook the potential of new technologies, trends, and ideas. This creates an opening for scrappy outsiders to offer cheaper, simpler, and more accessible products to a wider array of customers who are less demanding. As the new technology improves, the newcomer's market share grows until it eventually overtakes the incumbent.

When disruptive technologies debut, they're often dismissed as toys because they undershoot user needs. The first telephone, invented in the 1870s, could carry voices only short distances. The leading telco of the time, Western Union, famously passed on acquiring the phone because it didn't see how the device could possibly be useful to the company's primary customers, which were businesses and railroads. What Western Union failed to anticipate was how rapidly telephones and their underlying infrastructure would improve. The same thing happened a century later when minicomputer manufacturers, like Digital Equipment Corporation and Data General, ignored PCs in the 1970s and, in ensuing decades, when desktop computing leaders, like Dell and Microsoft, missed out on smartphones. Time and again, a sling and rock beat a lumbering swordsman.

Yet not every product that looks like a toy will become the next big thing. Some toys remain just that, toys. To distinguish the duds from the disrupters, products need to be evaluated as processes.

Disruptive products ride exponential forces that cause them to improve at surprising rates. Products that get better incrementally are not disruptive. Bit-by-bit improvements yield weak forces. Exponential growth comes from stronger forces that have compounding effects, including network effects and platform-app feedback loops. Software composability—a property describing code that is reusable so developers can more easily extend, adapt, and build on what exists—is another source of exponential growth. (Much more on this in "Community-Created Software.")

The other critical feature of disruptive technologies is that they are misaligned with incumbent business models. (I discuss in detail how tokens fit this mold in part 5, "What's Next.") You can be sure that Apple is working on phones with better batteries and cameras. It would be foolish for a startup to try to compete with the company on that basis. Apple knows that improving its phones will make the phones more valuable and help it grow its core business: selling phones. A more interesting startup idea would be something that makes phones *less* valuable. This is something Apple is far less likely to pursue.

A product doesn't have to be disruptive to be valuable, of course. There are plenty of products that are useful from day one and continue being useful long-term. These are what Christensen calls sustaining technologies. When startups build sustaining technologies, they are often acquired or copied by incumbents. If a company's timing and execution are right, it can create a successful business on the back of a sustaining technology.

Few people doubt the significance of many modern technology trends, including artificial intelligence and virtual reality. These inventions play to the advantages of companies like Meta, Microsoft, Apple, and Google, which have the computing power, the data, and the resources to fund their costly development. Big Tech is investing heavily in these areas. Upstart competitors, like OpenAI, need to raise billions of dollars just to compete. (OpenAI has reportedly raised $13 billion from Microsoft.) While some people question how these technologies will square with the traditional ways these companies make money, it's likely that they will extend preexisting business models. In other words, they're sustaining technologies.

To be clear: I believe AI and VR have profound potential, so much so that I co-founded an AI startup back in 2008 and was an early investor in Oculus VR (which Facebook bought in 2014). My point is just that Big Tech recognizes the potential of these technologies too, which makes them less disruptive in the strict sense intended by Christensen. Although people now use "disruption" casually, the term has a precise academic meaning. Disruptive technologies are, by definition, harder to spot than sustaining ones. They elude experts—and that's the point. Incumbents missing disruptive innovation is what makes it disruptive.

One might be forgiven for mixing up the categories. Even Christensen, the expert on the matter, erred. He famously misread the iPhone as a sustaining technology, miscalculating that the device would merely extend the market for phones when, in fact, it would disrupt a much bigger potential market—the market for computers. Such is the innovator's dilemma; even innovators nod.

Incumbents are opening themselves to disruption yet again. Few big companies have taken blockchains and tokens seriously to date, unlike what they've done with AI and VR. Established players don't recognize their significance. In the years since Bitcoin and Ethereum debuted, only one tech giant has made a real run at tokens. Meta started a blockchain project called Diem, formerly Libra, in 2019. Two years later the company sold off its assets and shut down its related digital wallet product, Novi. It's no coincidence, in my view, that Meta also happens to be the only Big Tech company still led by its founder. It takes a visionary to even try to buck convention.

Tokens have all the earmarks of a disruptive technology. They are multiplayer, like websites and posts, the disruptive computing primitives of earlier internet eras. They become more useful as more people use them—a classic network effect that primes them to be much more than mere playthings. The blockchains that underpin them are also improving at a rapid rate, driven by platform-app feedback loops that generate compound growth. Tokens are programmable, so developers can extend and adapt them for myriad applications, such as social networks, financial systems, media properties, and virtual economies. They are also composable, meaning people can reuse and recombine them in different contexts, amplifying their power.

Skeptics who once dismissed websites as "dot-bombs" and who similarly derided social media posts as nothing more than idle chatter failed to see their power. They misunderstood—and missed out on—the extraordinary forces that network effects unleash. New trends and inventions take hold when the networks that sprout around them kick off compound growth. Websites rose in tandem with the read-era protocol network of the web. Posts rose in tandem with read-write-era corporate networks like Facebook and Twitter.

Tokens are, in the read-write-own era, the latest computing primitive to grow and flourish amid a new kind of internet-native network.

6. Blockchain Networks

Cities have the capability of providing something for
everybody, only because, and only when, they are
created by everybody.
—Jane Jacobs

What makes a great city?

The world's best metropolises are a mix of public and private
spaces. Parks, sidewalks, and other shared spaces attract visitors
and improve daily life. Private spaces create incentives for people
to build businesses, adding variety and essential services. A city
with only public spaces would lack the creative vitality that entrepreneurs bring. A city owned by a private company would, in contrast, be a soulless simulacrum.

Great cities are built from the ground up by many different
people with varying skills and interests. The public and private
depend on each other. A pizza shop attracts pedestrians off the
sidewalk, converting them into customers. But it also brings more
people to the sidewalk and helps pay for its maintenance with its
contribution to city revenues through taxes. The relationship is
symbiotic.

Urban planning provides a helpful analogy for the design of
networks. Of the existing large networks, the web and email are

the closest to great cities. As we've said, the communities that build on these networks govern them and receive their economic benefits. Communities, not companies, control the network effects. Entrepreneurs have a strong incentive to build on top of these networks because of predictable rules that guarantee they own what they build.

The internet should feature the same balance between public and private spaces as seen in healthy cities. Corporate networks are like private real estate that entrepreneurs can develop. They are nimble and resourceful. But their success can subsume the commons, crowd out alternatives, and reduce opportunities for users, creators, and entrepreneurs.

An alternative to protocol and corporate networks is needed to restore the internet's balance. I call these new networks blockchain networks because they have blockchains at their core. Bitcoin was the first blockchain network. Satoshi Nakamoto and the project's other contributors built it for a specific purpose: cryptocurrency. But more generalized constructions are possible. Technologists have since extended the underlying design of blockchain networks—and the closely related concept of tokens, which enable distributed ownership—to many more kinds of digital services. They've extended it not just to financial networks, but also to social networks, game worlds, marketplaces, and more.

Before blockchains, network architectures were more limited. With traditional computers, the people who own the computer hardware are in charge. They can change the software however and whenever they like. Therefore, when designing networks for traditional computers, one must assume that any software acting as a network node can potentially "turn evil"—changing behavior to serve the interests of the owner over the interests of the network's users. This assumption restricts the range of feasible network designs. Historically, only two have worked: (1) protocol networks, where a long tail of weak network nodes limits power to the point that it doesn't matter if some nodes turn evil; and (2) corporate networks, which invest all power with the corporate owners in the hope that they don't act badly.

Blockchain networks take a different approach. Recall that blockchains put software in charge, inverting the traditional relationship between hardware and software. This allows network designers to take full advantage of the expressivity of software. They can engineer blockchain networks to have persistent rules encoded in software that are resilient to changes in the underlying hardware. The rules can cover every aspect of the network, including who gets access, who pays fees, how much gets charged, how economic incentives are allocated, and who can modify the network under what circumstances. Blockchain network designers write the core network software but don't need to worry about nodes in the network turning evil and undermining the system. They can instead rely on built-in consensus mechanisms to keep nodes in check.

Blockchains make network design as rich and expressive as software, and they do so on top of solid, persistent foundations. The designs I describe ahead represent what I believe to be the emerging best practices for blockchain networks, but the breadth of opportunity afforded by software's design space could have broader implications than what I discuss. It is possible that there will be other network designs—ones not yet even considered—that will improve upon the ideas presented here. In fact, I expect that to be the case, since almost any network design one can imagine can be encoded in software.

I should note that I use "blockchain networks" as an umbrella term to describe both infrastructure and application layers of the tech stack. If you recall, the internet is like a layer cake. Networking across devices comes at the bottom of the stack. Infrastructure blockchain networks build on top of this. Some of the most popular general-purpose infrastructure networks include Ethereum,

Solana, Optimism, and Polygon. Above this layer are application blockchain networks, including DeFi networks like Aave, Compound, and Uniswap, and newer networks that power things like social networks, games, and marketplaces.

(A quick note about terminology. Many industry practitioners refer to application blockchain networks as "protocols." As I've said before, I avoid this naming convention to prevent confusion with protocol networks, like email and the web, which are, in my framework, a separate category. It doesn't help that some blockchain-related companies take their names from the underlying application networks that they're built on. Compound Labs,

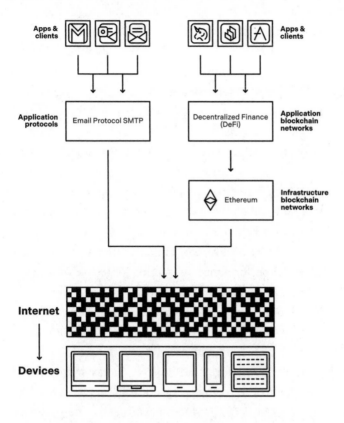

Comparison of email stack to an example blockchain stack

a company that makes client software, is distinct from Compound, the underlying application network, for example. Compound Labs develops websites and apps that provide access to Compound, the underlying network, similar to the way Google develops Gmail to access email.)

Although blockchains have been around for more than a decade, they have started operating at internet scale only in the past few years. This is due to improvements in blockchain scaling technology, which lowers the usage fees blockchains charge and increases the throughput and speed of transactions. In the past, blockchain transaction fees were too unpredictable and steep for high-frequency activities like social networking. Imagine paying a few dollars every time you want to upload a post or click "like"— it would be impractical. In contrast, DeFi networks succeeded despite scaling limits because they generally perform low-frequency, high-volume transactions. If you're dealing with tokens valued at tens, hundreds, or thousands of dollars, paying a few dollars in fees is less of an imposition.

Blockchain performance is steadily improving, following the same platform-app feedback loop that has propelled past computing waves. New infrastructure enables new applications, which in turn drives investment back into infrastructure. Early blockchains like Bitcoin and Ethereum currently process 7 to 15 transactions per second (TPS) on average. Higher-performance blockchains have increased performance by multiple orders of magnitude, including Solana (65,000 TPS), Aptos (160,000 TPS), and Sui (11,000–297,000 TPS). In addition, Ethereum has continued to deliver on its road map of technology updates, which has the potential to scale throughput by more than a thousand times. Evaluating blockchain performance fairly and accurately can be a challenge due to the particularities of each network and the nuances involved in benchmarking; nevertheless, the progress here has been promising.

A variety of technologies have contributed to these performance improvements. One example, in Ethereum's case, is "rollups": second-layer blockchain networks that shift heavier computations "off chain" to traditional computers and then send the results back to the blockchain so that it can verify their correctness. These "layer two" systems build on developments in theoretical computer science that make it so computers can verify computations more efficiently than they can perform those same computations. They depend on advanced cryptographic and game-theoretic methods that have taken technologists years to perfect. Rollups increase the processing power of blockchains while maintaining the strong commitment guarantees that make them useful in the first place.

Today, many applications that can be built using corporate network architectures can also be built using blockchain architectures. But elaborate infrastructure optimizations are often required, meaning that development teams need to have both application and infrastructure expertise, which makes development more difficult and expensive.

As we've seen in past computing cycles, a key moment will be when the infrastructure becomes good enough that application developers no longer need to think about infrastructure. If a team is building a blockchain-based video game, it shouldn't have to worry about esoteric infrastructure scaling issues. Its exclusive focus should be on making the game fun. Similarly, before the iPhone, developers had to be experts in both application design and GPS technology to build location-based applications. The iPhone abstracted away the infrastructure complexity and let developers do what they do best: build great user experiences. Based on current trends, blockchains should reach a point where division of labor acts as a force multiplier in the next few years.

The benefit of building on blockchain networks is that they combine—and improve on—the most desirable properties of earlier network designs. Like corporate networks, blockchain networks can run core services that enable advanced functionality, but they do so on decentralized blockchains rather than on private company servers. Like protocol networks, blockchain networks are governed by communities. And both protocol and blockchain networks have predictability—as well as low or no take rates—which encourages innovation at the network edges.

Yet the built-in economics of blockchain networks make them more powerful than protocol networks could ever hope to be, and I say that as a longtime believer in and supporter of protocol networks. The revenue-generating take rates of corporate and blockchain networks can fund core services and allow these networks to attract capital and make investments to accelerate growth. Unlike corporate networks, though, blockchain networks have weak pricing power, meaning they cannot easily raise take rates (for reasons we'll discuss in depth in "Take Rates"). This constraint—hard-capped pricing power—benefits the community and further encourages people to build on, create for, and participate in the network.

Each network type has a distinct shape and structure based on its unique qualities. We've already seen how protocol networks distribute power broadly among participants and how corporate networks are lorded over by, well, corporate overlords. The architecture of blockchain networks is different from both. Blockchain networks inhabit the "Goldilocks zone." They consist of small core systems surrounded by rich ecosystems of creators, software developers, users, and other participants. Whereas corporate networks centralize most activities in a bloated core and protocol networks have no core, in blockchain networks the core is just right—big enough to support basic services, but not so big as to monopolize the network.

Blockchain networks are *logically* centralized but *organizationally* decentralized. Logical centralization means that centralized

Network Architecture	Strengths	Weaknesses
Corporate Network (e.g., Facebook, Twitter, PayPal)	Can raise, hold, and deploy capital. Centralized services: easy to upgrade, advanced functionality.	Corporate-controlled network effect; high take rate, unpredictable rules. Once at scale (extract phase), weak incentives for users to participate and creators and developers to build on top.
Protocol Network (e.g., web, email)	Community governance and community-controlled network effect. Strong incentive for users to participate and creators and developers to build on top. Zero take rate.	Can't raise or hold capital. Hard to fund core development. Can't provide network funding and incentives. Having no center of network where code and data can reside limits functionality.
Blockchain Network	Software core can raise, hold, and deploy capital. Maintains core services, upgradable, advanced functionality. Community governance and community-controlled network effect. Strong incentive for users to participate and creators and developers to build on top. Low take rate.	New and relatively early adoption, limited user interfaces and tooling. Performance limits sophistication of on-chain code.

code maintains the canonical state of the network. Blockchains allow rules to be encoded in software that can be overridden by neither the hardware nor the people who own the hardware. The core software runs on a blockchain (or "on chain") and contains basic system services that allow network participants to agree on the state of the virtual computer. Depending on the type of network, the core state can represent things like financial balances, social media posts, game actions, or marketplace transactions. Having a core makes it easy for developers to build around the network while also providing a mechanism—such as the ability to take a small cut of transactions—to accrue capital that can be reinvested in growth.

Corporate networks are logically centralized too. They run core code in privately owned data centers, rather than on distributed virtual computers. But corporate networks are also organizationally centralized. The design has advantages, but it comes at a price: company management controls the hardware and can change the rules of the network at any time, for any reason. This leads to the inevitable "attract-extract" pattern, which feels to network participants like a bait and switch, as discussed in "Corporate Networks."

Blockchain networks avoid this fate by placing control of the network in community members' hands. The communities can consist of a variety of stakeholders, including token holders, users, creators, and developers. In most modern systems, changes to a blockchain network can occur only by a vote, usually by users who hold tokens that represent governance rights. This provides assurances to those who depend on the network that the rules will change only when it's in the community's interest. (I cover blockchain governance, including its challenges and opportunities, in "Network Governance.")

Blockchain networks usually don't start out organizationally decentralized, though. In their embryonic stage, they almost always have a small founding team that is managed from the top down. Afterward, a larger, bottom-up community of builders, creators, users, and others takes on maintenance and development duties. There's no limit to how large these communities can get; many blockchain communities today number in the hundreds, thousands, or more. The job of the founding team is to design the core software for the network and an incentive system that encourages growth. After that, they hand control over to the community through a process of progressive decentralization.

An important consideration is deciding what should be centralized and what should be left to community development. The goal shouldn't be to pack everything into the core and mimic corporate networks. Too much centralization will re-create the same problems that corporate networks produce. There should be some central planning, but entrepreneurs should do the bulk of the development. As a rule, if a component of the system can be shifted to the community, it should be. The core should perform only basic services on chain, such as managing governance and community incentives.

One common aspect the community might control is the treasury, a blockchain network's financial core. The communities that control these treasuries are, as we've covered, sometimes called DAOs, or decentralized autonomous organizations. DAOs are somewhat misnamed. They're not autonomous like self-driving cars are autonomous. Rather, they're autonomous in the sense that they are blockchain based; the code that governs them runs on chain and can self-execute when certain conditions are met, such as when participants reach a consensus, usually through token voting. On-chain code can run in perpetuity, execute programmatically, and hold money without depending on outside institutions. DAOs are like the network equivalent of homeowners' associations, making and enforcing rules for communities, but with more automation.

Consider the city analogy again. In a well-designed city, you

Protocol Network

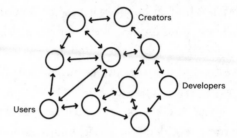

Corporate Network

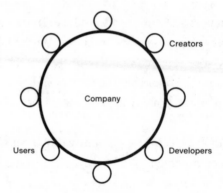

Blockchain Network

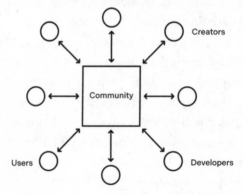

would expect to have a town hall, a police department, a post office, schools, sanitation crews, and other essentials. Residents and businesses depend on these services, which offer a foundation upon which to develop the rest of the city. Municipal services are centralized for efficiency, but they are still beholden to the populace. The community controls the services through elections.

Blockchain functions have neat analogues in urban planning. Starting a blockchain network is like building a new city on undeveloped land. The city designer constructs some initial buildings and then designs a system of land grants and tax incentives for residents and developers. Property rights—ownership—play a key role, providing strong commitments that property owners will get to keep what they own and can feel comfortable investing in it. As the city grows, so does the tax base. Taxes are reinvested into public projects like streets and parks, more land is given away, and the city grows.

In the case of blockchain networks, token rewards are like land grants, incentives given to contributors for various activities. Tokens confer ownership, enshrining property rights. Take rates are like city taxes, fees the network charges for access and transactions. DAOs are like city governments, responsible for overseeing the development of infrastructure, resolving disputes, and allocating resources to maximize the network's value. Through this combination of features, successful blockchain networks encourage bottom-up, emergent economies.

Imagine you are an entrepreneur looking to start a local business. The first thing you will want to know is the rules of the city you're in. Are they predictable? Will any rule change follow a fair process? Are the taxes reasonable? If your business succeeds, will you receive the financial upside? Fairness and predictability encourage you to invest your time and money. Your success and the city's success are mutually dependent. You have an incentive to help the city grow and prosper, and the city has an incentive for you to grow and prosper as well. The considerations are the same in a blockchain network.

The bottom-up, collaborative software development model of blockchain networks might seem strange to those more familiar with the top-down, corporate software development model. But bottom-up development is what built protocol networks and continues to build open-source software. It is also the same spirit of crowdsourced collaboration that powers websites like Wikipedia. Blockchain networks take this long-standing model and apply it to the killer app of the internet, networks.

In the next section, we'll explore the most compelling features of blockchain networks, starting with their embrace of openness. We'll dig into software composability and low take rates, which give blockchain networks competitive advantages over other network types. We'll tease apart blockchain networks' economics, including the incentives and strong commitments they offer to users, developers, and creators. And we'll see how these properties encourage the formation of real communities—inclusive and expansive sets of stakeholders who guide, govern, and share in the value these networks create.

Part Three
A New Era

7. Community-Created Software

Think Zen. The project belongs to no one and to everyone.

—Linus Torvalds

Until the 1970s, being in the tech business meant selling hardware, including microchips, data storage, and computers. Then a contrarian idea popped into the head of a shrewd kid. What if software could be a good business? In fact, what if it could be a great business—even *better* than hardware? Compelled to test the theory, the guy abandoned plans for law school, dropped out of college, and founded Microsoft.

I'm talking about Bill Gates, of course. Gates recognized that operating systems for personal computers could accumulate immense power through the harnessing of network effects. He foresaw that consumers would flock to operating systems and software applications instead of the hardware underneath. Application developers would build for the most popular operating systems, not the best-selling machines. This would create a self-reinforcing platform-app feedback loop. Software would be king.

Incumbents had no idea what was about to hit them. In 1980,

IBM agreed to license Microsoft's early crown jewel, the DOS operating system, in a deal that allowed Microsoft to continue to sell the software to other manufacturers. IBM failed to appreciate its oversight. More PC makers were entering the fray, copying IBM's designs, and turning computer hardware into a commodity. This was the context in which Microsoft flooded the zone, spreading its operating systems far and wide until they became the industry standard. For the next twenty years, software was the most lucrative business in technology.

But another turn of the tech cycle would arrive, and as Microsoft grew more powerful, a sect of programmer activists struck back by forming the open-source software movement. As Tim O'Reilly, the tech publishing magnate, described the situation in his 1998 blog post "Freeware: The Heart & Soul of the Internet," "Despite all Microsoft's efforts to convince the world that the capital city of the Internet is in Redmond, and Netscape's rival claims that it's in Mountain View, the real headquarters exist only in cyberspace, in a worldwide, distributed community of developers who build on each other's work by sharing not only ideas but the source code that implements those ideas."

The open-source movement would put downward pricing pressure on software. In particular, the movement would commoditize server-side software, the kind that runs in data centers—a shift that echoed the hardware-to-software upheaval Microsoft once led. Tech industry players responded by "moving up the stack," focusing on services instead of software. A new buzzword—"software as a service," or SaaS—soon took root.

Fast-forward to today and most tech companies are in the services business. They charge either for services or for advertising connected to services. Google, Meta, Apple, and Amazon are all in the services business. Tellingly, even Microsoft, the pioneer of the software model, now considers itself a services company.

In the 2000s, at the beginning of the read-write era, it seemed as if the shift to services might lead to greater openness and inter-operability across the internet. APIs, which connect internet services, were all the rage. Developers were creating services that remixed, modified, and reused other services into so-called mashups. YouTube gained popularity as a video widget to be embedded in blogs and other websites. Early delivery and ride-sharing apps hooked into Google Maps. Blogs and social networks bolted on commenting apps like Disqus and showcased third-party photos from sites like Flickr. They did this all for free; no one asked for permission.

At the time, it seemed as if a spirit of interoperability might suffuse the internet forever. In a retrospective for *The Atlantic* in 2017, the journalist Alexis Madrigal captures the decade-earlier optimism:

> In 2007, the web people were triumphant. Sure, the dot-com boom had busted, but empires were being built out of the remnant swivel chairs and fiber optic cables and unemployed developers. Web 2.0 was not just a temporal description, but an ethos. The web would be open. A myriad of services would be built, communicating through APIs, to provide the overall internet experience.

And then, in another turn of events, the iPhone debuted. The ground suddenly shifted with the rise of smartphones. Protocol networks lost their balance, and corporate networks gained the surer footing, as Madrigal relates:

> As that world-historical explosion began, a platform war came with it. The Open Web lost out quickly and decisively. By 2013, Americans spent about as much of their time on their phones looking at Facebook as they did the whole rest of the open web.

Blame the cruel logic of corporate extraction for what went wrong. As we've covered, the attract-extract cycle arises, inescapably, from an inherent tension in the design of corporate networks. The path follows the tech adoption S-curve. After a certain point, what's good for a network owner conflicts with what's best for network participants. In the early 2010s, mobile phones catalyzed a platform shift that accelerated the rise of corporate networks. As corporate networks gained ground, their optimal business strategy switched from attract to extract. With so many corporate networks switching to extract mode at once, power rapidly concentrated. APIs withered, interoperability fizzled, and the open internet got packed away into silos.

Modding, Remixing, and Open Source

Interoperability still persists in some categories of internet services. It thrives, notably, in video games where users create "mods": game remixes or DIY components that can consist of altered art, modified gameplay, randomized game elements, add-ons such as new weapons or tools, and other custom bits.

Modding has been around since the beginning of PC gaming in the 1980s. At the time, gamers were mostly programmers who liked to experiment with software—hackers, in other words. Game studios knew what their audiences craved and so embraced modding. id Software, maker of the hit first-person shooter game *Doom*, was perhaps the most famous example. In 1994, one *Doom* player went so far as to re-create inside the game the 1986 sci-fi movie *Aliens*, Xenomorph-grappling exoskeleton suit and all. The 1996 sequel to *Doom*, *Quake*, even included its own programming language to make modding easier.

Today, modding is mainstream in gaming on PCs, where the platforms tend to be more open than they are on consoles and mobile phones. The popular PC game store Steam has hundreds of millions of pieces of user-generated game mods and components. It's not uncommon for hit games to begin as mods of other games, including *League of Legends* (an adaptation of a *Warcraft III* mod called *Defense of the Ancients*) and *Counter-Strike* (a mod of the first-person shooter game *Half-Life*). Most of the content in the popular game *Roblox* is generated by users who create and remix existing game content. Making and remaking things is a big part of the game's appeal.

Many video games are playgrounds for modding, but the area where the activity has found the greatest success is open-source software. Contributors typically work as volunteers, often on a part-time basis. They're loosely organized and scattered around the world, and they depend on remote collaboration and knowledge sharing. Anyone can reuse open-source code in their own software, free of charge, with minimal restrictions.

Open source began as a radical idea, part of a fringe political movement in the 1980s. Proponents opposed the idea of copyrighting code on ideological grounds, believing that anyone should be allowed to tinker with software as they please. The campaign became a more pragmatic technology movement in the 1990s, yet still remained mostly at the edges of the software industry. It wasn't until the 2000s that open source started going mainstream, particularly following the rise of the now ubiquitous open-source operating system Linux.

Given open-source software's humble origins, it might surprise you to learn that most software running in production around the world today is open source. When your phone connects to the internet, it talks to computers in data centers, most of which are running open-source software like Linux. Android phones run mostly open-source software, including Linux. Most next-generation devices like self-driving cars, drones, and VR headsets run Linux and other open-source code. (iPhones and Macs run a mix of open-source and proprietary software from Apple.)

How did open source take the world by storm? One of the main reasons the movement has been so successful is a feature of software known as composability.

Composability: Software as Lego Bricks

Composability refers to a property of software that allows smaller pieces to be assembled into larger compositions. Composability depends on interoperability, but it takes the idea further by combining systems the way one builds using Lego bricks, as mentioned in "Tokens." Composing software is like making music or writing, where larger creations, like symphonies or novels, are composed of smaller parts, like strings of notes or words.

Composability is so central to software that most computers assume all code is composable by default. Computers enact this assumption via a two-step process when preparing to run code. First, a program called a compiler converts the software's source code, written in a human-readable language, into a lower-level, machine-readable language. Then all the other composable bits of code referenced by the software are brought in by a program called a linker. The linker links—or composes—all the pieces of code into one big executable file. And so software is an art of composition.

Composability unlocks the best humanity has to offer. Almost every project on GitHub, an online code repository for open-source developers, contains references to other open-source projects hosted there. For most projects, the bulk of their code is new compositions of other code. The collective set of code repositories make up a branching tree of billions of interconnected ideas created by millions of people, most of whom have never met, yet who work collaboratively to advance the global store of knowledge. (And if you need more proof of open source's mainstream arrival: GitHub is now owned, ironically, by the movement's formerly biggest adversary, Microsoft.)

The power of composability is that once a piece of software is written, it never needs to be written again. If you browse GitHub, you'll see free open-source code for almost anything you might want to do, from math formulas to website development to video game graphics. The code can simply be copied and reused as a component in other software. Then the other software can be copied and reused, ad infinitum. When this happens inside a company, it makes the company more productive. When this happens in open-source repositories, it speeds up software development everywhere.

Albert Einstein once purportedly said that compounding interest is the eighth wonder of the world. Whether or not Einstein actually said this (he probably didn't), the wisdom holds true. Principal generates interest, which grows the principal, yields more interest, and piles up ever greater returns. The remarkable effects of compound growth are not limited to finance. Many things in the world that grow exponentially do so because of underlying compounding processes. For instance, exponential improvements in computing hardware are described by Moore's law, as discussed in "Blockchains." Composability is software's version of compounding interest.

The reason composability is so powerful is that it combines multiple forces, each of which is powerful on its own:

- **Encapsulation.** One person can create a component and another person can use it, without understanding the details of how it's made. This allows a software code base to grow quickly while the complexity, and likelihood for errors, grows much more slowly.

- **Reusability.** Every component needs to be created only once. As soon as something like a game element or open-source software component is created, it can be reused over and over without needing anyone's permission. It becomes a building block, forever. When this occurs in permanent repositories on the open internet, collective software development advances through the contributions of a global hive mind.

■ **The wisdom of crowds.** Recall Bill Joy's quip that no matter how smart you are or how many smart people work for you, most of the smartest people work somewhere else. Reusing software means you can tap the intelligence of all those other people. There are tens of millions of smart developers with varied areas of expertise. Composability lets you absorb that expertise as much as you like.

For all its power, software composability hasn't yet reached its full potential. It has been mostly limited to static code sitting in repositories as opposed to services in which code is live and running. The reason is that computation costs money. The contributor model that sustains open-source software—namely, reliance on charitable donations and ad hoc volunteers—doesn't work so well for open-source services. Developers can lend time writing software, but they need financial resources to host and run the software. What's missing is a business model that provides ongoing funding to pay for bandwidth, servers, energy, and other costs.

Composability for software services stalled out when corporate networks stopped interoperating. You can still find APIs for Big Tech corporate networks like YouTube, Facebook, and Twitter, but these APIs have restrictive rules and limited features. The providers decide what information they send, to whom, and on what terms. In the switch from attract to extract mode, corporate networks tightened their grip and left third-party builders in the lurch. Outside developers learned not to depend on them.

It's worth noting there are still popular APIs in the business-to-business enterprise software space. Successful API providers include Stripe for payments and Twilio for communications. These APIs hide complex code behind simple interfaces, so they offer one benefit of composability, encapsulation. But they miss out on the other two benefits. The code powering the APIs is mostly closed source, which means it neither benefits from crowdsourced wisdom nor contributes back to the global knowledge base of coders everywhere. Moreover, these APIs can be used only with permission, and their providers can change the fees and rules at will. Permissioned APIs are useful in corporate contexts, but they don't advance the vision of an internet built from open and remixable services.

Ideally, anyone building on other services and APIs will receive strong commitments that the services not only are open but will remain open, indefinitely, so they can be depended on. You can't get guarantees of openness unless services are financially independent.

Where corporate networks failed, blockchains provide a solution. Blockchain networks make strong commitments that the services they offer will stay remixable, without needing anyone's permission, in perpetuity. They do this in two ways. First, they provide strong, software-encoded assurances that their prices and access rules won't change. Once the initial development team behind a blockchain network deploys its code, the services they push live are either fully autonomous or, in some network designs, amendable only by a community vote. The platform is dependable.

Second, blockchain networks fund hosting expenses through sustainable financial models that use tokens. Ethereum has tens of thousands of validators, or network-hosting servers, spread around the world. The network itself covers its own hosting costs—servers, bandwidth, energy—by distributing token rewards to validators. So long as there is demand for the Ethereum network, and users and applications pay transaction fees to use it, the validators get paid for the hosting services they provide. So the ground to build on isn't just solid and stable; it's rich in renewable resources.

The Cathedral and the Bazaar

Composability is a time-tested force that demonstrates its power again and again, most strikingly with the success of open-source software. Yet the vision for an open internet built from composable services has fallen short because corporate networks have always pulled back. As corporate networks grow, their interests shift away from being open to being closed. It's naïve to count on a company not to be evil just because its motto is "Don't be evil." Companies will generally do whatever it takes to maximize profits. If they don't, they won't last long as they'll fall behind other companies that do.

Blockchain networks turn "Don't be evil" into "Can't be evil." Their architecture provides strong guarantees that their data and code will forever remain open and remixable.

The debate between the monolithic design of corporate networks and the composability-friendly design of blockchain networks mirrors a similar debate in the 1990s over the design of operating systems. In his famous 1999 essay, "The Cathedral and the Bazaar," the programmer and open-source software advocate Eric Raymond contrasts two models of software development. In the first model, popularized by closed-source companies like Microsoft, software is "built like cathedrals, carefully crafted by individual wizards or small bands of mages working in splendid isolation." In the second model, popularized by open-source projects like Linux, the community seems "to resemble a great babbling bazaar of differing agendas and approaches," and the guiding philosophy is "release early and often, delegate everything you can, be open to the point of promiscuity."

Raymond favored the promiscuity of the bazaar to the isolation of the cathedral. In an open-source community, "every problem will be transparent to someone," and the crowd can work together to outperform centralized competitors:

> The Linux world behaves in many respects like a free market or an ecology, a collection of selfish agents attempting to maximize utility which in the process produces a self-correcting spontaneous order more elaborate and efficient than any amount of central planning could have achieved.

Since the advent of computer programming almost eighty years ago, the pendulum has swung back and forth between these two modes of software development. Corporate networks are today's cathedrals, and blockchain networks are the bazaars. Blockchain networks bring the power of software reuse and remixes to a modern form that can rival corporate networks. The networks of the future can be like great cities, built through the creative collaborations of millions of people with diverse skills and interests who share resources and work together, brick by brick, toward common goals.

8. Take Rates

Your margin is my opportunity.

—Jeff Bezos

If you were an executive at an established business and you heard some hotshot dot-com founder utter the above threat in the mid-1990s, you might have laughed at the hubris. Later you would regret doing so.

Jeff Bezos, the founder of Amazon, was referring, without embellishment, to his strategy for seizing market share. The plan: minimize overhead, slash prices, eat rivals' profits. Be lean, be mean. Be relentless.

The cost structures of the physical retailers that were Amazon's competitors at the time prevented them from matching Amazon's price cuts. Brick-and-mortar expenses, like rent, utilities, and shopkeepers' wages, set hard limits to incumbents' pricing. With no physical stores to support, Amazon could keep prices low. So Amazon pressed its advantage, undercut many of its competitors, and put them out of business.

Amazon's lower cost structure lent itself to a deflationary business model, one that maintains or increases the value of a service while decreasing the cost to consumers over time. This combination of tactics has been popular since the early days of the commercial internet. It explains how Craigslist absorbed newspaper classifieds businesses, how Google and Facebook swallowed advertising-based media, and how Tripadvisor and Airbnb tackled the travel industry. In each case, the disrupters slashed costs and upended incumbents that were attuned to the cost structures of an earlier era.

Blockchains are the natural successors of this strategy. Just as internet startups undercut the high prices of traditional businesses, blockchain networks expose the soft underbelly of corporate networks: high take rates.

Network Effects Drive Take Rates

Networks make money by charging fees on network activities like commerce or advertising. The percentage of revenue passing through a network that the network owner takes for itself, as opposed to passing on to network participants, is, as you'll recall, the network's take rate. Absent other checks on a system, strong network effects usually mean high take rates because they lock in network participants who have few, if any, alternatives to turn to.

In the pre-internet era, scale was the main driver of pricing leverage. On the internet, it's network effects that drive pricing leverage. Today's biggest social media companies have very high take rates, demonstrating the strength of corporate network lock-in.

Of the large social networks, YouTube is the most generous with creators, taking 45 percent of revenue for itself and passing 55 percent to creators. In its early days, YouTube faced stiff competition from other up-and-coming video platforms that were offering to share half their ad revenue with creators. Feeling threatened, YouTube set up its revenue-splitting "partner program" at the end of 2007, and it has stuck to it ever since.

Such generosity is uncommon, though. Facebook, Instagram, TikTok, and Twitter extract about 99 percent of their networks' primary revenue source, advertising. These networks have all recently created cash-based programs to give creators kickbacks. Most of these programs take the form of time-bound "creator funds" and static pools of money rather than YouTube-style revenue shares. Creators receive mere fractions of these networks' take-rate revenues, usually less than 1 percent, and the companies are under no obligation to continue supporting these funds over the long term. Worse, the fixed-pot model can make the relationship between platform and creator zero-sum since it forces people to fight over limited resources. As Hank Green, a longtime YouTuber points out, "When TikTok becomes more successful, creators make less per view."

Even after accounting for their creator funds, the biggest social networks share almost nothing with network participants. This is great for the networks, but not for creators, who provide content without receiving their fair share of revenue in return. On the other side of the networks, these companies use their leverage to extract personal user data instead of money, which helps them earn more through better ad targeting. Network effects with lock-in amplify pricing power.

Apple has extraordinary pricing power thanks to its captive audience of iPhone users combined with the network effect derived from the iOS developer ecosystem. Apple exercises this power through strict rules around payments, which the companies subject to them loathe. Ever try to subscribe to Spotify or buy an Amazon Kindle book via an iOS app? You can't. These businesses don't want to pay Apple's take rate, which can run as high as 30 percent. A common work-around app developers use to circumvent Apple is to accept payments only in mobile web browsers, not in apps. (The web and email are the last free havens on mobile phones.) On a technical level, Apple could override this bypass and force all transactions to route through the App Store, but Apple hasn't dared to clamp down here. No doubt there would be a strong backlash, and probably legal and regulatory ramifications.

Some companies would rather go to war than fork over so much of their revenue to Apple. In fact, app developers are so fed up with Apple's take rates that they've banded together to sue Apple over its dominant market position. But unless courts and regulators say otherwise (and barring some other unexpected business comeuppance), Apple can—and will—keep charging remarkably high fees. It has that power because it has a captive network.

If monopoly exacerbates rate taking, competition keeps it in check. Fees on payment networks remain relatively low thanks to the prevalence of interchangeable payment options. Multiple payment networks offer similar services, including Visa, Mastercard, and PayPal. The abundance of choice reduces businesses' pricing power, to consumers' benefit. As a result, credit card networks charge 2 to 3 percent on every transaction, a relatively low take rate, and much of that goes back to consumers in the form of points and other incentives. (One could argue these rates are still too high, a point I discuss later in "Making Financial Infrastructure a Public Good.")

Physical goods marketplaces tend to have take rates in the midrange, higher than payment networks but much lower than social networks. For example, eBay (mostly secondhand goods), Etsy (handmade items), and StockX (sneakers) have take rates between 6 and 13 percent. Users can choose where to sell items and can cross-post listings on multiple sites. The take rates are lower partly because sellers earn lower margins from these goods, but also because of weaker network effects. Buyers discover items mostly through search results rather than social feeds, which lowers the cost for sellers to switch networks. Sellers can take their wares to any network they want because they own the physical goods they're selling. When network participants own what's valuable to them, switching costs drop and bring take rates down.

Protocol networks have no companies in the middle taking a cut of revenue, so they have no take rates. You own your domain name, and you can take it to any hosting provider you wish, no questions asked. Some access points, such as email and web hosting providers, charge for certain services; however, because protocol networks don't have network effects that accrue to a central entity, as corporate networks do, hosting providers have little pricing power and must charge based on the costs of storage and networking, rather than as a percentage of revenue. As a result, even with these fees, the *effective take rate*—the actual price network participants end up paying to use the network—stays very low.

Effective take rates can be sneaky, like hidden fees that crop up at the checkout counter. Corporate networks often have effective take rates that exceed their apparent take rates. These networks raise rates by dialing down the organic reach of network participants in algorithmic social feeds and search results. Once creators, developers, sellers, and others attain a certain scale, corporate networks force them to buy ads to maintain or grow their audience.

You may notice, for instance, how a search on Google or Amazon yields an ever-increasing number of sponsored results (look for the "sponsored" label). Big companies use this technique to raise the effective rates on the supply side of the network, which for Google is websites and for Amazon is sellers. On Google, a website doesn't pay for organic links, but it has to bid in an auction for sponsored links. On Amazon, sellers are charged a fee, but if they want sponsored placement, they're charged additional fees. Google and Amazon know that users tend to click on the top links in search result rankings so, as they push organic links down, they are effectively forcing websites and sellers to pay more for the same exposure. As if that weren't bad enough, these companies also use valuable screen real estate to promote their own products, which compete with those of their suppliers.

Google, Amazon, and other big companies were disrupters in their early days, when they were in the attract phase. Today, in their extract phase, they're focused on squeezing as much revenue as they can out of the networks they own. Thus, corporate network owners not only suck up almost all network revenue, but they find ways to extract additional fees on top of that. Network participants get left high and dry. They spend years cultivating followings; then the rules change, and they are forced to pay even more to reach the audiences they built.

Big Tech's high take rates are bad for network participants, but they're great for their own profit margins. Meta has gross margins of over 70 percent, meaning that for every dollar in sales, it keeps more than 70 cents for itself (with the remainder paying costs related directly to revenue generation, like running data centers). Big Tech companies that own networks spend some of this windfall on fixed costs such as head count and software development. They realize the rest as profit. Inside these companies, thousands of employees work in management and sales, and some work on new R&D projects. But they also have layers of middle managers and wasteful bureaucracy enabled by the excess.

Where bean counters see fat margins, entrepreneurs should see blood. *Your take rate is my opportunity,* as Bezos might say.

Your Take Rate Is My Opportunity

Blockchain networks disrupt rent-seeking intermediaries, allowing them to take market share from extortionary corporations by lowering prices. Networks with a greater ability to lock in consumers have more pricing power. More pricing power translates into higher take rates. The higher the take rate of an incumbent network, the more opportunity there is for disruption.

Popular blockchain networks have very low take rates, ranging from below 1 percent to 2.5 percent. That means the rest of the money flowing through the networks goes to network participants, including users, developers, and creators. Compare the take rates of popular corporate networks with Ethereum and Uniswap, popular blockchain networks, and OpenSea, a marketplace built on top of blockchain networks:

Corporate Networks	Take Rate		Blockchain Networks/ Applications	Take Rate
Facebook	~100%		OpenSea	2.5%
YouTube	45%		Uniswap*	0.3%
iOS App Store	15-30%		Ethereum**	0.06%

*Most popular fee tier. **Calculated as total gas fees paid by users divided by total transfer value of ETH and top ERC20 tokens in 2022 (source: Coin Metrics)

Blockchain networks have low take rates because of rigid constraints set by their core design principles, namely:

- **Code-enforced commitments.** Blockchain networks commit to take rates up front at launch that cannot be changed except by the consent of the community. This forces networks to compete for network participants by offering commitments to lower take rates. In competitive markets, take rates will trend close to the cost of maintaining and developing the network.

- **Community control.** In well-designed blockchain networks, take rates can be increased only if the community votes to do so. This contrasts with corporate networks where the owner can raise take rates unilaterally, at the expense of the community.

- **Open-source code.** Because all blockchain code is open source, it is easy to "fork," or create a copy of it. If a blockchain network raises take rates too high, a competitor can create a forked version with lower rates. The threat of forks helps keep take rates in check.

- **Users own what they value.** Well-designed blockchain networks interoperate with standard systems that guarantee that users own the things they care about. For example, many blockchain networks interoperate with the Ethereum Name Service (ENS), a popular naming system on the Ethereum blockchain. That means I can use my ENS name (cdixon.eth) across many different networks, and if the networks change the rules or raise the take rates, I can easily switch to a new network without losing my name or network connections. Lower switching costs mean reduced pricing power for networks, thus lower take rates.

One critique of blockchain networks is that their low take rates might be temporary: as blockchain networks proliferate, new intermediaries will pop up that raise the take rates, skeptics say.

Moxie Marlinspike, a respected security researcher and founder of the Signal messaging app, wrote a widely read blog post arguing that because users are averse to even tiny user-interface frictions, they will end up clustering around easy-to-use front-end applications that siphon users away from blockchains. If these applications are run by companies, then we end up with the same problem we have today: a few companies with strong pricing power in control.

This is an insightful critique, sometimes known as the risk of recentralization. A similar dynamic undermined RSS, as discussed in "The Fall of RSS." Twitter and other corporate networks siphoned users away from the protocol by offering lower-friction user experiences. This dynamic is also a risk for poorly designed blockchain networks.

Blockchain networks can avoid this fate if they can guarantee that users retain the credible threat of switching front-end clients even if users cluster around a few popular ones. To ensure this, the network must be designed to include the following:

- **Low-friction user experiences that match those of modern corporate networks.** This is why blockchain networks need a mechanism for funding much of what corporate networks fund, including ongoing software development and user subsidies like free hosting and name registration. Protocol networks never had a sufficient funding mechanism, a key reason RSS failed. (See "Building Networks with Token Incentives" for more on blockchain funding mechanisms.)

- **Network effects that accrue to community-controlled blockchains rather than to company-controlled front-end applications.** This means the things users care about—their names, social relationships, and digital goods—need to be blockchain-based and user owned. Applications are unable to acquire pricing leverage if users can easily switch from one application to another. When users own what matters, lock-in is much less likely.

Marlinspike cited the NFT marketplace OpenSea as an example of a corporate-owned application that could wrench control away from blockchain networks. But the blockchain networks that OpenSea interoperates with are well designed. When you sign up for OpenSea, you do so using a name that you own, tied to a blockchain like Ethereum. All the NFTs you own are also stored on a blockchain, not company servers. This makes it easy to switch to another marketplace while taking all the things you care about with you.

Marlinspike wrote his post in early 2022. Since then, new marketplaces like Blur have exploited the low switching costs of NFT platforms to take market share from OpenSea. In response, OpenSea lowered its take rates, demonstrating that blockchain-based ownership does, in practice, compel lower prices. In contrast, downward price competition is something you almost never see between corporate networks.

The low take rates of blockchain networks create strong incentives for developers and creators to build on top of them. For example, third-party startups add features and applications to DeFi networks without fear that they'll regret having done so later. These startups know they can invest in and grow their businesses without the risk that the DeFi networks will change the rules, undermine them, and extract their profits later. Very few software developers are willing to become dependent on corporate financial networks like Square or PayPal. They may offer these services as one of multiple payment options, but they know better than to become reliant on them.

Blockchain networks should be designed to have take rates

that are high enough to fund essential network activities but low enough to undercut corporate competitors. Blockchain networks offer a new model where far more of the economic surplus goes toward network participants and far less of it goes to bottom lines and bureaucratic bloat.

Squeezing the Balloon

To understand the tech industry, it is essential to understand that when one layer in a "tech stack" becomes commoditized, another layer becomes more profitable. A tech stack is, in this context, a set of technologies that work together to generate revenue. Think of the combination of a computer, an operating system, and software applications as a tech stack of layers built one on top of another.

When layers get commoditized, that means they lose their pricing leverage. In the physical world, this usually means competition is so fierce, and the resulting products so undifferentiated, that profits trend toward zero. Such is the case among actual commodities, like wheat or corn. In a tech stack, it's more common for a layer to become commoditized when products and services are (1) given away for free, like the calculator app on an iPhone; (2) made open source, like the Linux operating system; or (3) controlled by a community, like the email protocol SMTP.

Clayton Christensen, whom we last heard from in the discussion of disruptive innovation in "Tokens," generalized these ideas in his "law of conservation of attractive profits." The theory is that commoditizing a layer in a tech stack is like squeezing a balloon. The volume of air stays constant but shifts to other areas. The same is true for profits in a tech stack (roughly, at least, since business isn't as deterministic as physics). The overall profits are conserved but shift from layer to layer.

Let's look at a concrete example. Google search makes money

when a user clicks on a search ad. In between the advertiser paying and the user clicking, a stack of technologies intervenes: a device like a phone or PC, an operating system, a web browser, a telecom carrier, a search engine, an ad network. All these layers compete to capture a portion of each dollar that passes through the stack. The overall market can grow or shrink, but at any given time the competition between layers is zero-sum.

Google's strategy with respect to search is to either own or commoditize the layers in the stack so that it can maximize its own revenue. Otherwise, a competitor that controls another layer could take away its profits. This is one reason why Google created products in each layer of the stack: devices (Pixel), operating systems (Android, mostly open source), browsers (Chrome plus the open-source Chromium project), and even carrier services (Google Fi). When a company like Google contributes to open-source projects or releases lower-priced versions of competing platforms' products, it does not do so out of charity. It does so out of self-interest.

Here's how this competition plays out on phones today. Because Apple controls the iPhone operating system and its default web browser, Safari, the company can charge Google a reported $12 billion per year for Google to remain the iPhone's default search engine, and Google accepts this as the cost of doing business. Apple is using the popularity of the iPhone to squeeze Google's search balloon. The payment would have been a lot higher if Google hadn't had the foresight to build Android, giving it a big chunk of mobile market share. Google doesn't even need to make money on Android. It just needs that part of the mobile market to be commoditized so it isn't controlled by a competitor, like Apple, which could limit people's access to Google's search product. Thus, the fight for operating systems spills over to the fight for search profits.

By making Android open source (and bundled for free on

many hardware makers' phones), Google pursued a classic tech strategy known as "commoditize your complement." Joel Spolsky, co-founder of Stack Overflow and Trello, coined the phrase in 2002, drawing on the work of economists such as Carl Shapiro and Google's Hal Varian. Google commoditized a large share of the mobile operating system market, thus ensuring its search engine—its real moneymaker—could flourish, unimpeded, on a new computing platform. The move lessened Google's platform risk in the industry-wide shift from PCs to mobile and improved its negotiating power, removing threats to its search profits.

Intel pursued a similar strategy by becoming the biggest code contributor to the open-source operating system Linux. Operating systems are complements to the processors Intel makes. When someone buys a Windows machine, Microsoft captures a share of profits that would otherwise have gone to Intel. When someone buys a Linux machine, more of that money goes instead to Intel. Intel supports Linux to commoditize operating systems, which complement its moneymaking processors.

Applying Christensen's theory to social networks, one can think of the path money takes from users to creators, software developers, and other network participants as a tech stack. High take-rate corporate networks squeeze the balloon at both ends. They capture value at the center of the network, on behalf of the network owner, at the expense of complementary layers that build on top of the network, like creators and software developers. Network effects that result in lock-in force creators to work for free and developers to behave as they are told.

In the case of ad-supported media, the advertiser is the customer and source of the money flow, and users are a complementary layer to be squeezed. People give up their attention and personal data in exchange for network access. Protocol and blockchain networks, by contrast, have low take rates and therefore allow value to flow to users, creators, developers, and other network participants. They squeeze the balloon in the middle, to the benefit of the network edges.

In this sense, you can think of corporate networks as thick and protocol and blockchain networks as thin. Thick networks claim more profits for the center of the network and create thin complementary layers, with lower profits, for creators and software developers. Thin networks do the opposite, generating less profit for the network core and more profit for complements.

Let's imagine you're designing a social networking stack from scratch. Your goals might include some concept of fairness, such as that people deserve to earn money proportionate to how much value they create. You might also have societal goals in mind, like more uniform wealth distribution. But let's just suppose, putting other concerns aside for a moment, that you merely want a network that encourages innovation and creativity. That means you will want social networks to be thin, the opposite of what we have today.

Think about it in terms of the infrastructure of a city, an analogy to which I'll continually return. Roads should perform basic functions, but you don't need them to be hotbeds of innovation. There isn't that much creativity required; they just need to convey cars. On the other hand, you do want lots of creative entrepreneurs building *around* the roads: creating new shops and restaurants, constructing new buildings, expanding neighborhoods, and so forth. Roads should be thin, and their surroundings should be thick.

Social networks should be thin utilities, like roads. They need to support basic features and be reliable, performant, and interoperable. That's about it. The rest of the features can be built around the network. The layers on top should be innovative, diverse, and thick. There should be boundless room for creativity in the media and software that complements social networks. (We'll cover this at length in part 5, "What's Next.")

The web developed as a thin network—and look at the results. The network itself is a simple protocol (HTTP), and all the innovation happens on top, at the level of websites. This structure has led to a thirty-year run of explosive innovation across the internet.

Today's corporate social networks are designed the opposite way, as thick networks. Almost all the value flows to the networks themselves—Facebook, TikTok, Twitter, and others. To the extent there is innovation, it involves startups trying to build competing social networks, rather than building businesses on top. In other words, startups have to build entirely new, proprietary roads in order to support new cities on top, instead of simply building on top of preexisting public roads. Social networks squeezed the balloon in a way that stifles innovation.

The same is true for modern financial networks. Payments should be an easy and inexpensive commodity, a basic utility, like sending email. We have the technology to do it, as we'll cover in "Making Financial Infrastructure a Public Good." This would make payments a thin layer in the finance and commerce stack. Today, it's inverted: there are some very profitable payments companies, and the field remains an active area of entrepreneurship where startups and venture capital are lured by the industry's persistent take rates. Again, the balloon got squeezed in the wrong places.

Blockchain networks are like a rubber band. They reshape the balloon, making the thick belly thin. DeFi makes payments, lending, and trading thin. The same is true for blockchain networks in areas like social networking, gaming, and media. The broader societal goal should be to build new tech stacks where users, creators, and entrepreneurs are not squeezed but rewarded.

Take rates are only half the economic equation for blockchain networks, though. The other half is token incentives that fund software development and other constructive activities. Tokens are a powerful tool that, like all tools, can be put to good or bad uses. Designed properly, they can make a network an attractive place to build a career or business. Achieving these design goals requires careful planning.

If take rates are the stick, token incentives are the carrot.

9. Building Networks with Token Incentives

Show me the incentives and I will show you the outcome.
—Charlie Munger

Incentivizing Software Development

It's telling that the most successful protocol networks were funded by government programs in the 1970s and 1980s, before the arrival of the commercial internet. Email and the web prospered absent corporate network competition. To quote *The Cluetrain Manifesto*, a book published in 2000 that describes how the internet had changed business (and much else): "The Net grew like a weed between the cracks in the monolithic steel-and-glass empire of traditional commerce." The internet flourished, the authors continue, "largely because it was ignored."

Imagine if email and the web had, in their nascency, faced off against corporate startups. The protocol networks might never have endured. Probably, they would have gone the way of other fizzled protocol networks, like RSS. Corporations were able to steamroll protocol networks in part because they had so much more funding to support software development. Tech companies could build large teams of world-class developers by offering them attractive compensation and financial upside that protocol networks couldn't match.

Networks don't build themselves. Any network design that seeks to challenge corporate rivals needs to offer competitive compensation and financial upside. Someone needs to put in the work; that this is a truism doesn't make it any less true. Incentives matter.

Protocol networks generally don't have the resources to provide developers with competitive compensation. They lack self-sufficiency and depend on the goodwill of volunteers instead. Like protocol networks, blockchain networks rely on third parties, either individuals or companies, to build most of their software components, but there's a key difference between the two: Blockchain networks don't rely solely on volunteers. They have a built-in mechanism for funding developers.

Blockchain networks use token incentives to motivate developers. Recall that tokens are general computing primitives for representing ownership and that they can represent units of value underpinning the economies of blockchain networks. (We'll cover principles for designing blockchain-based economies in "Tokenomics.") Tokens used for this purpose are usually called native tokens; for example, ether is the native token of the Ethereum blockchain. Sometimes, in addition to being a financial incentive, native tokens can confer governance rights to their holders. (More on this in "Network Governance.")

By doling out token incentives, blockchain networks bring outsiders into their fold, encourage software development, and stay competitive. The funding source enables blockchain networks to create modern software experiences that rival those of corporate networks.

In corporate networks, employees perform almost all software development. Work to be done at a company like Twitter includes developing and maintaining the app, tweaking algorithms that sort and rank tweets, and creating filters to fight spam. Blockchain networks, by contrast, externalize these tasks. They get outside developers and software studios to do the work. Jobs held captive in corporate networks become external, market-based tasks in blockchain networks. These outside developers are often compensated with tokens, turning them into stakeholders with partial ownership and governance rights in the network.

Token incentives for developers have multiple benefits. First, anyone in the world can contribute, widening both the talent funnel and the base of network stakeholders. As contributors earn tokens and become partial owners, they have an incentive to help the network succeed, by building software, creating content, or helping the network in other ways. Second, token incentives create competition for each task, which means users get to choose from multiple software options, the way they get to choose from multiple web browsers and email clients. Third, the tokens can be disbursed transparently and programmatically, unlike corporate stock, in a way that's fairer, more open, and more frictionless than analog systems. (More on this in "Regulating Tokens.")

The goal of any project is to recruit a broad community of contributors, but it takes time to get there. At the earliest stage, projects usually consist of a small group of developers pursuing a new idea. Sometimes the early contributors collaborate informally, and other times they create formal relationships using legal entities. The early developers are usually compensated, at least partially, with tokens. A well-designed network distributes these token rewards such that the team will have some ongoing influence and upside after the initial work is done, but not too much.

When the semiautonomous code is ready to run on a blockchain, the early developers launch the network. In doing so, they relinquish control. Early developers often continue to work on apps that provide access to the network, but these are typically just one of many such apps. Networks work best when they are supported by a broad and diverse community. Blockchain networks are permissionless, and when designed properly, they privilege no app developers—even the original inventors of the network—above any others.

Postlaunch, blockchain networks fund ongoing development through token grants. Several blockchain networks have treasuries worth hundreds of millions of dollars from which grants can be distributed either by community decision or in an automated way based on predetermined metrics. Grants can go, for example, to independent software developers for building front-end applications, infrastructure, developer tools, analytics, and more. In a healthy ecosystem, for-profit investors will supplement these grant programs with additional funding for new projects, apps, services, and other businesses that build on the network. (Recall from the last chapter how predictably low take rates encourage blockchain network investment because builders and investors know that if they succeed, they will receive the upside of what they build.)

Blockchain networks' ability to disburse token incentives to software developers puts them on a level playing field with corporate networks. Grants, plus outside investments, allow blockchain networks to credibly compete with the sizable investments that corporations make in software development. But token incentives can have other advantages too. The same rewards that attract developers can also attract users, creators, and other network participants.

Overcoming the Bootstrap Problem

Early network participants create significant value for corporate networks, yet they rarely receive fair compensation for their efforts. Just look at the video creators who built YouTube, the social groups who built Facebook, the influencers who built Instagram, the homeowners who built Airbnb, the drivers who built Uber—the list goes on. Without participants, there's no network.

Almost invariably, corporate networks consolidate wealth and power in the hands of a small group: investors, founders, some employees. To a lucky few go the spoils. The network effects accrue to the company that owns the network, often resulting in winner-take-all outcomes at the expense of other contributors. As corporate networks grow, early users get burned. A few corporate affiliates make money while everyone else who helped build the network gets passed by. Early participants become embittered. They're left out.

Blockchain networks take a much more inclusive approach. They grant tokens to early users who build and participate in networks. A blockchain social network might reward users for creating content that is popular with other users, for example. A game might reward users who play well or contribute interesting mods. A marketplace might reward early sellers who bring in new buyers. The best designs reward users not for paying fees or buying anything but for making constructive contributions to the network.

As the network grows, token rewards should taper off. More participants make a network more useful; once enough people are participating and network effects kick in, the need to offer incentives decreases. People who take a risk by contributing early, when a network's success isn't assured, gain the most.

This isn't good just for users and contributors. It's also good for the networks. A key challenge when building networks is overcoming the "bootstrap" or "cold start" problem: attracting users and contributors before enough of them are participating to make the network intrinsically useful. This is because network effects cut both ways: they can accelerate growth, but they can also handicap it. Scaled networks attract new users without much effort. Conversely, subscale networks struggle just to survive.

Token rewards can help overcome the bootstrap problem. DeFi networks like Compound pioneered this approach after recognizing that token incentives can recruit users during the bootstrap phase, when network effects are weak, as the chart below shows.

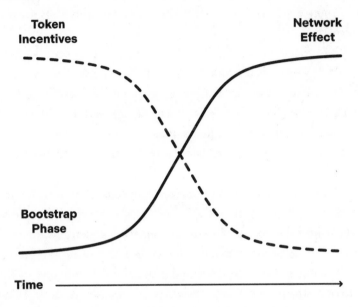

Corporate networks used similar techniques to overcome the bootstrap problem, although instead of token incentives they offered subsidies. As you'll recall, when YouTube started out, it subsidized video hosting costs as an incentive for people to contribute videos to its network.

But subsidies go only so far. There are many networks that would be broadly useful and should exist yet do not because it is so hard to overcome the early hurdles to network effects. Token incentives offer a new technique for building networks in categories where previous attempts got stuck.

Take telecom, for instance. For decades, technologists have dreamed of building a grassroots internet access provider. Instead of a corporate network owner building out and owning the infra-structure, users would voluntarily install access points, like wireless routers, at their homes or offices. Another set of users would tap these access points (rather than, say, corporate cell towers) for network connectivity. The goal would be to displace incumbent telecom companies like AT&T and Verizon with community-owned alternatives.

Over the years, people have tried repeatedly to start a grassroots telecom service. Students at MIT (Roofnet), employees at a venture-funded startup (Fon), and neighbors in New York City (NYC Mesh) all took a crack at the challenge, and they all learned how hard it can be to install a sufficient number of access points for broad network coverage. Most projects stalled at the bootstrap phase.

That is, until one. An experimental blockchain project, Helium, got further than anyone else. The network encouraged people to install and run access points in exchange for token rewards, enabling it to reach nationwide coverage in a few years. The project still has lots of work to do to build out the demand side of the network. (The initial network was based on an esoteric networking standard, but it has since upgraded to 5G cellular, a much more popular option.) But Helium built the supply side of the network for a grassroots telecom service much more successfully than previous attempts—proof of token incentives' potential.

Already, other projects are using similar methods to build out networks for electric car charging, computer storage, artificial intelligence training, and more. These are all networks that would be useful for the world but that have gotten tripped up by the bootstrap problem. Token incentives provide a powerful new tool for overcoming hurdles to building new networks. They can also help break the rich-get-richer tendency in corporate networks, where only the employees and investors, not the users, see upside when a network succeeds.

Tokens Are Self-Marketing

Achieving a word-of-mouth chain reaction is the dream of any marketer. One person tells the next two people, who tell the next four people, who tell the next eight people, and so on, exponentially. Such testimonial-driven marketing is the most effective and cost-efficient way to grow a product, a brand, a community, a network. The trick is to be contagious.

Ever since Hotmail added a default footer to emails—*PS: I love you. Get your free email at Hotmail*—founders have obsessed over finding the right viral loop to make their services infectious. Facebook figured it out for socializing on college campuses. Snap got through to teenagers who were tired of having a permanent digital record. Uber found the secret in a magic button to make rides and food instantly appear.

But many users have settled into habits since these corporate networks first appeared. For evidence, look at the top apps in the Apple or Google mobile stores. Almost all the products that consistently stay in those top lists were founded more than a decade ago: Facebook (2004), YouTube (2005), Twitter (2006), WhatsApp (2009), Uber (2009), Instagram (2010), Snap (2011), and so on. Even the parent company of TikTok (2017) has been around for longer than you might expect: ByteDance (2012).

I'm not saying new services will never hit it big. There will always be exceptions. Maybe AI apps like ChatGPT will have staying power and become the new top apps. But for the most part the game has changed. If you talk to consumer internet investors, they'll tell you that users have filled up the home screens of their phones and it's much harder for new apps to break out. People's routines are set.

Big Tech companies are now the gatekeepers. For startups to reach people, they first need to go through these services. Corporate networks in the extract phase throttle how much free traffic startups receive and force most startups to advertise to continue growing, as discussed in "Take Rates." To get noticed and stay relevant, many startups need to pay for promotion.

Startups justify the increased marketing expenses under the theory that if they retain enough customers, the long-term economics will work out. They convince themselves that they will, someday, become profitable. In practice, the marginal profitability of advertising declines as startups scale. Many later-stage startups—whether they're selling mattresses, meal kits, movie streaming, or whatever else—have high user acquisition costs and negative margins. They devolve into bad business prospects, in other words.

Tokens provide a new way to skip advertising and acquire customers through peer-to-peer evangelism. Tokens empower individuals to become stakeholders in networks, not just participants. When users feel a sense of ownership, they are motivated to contribute even more and spread the word. These user-evangelists are more authentic and effective than corporate marketing programs run by hired teams. They win hearts and minds through blog posts, tweets, and code. They participate in forums. They sing praises and shout from the desktops. Thanks to their economic and other benefits, tokens don't need marketing, per se; tokens are *self-marketing*.

Blockchain networks depend on community-led evangelism, not advertising. This allows them to grow without having to pay Big Tech gatekeepers. Bitcoin and Ethereum don't have companies behind them, let alone marketing budgets, and yet tens of millions of people own their tokens. Evangelists use word of mouth. They organize meetups, chat online, trade memes, and write posts. The same happens with many other networks. Almost none of the top blockchain networks have spent materially on advertising. They don't need to; they're contagious. Users do the marketing.

Tokens are a powerful tool, but they need to be used responsibly. The networks they are part of should provide useful services. Marketing should be a means to building a network, not an end in itself. Otherwise, projects evaporate as empty marketing schemes. (This is also why thoughtful regulation is important, something I discuss in "Regulating Tokens.")

Again, the city analogy is useful. Homeowners are incentivized to build and promote their cities. They develop real estate and start businesses, support local schools and sports teams, get involved in organizations and civic causes. They are true community members with financial upside and a say in governance.

Building true communities is the best way to go viral.

Making Users Owners

Perhaps the purest example of the self-marketing phenomenon in action is Dogecoin, a well-known "memecoin," or joke token.

Like many memecoins, Dogecoin sprang from the open-source ethos of blockchains. Creating a blockchain network is easy because anyone can "fork," or copy, another project's code. Dogecoin is one such derivative. In fact, it's a copy of a copy . . . of a copy. Dogecoin is a fork of another project, Luckycoin, which is a fork of Litecoin, which is a fork of Bitcoin. (That's composability for you.)

The founders of Dogecoin intended the project to parody cryptocurrencies like Bitcoin. Yet, despite being a spoof with no practical applications, Dogecoin has maintained a market capitalization in the billions of dollars for years. Only a few places accept the coin as payment, but it has developed a passionate following anyway. More than two million users subscribe to the Dogecoin Reddit discussion forum, with Elon Musk as the project's most famous supporter. After meeting at Dogecoin meetups, some people have even gotten married.

Dogecoin's creators are sour about what they built and periodically disparage crypto in an attempt to tamp down the mania over their invention. Despite the founders' criticism, the coin has taken on a life of its own—like Frankenstein's monster, only cuter.

Dogecoin's tenacity proves how a grassroots community can propel a blockchain network long after the original team departs—or even turns hostile. To its users, Dogecoin may be a silly network, but at least it's *their* silly network. Users own and control the network. If there were meaningful decisions to be made about the network's development, the users would get to make them. If the network were to grow, Doge holders would see the upside, which is not the case in corporate networks. Dogecoin is the closest one can get to a clinical experiment demonstrating the power of tokens absent confounding factors.

To be clear, I'm not a fan of Dogecoin, at least in its current state. I'm not a fan of most memecoins, for that matter. The majority exist solely for financial speculation, and at worst they can be Ponzi schemes that enrich their promoters. (The beauty of permissionless innovation is, of course, that if you disagree, you don't have to get my blessing or anyone else's.)

Despite its frivolity, the Dogecoin community has remained vibrant for more than a decade. Other memecoins have remained strong for similarly long periods. For thirty years users have been contributing to the growth of internet networks but have received little in return. Corporate networks forgot them. Dogecoin and other tokens actually include them, making them owners and granting them real control and upside for the first time. Clearly, ownership has a powerful and lasting effect.

Now imagine pairing that effect with a network that provides useful services. Uniswap combines a useful product—a decentralized token exchange—with a dedicated community that benefits from the network's success. More than $1 trillion in assets has flowed through the network since its debut in late 2018. In 2020, Uniswap distributed free tokens—15 percent of its total supply—

as a reward to anyone who ever used the network. At the time, roughly 250,000 users received an "airdrop" worth thousands of dollars per user, plus network governance rights. Additionally, the network set aside another 45 percent of its tokens for community grant programs, thereby allocating in total 60 percent of the network's tokens for its community.

Turning users into owners at this scale is unprecedented in the history of tech startups. Uniswap's community received a majority of the network's financial upside *and* governance power. Most corporate networks are much stingier when it comes to sharing anything of value with network participants, beyond a narrow set of employees. Facebook, TikTok, Twitter, and most other large corporate networks set aside no shares for the users who built, grew, and sustained these networks.

Throughout this book, I've discussed the drawbacks that arise from the corporate network model. Corporations have done a lot of good too, of course. As noted in "Take Rates," the deflationary business models of companies like Amazon, Airbnb, and Google lowered the price of services for consumers while maintaining or improving product quality. Users voted with their feet, awarding money, attention, and data to companies whose offerings were better than what came before.

But we should expect more from the internet. Cost savings are nice, but wouldn't it be nicer if companies let users, not just shareholders, participate in their financial success? The market cap of Big Tech companies totals in the trillions of dollars. Users, especially early ones, contribute much to this success. They sell products on Amazon, publish videos on YouTube, share content on Twitter, and so on. Users make early bets, just as founders and investors do. And yet in most corporate networks, users are treated as second-class citizens at best, or as a product to be served up to real customers, like advertisers, at worst.

There are glimmers of hope. Some companies have managed to

set aside equity for users as part of their initial public offerings. Notably, Airbnb, Lyft, and Uber reserved portions of their initial public offerings for some homeowners and drivers and encouraged them to buy shares with onetime cash bonuses. These programs are a step in the right direction. But they account for only a fraction of these companies' total ownership—in the low, single-digit percentages.

Blockchain networks are, meanwhile, much more generous. In most popular blockchain networks, the community receives more than 50 percent of the total tokens, which are distributed in various ways, including through airdrops, developer rewards, and early-adopter incentives. Instead of being concentrated in the hands of a small group of insiders, ownership is broadly distributed among users according to how much they contribute to the network.

This is how all networks should work. If corporate networks can figure out how to give their communities significant ownership, as many blockchain networks already do, that would be good for the world and a far better outcome for users. But corporate networks haven't done this so far and don't seem likely to. Besides, even if corporations do find some way to make it happen, they will still come up short in other areas, like making strong commitments to users, guaranteeing low take rates, and ensuring always-open, composable APIs.

Blockchain networks bake community ownership into their core design. It's in their DNA. While memecoin mutations, like Dogecoin, may seem like a joke, they show how users are embracing all sorts of tokens—some silly, some serious—in search of community, to fill the void left by corporate networks. The internet was originally envisioned as a decentralized network owned and controlled by its participants. Tokens restore that vision.

10. Tokenomics

Prices are important not because money is considered
paramount but because prices are a fast and effective
conveyor of information through a vast society in which
fragmented knowledge must be coordinated.

—Thomas Sowell

Designing systems of incentives to underpin blockchain networks
is sometimes known as tokenomics—a blend of, you guessed it,
"tokens" and "economics."

While tokenomics may sound like something entirely new,
it's novel only insofar as it applies old concepts to the context of
the internet. Conceptually, there's nothing that groundbreaking.
Tokenomics mostly just encompasses economics. (Practitioners
also call the discipline protocol design, but I avoid this to prevent
confusion with early internet-style protocol networks.)

Blockchain networks didn't invent the idea of virtual economies with built-in, or native, currencies. Games have had virtual
economies for years. In the 1970s and 1980s, arcades started swapping out the usual coin-operated games with cabinets accepting
proprietary tokens. As arcades expanded, grew in popularity, and
added more games, they often raised the price of their tokens. Old
tokens would still be usable, so if you bought a bunch of tokens

early and held on to them, you would have a lower effective cost to play games than others.

A more sophisticated version of the same idea exists today within video games. *Eve Online,* which has been around since the early 2000s, is probably the game most famous for its virtual economy. *Eve* has millions of players who trade and battle across a fictional galaxy called New Eden. The game maker, CCP Games, publishes a data-rich monthly economic report about conditions within the game, such as what market prices fictitious ores like "veldspar," "scordite," and "pyroxeres" are fetching. The studio takes its economy, based on so-called InterStellar Kredits, very seriously. It made headlines in 2007 when it hired a respected PhD to run its in-game monetary policy.

Eve's success inspired a generation of followers, from simple mobile games like *Clash of Clans* to hard-core games like *League of Legends.* These games all have in-game currencies and ways players can earn and spend those currencies. The game makers create demand for their digital currencies with fun experiences that attract millions of players, who then use the native currencies to buy in-game virtual goods. Demand drives up the currencies' value; ebbing interest sends it downward.

Tokenomic designs in blockchain networks build on lessons learned in video games. A blockchain economy, like any healthy virtual economy, should balance the supply and demand of native tokens to fuel sustainable growth. A well-designed token economy helps the network flourish. The right incentives turn users into communities of owners and contributors.

But incentives must be designed with intention, otherwise there can be unintended consequences. "Incentive structures work, so you have to be very careful of what you incent people to do," as Steve Jobs once observed about corporate incentives. Sounding a note of caution, he added, they can "create all sorts of consequences that you can't anticipate."

Faucets and Token Supply

A common metaphor for thinking about the design of token economies is to imagine tokens as water that flows through the plumbing of a house. Sources of supply are "faucets," which provide water, and sources of demand are "sinks," which drain water.

The network designer's first goal is to balance the faucets and sinks so water doesn't over- or under-flow. Faucets that are too strong can lead to more supply than demand—and therefore downward price pressure. Sinks that are too strong can lead to less supply than demand—and therefore upward price pressure. Without the right balance, token prices can swing too far up or down, causing a bubble or crash. Such events distort incentives and decrease a network's utility.

Much of the discussion in the last chapter concerns faucets: token grants for developers, bootstrapping networks with token rewards, air-dropping tokens to early users, and other activities. Ideally, faucets optimize for positive behaviors that grow the network. They should incentivize software developers to build new features and experiences, and they should turn other participants, such as creators and users, into a community that's motivated to cultivate and grow the network.

Common examples of faucets include the following:

Faucet	Description
Sale to Investors	Selling tokens for cash to help fund initial operations.
Founding Team Award	Rewards with potential upside for building the initial network. Allows the network to compete for top talent.
Ongoing Development Awards	Community-controlled grants to fund ongoing development. Allows the network to compete for top talent.

Faucet	Description
User Bootstrapping Rewards	Incentives to help the network get past the "bootstrapping" phase. Tapers out as a network's intrinsic utility increases.
Airdrop to Users	Rewards for early community members. Builds goodwill and expands the base of network stakeholders.
Security Budget	Incentives that increase the security of the system. Rewards for blockchain validators are an example.

Faucets are a powerful tool for building networks. The token incentives they distribute can help overcome the bootstrap problem, recruit early contributors, fund ongoing development, share upside with a broad community of users, and keep networks secure. They are analogous to land grants in early cities that align incentives and encourage real estate, business, and other development.

Sinks and Token Demand

The best sinks tie token demand to network activity, thereby aligning the token price to the network's usage and popularity. Useful networks generate more token demand, while less useful networks generate less demand.

Sinks that charge fees for network access or usage are known, aptly, as access or fee sinks. You can think of them as the digital equivalent of highway tolls, collecting just enough for network upkeep. Ethereum and certain DeFi networks take this approach. The Ethereum network has a maximum capacity and can run a limited amount of code at any given time. To avoid overload, the network charges for computing time. (Recall that Ethereum behaves like a public computer, reminiscent of time-sharing main-frame computers from decades ago.)

The cost of compute on Ethereum is called gas. The price of gas is a small denomination of the native token ether, which varies according to supply and demand. The Ethereum network collects some of its gas fees to buy and "burn" (read: destroy) tokens. This collection and burning activity reduces the token supply and, in theory, increases the price of ether (assuming constant demand). Similarly, DeFi networks like Aave, Compound, and Curve take fees and save the proceeds in their network treasuries, which can later be redistributed via faucets. All of this happens automatically, powered by immutable code embedded in each blockchain network.

Another common sink for base-layer blockchains is a "security" sink that rewards token holders for "staking," or locking up tokens in validators. As discussed earlier in "Blockchains," validators are computers that maintain the security of a network by verifying the validity of proposed transactions. Staking is the process by which users lock tokens in code-enforced escrow accounts. If a validator behaves honestly, it gets rewarded with more tokens. In some network designs there can also be a penalty if the validator behaves dishonestly. Staking is a double-edged sword: it creates both a sink, which locks up (and sometimes confiscates) tokens, and a faucet, which rewards honest stakers with tokens.

Security sinks have pros and cons. On the pro side, they promote network security. The more money that's at stake, the more secure the network and its applications. As applications running on the network become more popular, more people pay to use them and network revenue goes up. This puts upward pressure on the token price, which raises the staking rewards. This, in turn, encourages more staking and, thus, improvements in network security.

On the con side, security sinks can be expensive. Designed with built-in faucets to reward staking, they can counteract demand pressure by adding to the token supply, potentially depressing prices. This is why blockchain networks like Ethereum combine access sinks with security sinks, and why their communities fine-tune token inflows and outflows to ensure balance. Too much of one or the other can throw a system out of whack.

The last common type of sink we'll cover here is "governance" sinks. Some tokens give users the power to vote on changes to the network. Users will buy tokens, so the thinking goes, to gain more influence. The incentive to vote gets people to acquire and hold tokens, taking them out of circulation, therefore generating demand for tokens and a resulting sink. Governance sinks can, however, suffer from free-rider problems. Free ridership happens when people don't vote. They might skip out because they think the outcomes of the vote don't matter, or because they believe an election will swing their way regardless of whether they participate. Governance tokens help keep networks democratic, but they are unlikely to sustain token demand all by themselves.

Sink	Pros	Cons
Access/Fee Sink	Aligns well with network usage, incentivizes token holders to build useful apps that grow the network.	If too high, can discourage network use.
Security Sink	Increases network security as the token becomes more valuable.	Can be expensive as it requires faucets to reward for honest behavior.
Governance Sink	Gives stakeholders a way to participate in governance.	Subject to free-riding; only partially aligned with growing the utility of the network.

Well-designed sinks correlate with network usage. As usage increases, more tokens drain away, which creates upward price pressure. Upward price pressure increases the value of token rewards used for security, software development, and other constructive activities. Designed correctly, sinks create a virtuous cycle.

Badly designed faucets and sinks can, however, fuel a speculative environment that destroys the spirit of the community. Some blockchain communities focus almost exclusively on token prices. Paying excessive attention to prices is a bad sign—a hallmark of casino culture. Well-designed token incentives focus communities on constructive topics, like new applications and technology improvements. The quality of a project's discussions often reveals the health of its community.

Tokens Can Be Valued Using Traditional Financial Methods

A common argument against blockchain networks is that tokens are purely speculative and have no intrinsic value. Newspaper columnists routinely refer to them as scams. Warren Buffett branded them "rat poison." Michael Burry, the contrarian trader of *The Big Short* fame, has labeled them "magic beans." The implication is that networks that depend on tokens can't be useful. It's all just a speculative mirage.

Cherry-picking the worst examples of an emerging technology to dismiss a promising new industry out of hand may make for catchy headlines, but it is a disingenuous form of criticism. The railroad wasn't worthless just because many unviable railroad companies fed early stock market mania. When automobiles made their debut, they were considered impractical, inefficient, and life threatening. The early internet featured content that was silly, offensive, even dangerous, and many people who thought they knew better regarded the industry as either unserious or, at the other extreme, morally hazardous.

Understanding new technologies takes work. Critics who focus on the bad while dismissing the good fail to foresee the long-term potential of disruptive innovation. While it is true that there are plenty of poorly designed tokens driven purely by speculation (see: most memecoins), this is not true of all tokens. What the criticisms miss is that software is a highly plastic medium and that almost any economic model that can be dreamed up can be implemented in software. An honest assessment would look at the details of token designs instead of generalizing from a few bad ones.

There are plenty of well-designed tokens that have sustainable sources of supply and demand. Take Ethereum, for example. Recall how the system collects fees on transactions, or network usage, and how it uses these funds to buy and burn tokens, thereby taking them out of circulation. Reducing the supply of tokens can increase the value of existing ones, benefiting token holders. All of this happens automatically as part of the system's transparently encoded rules, with no company making decisions about the process behind the scenes. The design makes sense.

Put another way, Ethereum generates the token equivalent of cash flow. The more applications written for Ethereum, and the more those applications get used, the greater the demand for computing time and for Ethereum's native token. The supply of ether varies but, generally, after all faucets and sinks are accounted for, has stayed relatively flat (in the past it increased slowly; recently it has been decreasing). This means the price of ether should roughly correlate with the popularity of applications built on the network. By studying the cash flows and burn rates of blockchain networks, you can value tokens like Ethereum's using traditional financial metrics such as price-to-earnings ratios.

Ethereum shows what good token design can be, but it is not the only well-designed blockchain network. Others include DeFi networks that use similar models. The tokens these networks collect as fees go toward funding network activities, such as buying and burning tokens, or distributing money to token holders. If you understand a system's faucets and sinks, you can evaluate its tokens. Access and fee sinks generate network earnings, minus any costs. The price of tokens times the supply (with some discount rate applied to future token issuances) yields market capitalization. All of this is standard finance.

Compare what we're talking about with real estate. Blockchain networks that charge for access have characteristics similar to property holdings. "Price-to-rental" is a common valuation metric in realty, for example. You can calculate it by dividing home price by annual rent. The answer may inform whether you choose to buy or rent a house, or to live in or rent a house you own. That you can always rent out real estate and generate cash flow provides a model for valuing the assets. In the same way, you can apply fundamental analysis to blockchain networks to determine a fair value for tokens.

Whether tokens have value reduces, primarily, to whether they will have long-term demand. This depends, in part, on their economic design. The faucets and sinks of a blockchain network need to be designed such that network popularity converts into sustained token demand.

Of course, this raises a trickier question: Will the network be popular? It's impossible to know. Some networks will succeed, and some won't. This I can say for sure, though: the ones that succeed will offer useful services that attract users to the network.

A reasonable skeptic might doubt the viability of a specific network or whether the world needs blockchain networks at all. Maybe the internet has enough networks. Maybe corporate networks are sufficient and will keep winning, either because users are too locked in already or because they'll always outcompete blockchains in areas like user experience. That's not my view, but it's a valid stance for a critic to assume. What's unreasonable is to say that tokens are based on fanciful economic theories. Tokens are not magic beans. They are assets used to power virtual economies, and they can be valued using traditional financial methods.

Financial Cycles

Speculation exists everywhere property can be bought or sold, from equities and commodities to real estate and collectibles. Markets have always had speculation, and they always will. Tokens are no exception. Economic agents are excitable, especially in the presence of a promising new technology, business, or asset.

In her 2002 book, *Technological Revolutions and Financial Capital*, Carlota Perez, an economic historian, describes how tech-driven economic revolutions follow predictable cycles. First there is an "installation phase," involving an "irruption," or tech breakthrough, followed by a "frenzy" of speculation. Then comes a market crash: the bubble bursts. After that, a "deployment phase" takes place, including a period of "synergy," where the new tech gets adopted. Finally, industry consolidates and reaches "maturity," making once-groundbreaking inventions routine. And so, in fits and starts, capitalism progresses.

Another way of looking at the course of tech innovation is through the "hype cycle," a management framework the consulting firm Gartner made popular starting in 1995. Gartner's model builds on the work of other thinkers, like the economist Joseph Schumpeter, known for his theory of creative destruction. The model illustrates how when a new technology arrives, the excitement it generates can catalyze a financial bubble (the peak of inflated expectations). A crash usually follows (the trough of disillusionment). Then there's a long period of productive growth as the technology gets broadly deployed (the slope of enlightenment).

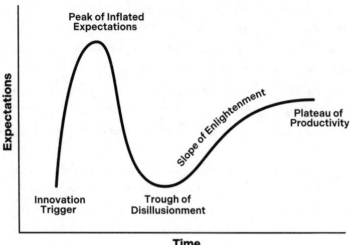

The hype cycle has played out many times across many technologies, including railroads, electricity, and automobiles. Take the internet, for instance. Dot-com mania climbed toward its "peak of inflated expectations" in the 1990s. A slew of overpriced IPOs came out of that era, but so did several legitimate and wildly successful companies. After the early 2000s' "trough of disillusionment," two steady decades followed along the "slope of enlightenment," bringing internet valuations back to new highs, this time driven by fundamentals. Any skeptic who dismissed dot-coms as magic beans would have missed out on the successes of Google, Amazon, and others.

Blockchain networks have already gone through multiple boom-and-bust cycles, each one bigger than the last. Some of the initial excitement was grounded in genuine tech breakthroughs. In 2009, Bitcoin pioneered the concept of a blockchain. In 2015, Ethereum expanded on the concept, creating a general-purpose programming platform. Both were technological advances that marked a classic period of irruption, in Perez's terms. As often happens, market excitement then got ahead of itself. The technological reality didn't support the outsized returns investors and entrepreneurs sought, at least not immediately. Crashes, sometimes precipitated by shocks, like macroeconomic events or the collapse of a prominent project, ensued.

One could argue that blockchains, more than other technologies, exacerbate speculative cycles because their key innovation is to enable digital ownership. When you own something, you can do what you like with it, including buying or selling it. If we lived in a world in which you could only rent houses, and one day someone invented a way for you to own houses, speculative real estate markets would almost certainly pop up. Smart policy and regulation can help tamp down speculation (a topic I discuss further in "Regulating Tokens"), but speculation also tends to quiet down naturally as people learn how to value new technologies based on fundamentals.

My colleagues and I have studied the ups and downs of token markets, and we call the pattern we've observed the price-innovation cycle. Token markets follow the same cyclical patterns economists have long studied, discussed above. New innovations kick off a period of interest and activity, which generates enthusiasm and price increases. This attracts more founders, developers, builders, and creators to the industry. If the market crashes because expectations overinflate, builders stick around and keep working on new ideas. Their efforts incubate further advances that eventually renew the cycle. As of the time of my writing, we've been through at least three cycles, and we expect the trend to continue.

Speculative manias don't just characterize tech revolutions; they often enable them. Many emerging technologies are resource intensive and depend on big capital inflows to fund the infrastructure required for the next rollout phase. Railroads require enormous amounts of steel production and spike-driving labor. Electricity flows only as far as a power grid can carry it, and automobiles roll only as far as roads can take them. The dot-com boom built out massive broadband infrastructure, which would later be essential for the industry's growth. Speculative investments don't always go to waste.

Blockchains need big investments too. They require tooling and infrastructure, and the networks and applications that are built on top of them require capital to fuel growth. Big Tech corporate networks spent tens of billions of dollars to scale to billions of users. Networks that intend to compete with them will require similar sums. A little exuberance, whether rational or irrational, goes a long way.

I expect the markets around blockchain networks will follow the same trajectory that markets around other technologies have followed throughout history. Over time, fundamentals will drive token prices just as they drive prices in other markets. Speculation will cool, replaced by a more sober evaluation of the sources of token supply and demand. To quote an old Wall Street adage attributed to Benjamin Graham, the father of value investing: markets are a voting machine in the short term and a weighing machine in the long term.

In other words, assets with actual substance or weight—fundamental value, in finance-speak—have the best prospects over the long term. The implication is that it may be prudent not to let any short term razzle-dazzle distract you. Just because something wins a popularity contest today doesn't mean it will age well.

11. Network Governance

Democracy is the worst form of government, except
for all the others that have been tried.
—Winston Churchill

The internet's core protocol networks approximate a democracy. At
their foundation, developers weigh in on and implement technical
standards. Many developers are independent and free to make their
own choices, or they are part of larger companies that make client
applications. If someone proposes to change an existing protocol or
invent a new one, it's up to developers and businesses to put the
ideas into practice. Proposals are just that, proposals.

It is in this sense that these protocols are owned and operated
by the internet community. Developers "vote" on proposals by deciding whether to include them in software. Users "vote" too, indirectly, by deciding on which products to use. Everyone more or less
has a say.

At a higher level, internet governance emerges from an organizational patchwork of technical standards coordinators. The World
Wide Web Consortium (W3C), an international nonprofit, provides a forum for hundreds of member organizations, including
research institutions, government groups, small companies, and

big corporations, to discuss web-related standards. The volunteer-only Internet Engineering Task Force (IETF), part of the separate nonprofit Internet Society, maintains standards for internet protocols like email. ICANN, yet another nonprofit, oversees the internet's name space, including by allocating IP addresses, accrediting domain name registrars, and adjudicating disputes over trademarks and other legal matters. Except for ICANN, these organizations are not really governing bodies. Yes, they set protocol standards and convene discussions but, for the most part, they issue recommendations, not edicts.

Governments are responsible for regulation and enforcement, though they generally do not interfere with underlying technology. Government groups participate in internet governance as advisers, providing input on protocols, but the policies that result are ultimately the product of a dialogue among industry, civil society, academia, and others. David Clark, an MIT researcher and internet pioneer, best captured the spirit of protocol network governance when he said, "We reject: kings, presidents, and voting. We believe in: rough consensus and running code." (The IETF would later adopt Clark's words as its unofficial motto.)

Historically, internet regulation has not targeted protocols, but instead has targeted the people and companies who interact with protocols. That includes businesses that make client apps. Authorities do not require that the email protocol, SMTP, block the transmission of spam, for example. Instead, governments regulate the misuse of email by fining any person or business that violates certain spam-fighting laws, such as false advertising or ignoring email opt-out requests. Software developers, businesses, and others can comply with such regulations (which target their apps, companies, and client software, rather than the underlying protocols) or suffer the consequences. It's their choice. By observing this simple setup—regulating apps, not protocols—governments help preserve the promise of the underlying technology.

If protocol networks are democracies, corporate networks are dictatorships. They're governed, absolutely, by their owners: effective at coordinating, but inherently unfair. When management issues a directive, everyone must obey. At the same time, nothing stops management from changing policies at will to suit corporate interests at the expense of other network stakeholders. The economic might of corporate networks and these networks' ability to make unilateral decisions give them a competitive edge over protocol networks. But corporate decision-making processes are usually opaque, capricious, and, as some users allege, discriminatory.

Most of today's popular internet products are corporate owned, meaning they're governed as dictatorships. Corporate networks have been a boon for big players in Silicon Valley, many of whom are happy with the status quo. The corporate model is so intertwined with how the internet operates today that people sometimes forget there are other ways to govern networks. But cracks in the edifice of corporate networks are beginning to show, and people are catching on to their harmful effects. The fissures are most pronounced in social networks, arguably the most significant class of corporate networks.

While questions of network governance might have seemed academic a few years ago, they've since become mainstream concerns. Debates over the governance of popular corporate networks like Facebook, Twitter, and YouTube are increasingly common. How should the algorithms rank content? Who should have access? What are the right moderation policies? How should user data be handled? How should ads and monetization work? For many businesses and creators, these questions directly affect their livelihoods; they may even affect democracy itself.

I believe there's a better way to govern networks—and I'm not the only one. People who share this mindset believe that network governance shouldn't depend on who might own a specific company, or the views of whoever happens to work there at any given time. Take Twitter, for example. Maybe you liked the way the company ran before Elon Musk took over, but do you like it now? Maybe you like the way your favorite network is currently governed, but will you like it in the long term? A growing number of people are coming around to the idea that networks are too important to leave to the whims of single, powerful companies or individuals.

The Nonprofit Model

Some people believe nonprofit legal entities provide a solution. The network would still be a dictatorship, but at least it would be controlled by an organization that has motives beyond financial success. Proponents of this approach cite Wikipedia, the crowdsourced encyclopedia owned and supported by the nonprofit Wikimedia Foundation, as a model. It's an interesting idea, but is it capable of being extended to other areas of technology?

Wikipedia is a special case: it is the only large-scale internet service structured as a nonprofit. Wikipedia was able to succeed this way due to a combination of factors, including the goodwill of its founders, its long-standing network effects, and its low upkeep costs. Unlike many other internet services, Wikipedia hasn't needed many product changes since its introduction in 2001. Consumer demand for encyclopedia information hasn't changed much as tech platforms have shifted. As a result, Wikipedia's expenses have remained relatively low and supportable through voluntary donations.

To the credit of its founders and board, Wikipedia hasn't wavered in its mission even when it might have been easy to get distracted or try to cash in. It would be great if Wikipedia's nonprofit model could extend to other areas, but it is exceedingly rare for modern internet services to need so little ongoing investment. Indeed, the two most prominent attempts to replicate Wikipedia's success in other domains have both since pivoted away from their founding nonprofit structures.

The first is Mozilla, creator of the Firefox web browser. Mozilla began in 1998 as an open-source project to steward code for the early web browser Netscape Communicator. In 2005, two years after spinning out Netscape assets as a nonprofit, Mozilla created a for-profit subsidiary, the Mozilla Corporation. This allowed it to pursue more aggressive business tactics that are prohibited for tax-exempt nonprofits, including inking a multi-hundred-million-dollar deal with Google and acquiring smaller companies to accelerate product development.

The second example is OpenAI, creator of ChatGPT and other tools. OpenAI originally started as a nonprofit in 2015. Four years later, it rolled out a for-profit subsidiary to raise the billions of dollars it needed to compete with Big Tech AI efforts. The startup went corporate.

It's hard to be a nonprofit in a for-profit world. Both of these organizations' transitions were probably necessary. The internet is a highly competitive place dominated by big companies with tens of billions of dollars in cash reserves. Competing without generating revenue or accessing capital markets immediately puts nonprofits at a disadvantage. The nonprofit model sounds good in theory, but it is very hard to make work in practice.

Federated Networks

Another solution to better governance is to return to protocol networks. Jack Dorsey, co-founder and former chief executive of Twitter, has advocated for this approach. No "individual or institutions should own social media, or more generally media companies. It should be an open and verifiable protocol," Dorsey tweeted in April 2022, after having stepped down as Twitter CEO. Later that year, asked to reflect on his tenure, Dorsey added that Twitter becoming a company was "the biggest issue and my biggest regret."

We've already discussed some attempts to revive protocol networks in "The Fall of RSS." There have been many others: Friend of a Friend, a 2000s-era decentralized protocol for social graphs. StatusNet, a distributed open-source social network, from 2009, which later merged with similar projects, FreeSocial and GNU Social. Scuttlebutt, a self-hosted social networking project, from 2014. Mastodon, a network built on the decentralized social protocol ActivityPub, from 2016. The web creator Tim Berners-Lee's Solid, short for "social linked data," in 2018. Bluesky, a Dorsey-backed Twitter alternative that uses a decentralized protocol of its own design, incubated in 2019. Meta's answer to Twitter, Threads, which launched in 2023 and will one day interoperate with ActivityPub, so the company says. Miscellaneous others: Friendica (decentralized Facebook), Funkwhale (decentralized SoundCloud), Pixelfed (decentralized Instagram), Pleroma (decentralized Twitter), PeerTube (decentralized YouTube), and more.

People keep trying to make the protocol approach to social networking work. Maybe one or more of these protocols will achieve mainstream adoption, but they have challenges to overcome, many arising from their network designs. Most implementations rely on a specific variation of protocol networks called federated networks. These protocols don't use centralized data centers to host people's data the way corporate networks do. Instead, people run their own instances of the software, called servers, to host the data. People refer to such efforts, collectively, as the Fediverse.

Several Twitter alternatives, including some mentioned above—Bluesky, Mastodon, Meta's Threads—either work or intend to work this way. Anyone can download open-source software and run their own server or apply for an account as a user at an existing server. Every server has its own admissions process and community standards. Cross-server communications protocols, the most popular of which is ActivityPub, allow users to follow the activity of users on other servers. This lets the system simulate some features of centralized systems without having a single company in control.

A physical analogy helps to explain the design. Think of a corporate network like Twitter as a large country with a single ruler. By contrast, federated networks are like a collection of smaller countries, each controlled by a single ruler. These countries are still dictatorships, but there are now many dictatorships to choose from. Users can decide where to spend time, which gives them some say over how they are governed. The system is an improvement over corporate networks, where there is no choice.

Federated networks have two main weaknesses, though. The first is friction. The impediments are due mainly to the boundaries between servers that are running independently. For example, searching for content and interacting with users across servers can be cumbersome because there is no central data repository. One server might store a user's post, and another server might store a reply to that post, but no central servers store the entire thread. This makes it difficult to provide a global view of what is happening across the network.

Because of their architecture, federated networks have difficulty matching the smooth user experiences of other networks. Corporate networks eliminate friction by storing data in centralized data centers while blockchain networks eliminate friction by storing data on a blockchain. (Recall that blockchains are distributed, virtual computers that can store arbitrary information, including social data.) Federated networks, like protocol networks, have no centralized components, and thus no central place to store data, which is a problem because, as history shows, even small amounts of friction can stymie adoption.

How might one fix this? Imagine another system on top of a federated network that collects data from the individual servers and aggregates that data into a single, centralized database. Sometimes servers will disagree, so the system needs a way to adjudicate disputes to decide which servers best represent the network's true state. Well, guess what? We've just invented a blockchain. Blockchains provide a mechanism for centralizing data while keeping control of that data decentralized.

Many proponents of federated networks refuse to use or even to consider blockchains, presumably because of the associations blockchains have with the casino culture of scams and speculation. This is unfortunate. Anyone who looks at blockchains dispassionately will see them as powerful tools that can help to compete with corporate networks. (See "The Computer versus the Casino" for more.)

To complicate matters further, some federated-network proponents will consider using blockchains, but only specific blockchains. For one, Dorsey has expressed interest in using Bitcoin as part of a decentralized social network. The problem is that Bitcoin has high transaction fees (typically more than $1 per transaction) and slow transaction times (usually ten minutes or longer, depending on various factors including network conditions). Some projects are trying to fix these limitations by building layers on top of Bitcoin. I hope they succeed. Without them, it's hard to see how Bitcoin can be a key component of a decentralized social network that can credibly challenge corporate networks.

Meanwhile, other systems already have sufficient performance to help power next-generation social networks. Newer blockchains and so-called layer-two systems built on top of Ethereum are among the existing options.

Protocol Coups

The second weakness of federated networks is the risk of protocol coups. That is, even if a federated network succeeds, it may spawn a new corporate network and thereby re-create the same problems discussed throughout this book.

As mentioned, federated networks are like a federation of countries. They have common rules but they still have cross-border frictions. Users tend to cluster in the most popular country (read: server), which gives that country's ruler (read: server owner) effectively unlimited authority to set and change rules. People who study such systems are aware of the risks. As one privacy researcher aptly put it in a 2018 blog post titled "Federation Is the Worst of All Worlds," "Without building consent and resistance into the protocol and infrastructure, we're just forcing most users to pick a new dictator for their data without any real basis for that choice."

Nothing binds a server in a federated network to its word. That's the problem. The system has no guardrails.

Similar coups have already happened. As discussed in "The Fall of RSS," people once viewed Twitter as an interoperable node in RSS's open network, even though it was, in fact, a corporate network. Eventually, Twitter pivoted and removed support for RSS. It switched from attract to extract mode, as is the fate of all corporate networks. A successful federated network would face the same coup threat from its largest nodes. Without stronger constraints in place, it would be only a matter of time before economic incentives superseded high-minded ideals.

Consider the typical life cycle of a server in a federated network. Running a server as a hobby works for a while, but if it grows to millions of users, the costs to run it go up too. Networks need money to grow, which is why most major social networks have raised billions of dollars in funding. The money can come from investors or from revenue sources like subscriptions and advertising. Since federated networks have no core by design, they have no easy way to raise money for the network itself. Instead, the money will find its way to popular servers. In time, the corporate network logic will take hold and interoperability will become a liability. The servers will clamp down, just as Twitter did—attract, extract.

Breaking a large dictatorship, like a corporate network, into smaller dictatorships, as in federated networks, works only if the countries stay small. But network effects ensure the opposite, that small advantages compound to create big winners. Thus, federated networks have a tendency, a fundamental by-product of their architecture, to evolve into corporate networks. The strongest nodes can co-opt the network.

It's worth noting that the risk of protocol coups exists even in classic protocol networks like email and the web. Nodes that acquire large user bases can exert outsized influence. Gmail and Chrome both have billions of users, which gives Google an outsized number of "votes" it can use to sway email and web governance in its favor. For example, Gmail's approach to spam filtering favors email sent by other large email providers. As a result, people sending email from personal or small-business-hosted servers get flagged as spam more often. This is a relatively minor issue affecting email purists, but Gmail has gotten so popular that Google could probably go much further and unilaterally modify core email standards if it wanted to. So far, Google hasn't tried this, partly because other large companies like Apple and Microsoft act as counterweights, and partly because the communities that have formed around email and the web have strong, deeply entrenched norms.

New networks don't have the same counterweights and historical norms. When governance is a function of network topology, as in protocol and federated networks, corporate takeover is always a risk. Communities need a network architecture that allows for growth while minimizing the risk of protocol coups. In the absence of rules explicitly enshrined in code, only custom—nothing more—keeps tyrants at bay.

Blockchains as Network Constitutions

Blockchains offer a new approach to network governance that gives people the ability to encode immutable rules in software. These rules can specify how networks are governed and in so doing build trust, improve transparency, and resist takeover.

National constitutions, like the U.S. Constitution, provide a helpful analogy. Constitutions formalized the shift of national governance from individual rulers to written law. In the same vein, blockchains shift network governance from corporate management to written code. Like legal documents, software can be extremely expressive. Blockchain governance systems are written in general-purpose programming languages that can codify virtually any governance system that can be written in English as a step-by-step procedure. They are constitutions for networks.

Even in the presence of a blockchain, forms of governance can vary widely. A blockchain constitution can emulate corporate networks by putting a single organization in charge. The leader can change whatever it wants, including algorithms, economics, and access rules. Alternatively, a blockchain constitution can restrict the powers of a leader, as in a constitutional monarchy. A blockchain constitution can also establish a light-touch republic with no single ruler, and it can set fees and controls to minimal levels in a way that takes inspiration from protocol networks. Most blockchain networks push decisions to the community, incarnating a governance design analogous to constitutional democracy. These are only a few points on a wide, multidimensional spectrum of possibilities: any system that can be written down can be realized.

Blockchain Governance

Blockchain governance tends to come in two flavors. Some blockchain networks use what's called off-chain governance, which is similar to protocol network governance in that the network is run by a coalition of developers, users, and other community members. The advantage of off-chain governance is that it is time tested, building on decades of lessons learned from protocol networks and open-source software projects. The downside is that, as with protocol networks, governance is a function of network structure. If certain nodes get too popular and gain too much power relative to others, they can take over the network.

Many newer blockchain networks use "on-chain" governance, where token holders explicitly vote on proposed network changes. They do this with voting software that lets them sign blockchain transactions associated with tokens they hold. These signatures indicate which way they are voting when proposals are made. The blockchain network automatically obeys the outcome of the vote. If you depend on a network, you'll probably want to cast a ballot.

Clout in on-chain governance is usually a function of how many tokens a voter holds. Divorcing governance from network structure removes the risk of large software providers gaining outsized influence. But tokens trading on open markets introduces a new risk: that a deep-pocketed actor could gain disproportionate influence. In other words, there is a risk of plutocracy, where big token holders could co-opt the network.

The best way to mitigate this risk is with a broad distribution of tokens. Token ownership should be widespread across the community such that no voting bloc has too much power. This requires thoughtful faucet design, as discussed in the previous chapter.

Some networks also have a second line of defense against plutocracy: splitting voters into two groups. The approach resembles the bicameral systems used by national governments, such as the U.S. Senate and House of Representatives. In a blockchain network, one house might consist of respected community members chosen by a foundation, while the other might consist of token holders. Sometimes the foundation house can veto proposals made by the token house if it deems the proposals overly self-interested. Other times certain responsibilities, such as technical and financial decisions, are split across houses.

Network	Governing Body	Governance Method	Pros	Cons
Protocol Networks and Blockchain Networks With Off-Chain Governance	Community	Informal, emergent from network structure	Changes slowly, mostly limited to technical upgrades	Risk of takeover by large nodes, slow moving
Corporate Networks	Company	Legal ownership	Fast, unilateral decision making	Opaque, undemocratic, serves company interests
Blockchain Networks With On-Chain Governance	Community	Formal, through token voting	Intentionally designed, resilient to network changes	Risk of plutocracy: big token holders with too much power

Blockchain networks vary in how much they can be modified through governance. At one extreme are networks where any participant can propose changes to core network code. Users submit proposals on discussion forums, either as informal proposals or as working code. Proposals with enough support go to a token-holder vote. If a proposal passes, the network implements the updates automatically. No further action is necessary.

At the other extreme are networks where the token holders don't have any control over core network code. Once the software is uploaded to a blockchain, that's it. It's immutable. The code just runs on autopilot. This means new versions of the software are released as entirely new networks, coexisting with older versions that remain indefinitely active. Token holders cannot tamper with the code, which limits what they're able to do and simplifies governance debates. Instead, token holders vote on more limited matters, such as supporting software development with treasury distributions.

None of these governance systems are perfect, but being able to formalize network governance at all represents a step forward in network design. The problem with informal governance is that rules and leaders inevitably emerge, but they are usually a product of inscrutable social dynamics rather than thoughtful design. The feminist author Jo Freeman calls this "the tyranny of structurelessness." In her 1972 essay of the same name, she describes how hidden, unaccountable hierarchies form within supposedly leaderless organizations. When you create formal rules, you can debate them, learn from them, and improve them. (This is also why when tech startups experiment with "holacracy" and other structureless management styles, it almost never ends well.)

This is one advantage corporate networks have over protocol networks. Someone is in charge, usually a CEO, and that person is chosen through a process that at least tries to pick good leaders and hold them to account. In protocol and federated networks, there are still rules and leaders, but they are usually the products of opaque interpersonal relations rather than well-considered processes that are designed to keep power dynamics in check.

Network designers can use blockchains to create formal rules that are enforced by code. These rules are like constitutions for networks. What these constitutions say is subject to debate, contention, and experimentation, but their very existence, the ability to enshrine rules in immutable software, is a meaningful advance that was not possible in previous network designs. Now is the time to think intentionally about network governance, a subject far too consequential to leave up to chance.

Blockchain constitutions enable users to share in the control of networks, just as composability enables developers to share in contributions to software and tokens enable participants to become owners with interests. By combining these tools, we can build a new generation of community-owned networks—digital cities that provide something for everybody, because they are built by everybody.

Part Four
Here and Now

12. The Computer versus the Casino

Technology happens. It's not good, it's not bad.
Is steel good or bad?

—Andy Grove

Two distinct cultures are interested in blockchains. The first sees blockchains as a way to build new networks, as described here throughout. I call this culture the computer because, at its core, it's about blockchains powering a new computing movement.

The other culture is mainly interested in speculation and money-making. Those of this mindset see blockchains solely as a way to create new tokens for trading. I call this culture the casino because, at its core, it's really just about gambling.

Media coverage exacerbates confusion over the two cultures. That blockchain networks are so transparent and tokens are tradable 24/7/365 means there is an abundance of public information for reporters, analysts, and others to draw from. Unfortunately, many news stories focus almost exclusively on short-term activity, like price action, to the exclusion of long-term topics, like infrastructure and application development. Tales of fortunes won and lost are dramatic, easy to explain, and attention grabbing. In contrast, the technology story is nuanced, slow to develop, and requires historical context to understand. (That's a big reason why I wrote this book.)

Casino culture is problematic. It takes tokens out of context, wraps them in marketing language, and encourages speculation in them. Whereas responsible token exchanges provide useful services, such as custody, staking, and market liquidity, reckless ones encourage bad behavior and play fast and loose with people's money. Many of these are offshore and feature leveraged derivatives as well as other speculative financial products. At worst, they're outright Ponzi schemes. In the most extreme cases, the casino culture's obsession with gambling has led to catastrophes like the bankruptcy of the Bahamas-based exchange FTX, which cost innocent customers billions of dollars.

In addition to hurting people, the excesses of casino culture have provoked a backlash, including reactions from regulators and policymakers that can be counterproductive. For the most part, regulators have ignored the more extreme casino-culture activity, partly because much of it is offshore and hard to reach. They have instead focused on the nearest and easiest targets: tech companies based in the United States. This has incentivized exactly the wrong behavior. Ethical entrepreneurs are afraid to build products, and development is increasingly moving abroad. Meanwhile, scammers operate in foreign jurisdictions mostly unchecked, further emboldening the casino culture.

Some critics say blockchain networks benefit from lack of regulation. This could not be further from the truth. Financial regulations can, when designed properly, protect consumers, aid law enforcement, and promote national interests, all while enabling responsible entrepreneurs to innovate and experiment. The United States led the way with smart internet regulations in the 1990s that helped make it the center of internet innovation. There's an opportunity to lead the way again in the new era.

Regulating Tokens

The area of regulation most often discussed with respect to tokens is securities laws. Financial regulations are complex and vary by jurisdiction, but it's worth briefly discussing securities laws and how they might relate to tokens.

Securities are the subset of the world's traded assets where investors are reliant on a small group of people, usually a management team, to generate a return on their investment. Securities laws are designed to reduce the risks that arise from this dependency by, among other things, applying disclosure obligations to securities issuers, as well as to certain other parties that transact in securities. These disclosures are designed to limit the ability of market participants with privileged information, including the management team, from taking advantage of others with less information. In other words, securities are assets where pockets of information exist that are accessible to some people but not to others.

The most familiar example of a security is corporate stock, like a share of Apple stock. There is a group of people at Apple, including the management team, who might have information that is material to Apple's stock price. These people might know things like the next quarter's earnings, information that could move the stock price. There are also vendors and commercial counterparties that might have material information about Apple's business dealings. Because Apple's stock is freely traded on public markets, anyone can acquire shares of the stock and, in so doing, would be trusting Apple's management team to generate returns. They would also be trusting that their trading counterparties don't have material information that might affect the stock price. Security regulations are designed to ensure that Apple fully discloses material information in a timely manner to the general public, thereby reducing or eliminating any potential information asymmetries.

Commodities are also a subset of the world's traded assets, but they are regulated differently than securities. The most familiar example of a commodity that is not a security is gold. Information about commodities like gold isn't uniformly distributed, but it is, for the most part, uniformly accessible. There are, of course, gold-related companies, like mining firms, and there are investors and analysts who might be skilled at predicting the price of gold. But there isn't a set of people who have special information that could affect the price of gold the way there is with a security like Apple stock. The ecosystem around gold and other commodities is decentralized enough that anybody can, in principle, conduct research and compete on a level playing field with other market participants.

When tokens are classified as securities or as being sold in a securities transaction, they are subject to securities laws. Most of these laws were created in the 1930s, long before the information technology revolution. Applying these laws, as written, would raise a host of issues, creating hurdles that would make it difficult if not impossible for users to transact directly in tokens. Absent changes, clarifications, or narrowing interpretations of these laws, transactions of tokens classified as securities would generally need to be intermediated by registered securities brokers and exchanges, a recentralization process that would destroy a large part of the value and potential of the technology—that is, decentralization.

Tokens are digital building blocks, analogous to how websites are digital building blocks. Imagine if every time you wanted to use an internet service that used tokens as securities you had to go through the process you currently go through when buying a share of equity. Rather than just opening a social media app and scrolling, you would first have to log in to your brokerage account and place an order to purchase tokens. Want to use that app? Sign this paperwork and wait for your order to settle.

Ultimately, for tokens to achieve their potential, they can't be regulated as conventional securities within current securities laws regimes. These regimes were designed for a world that used analog tools to transfer stock certificates representing interests in companies. Blockchain networks can compete with corporate networks only if they can offer comparable, state-of-the-art user experiences. Friction is a death knell.

The good news is that the fundamental goals of regulators and of blockchain builders are ultimately aligned. Securities laws try to eliminate pockets of asymmetric information with respect to publicly traded securities, thereby minimizing the trust that market participants need to place in management teams. Blockchain builders try to eliminate centralized pockets of economic and governance power, thereby reducing the amount of trust users must place in other network actors. Although the motives and tools are different, disclosure regimes and network decentralization have the same philosophical goal: eliminating the need for trust.

Regulators and policymakers generally agree that tokens that power "sufficiently decentralized" blockchain networks should be classified as commodities, not securities. It is widely agreed that Bitcoin has reached this threshold of sufficient decentralization. There is no group of people who have special knowledge that is material to the future price of Bitcoin. Therefore, Bitcoin is classified as a commodity like gold, instead of a security like Apple stock, and isn't subject to cumbersome processes.

Every software project starts small, with a founder or group of founders. Bitcoin started with Satoshi Nakamoto, Ethereum had a core founding team, and so on. At the early stages, by virtue of being small, these projects were centralized. At some point, however, the initial development teams behind Bitcoin and Ethereum faded into the background and the broader community became the driving force. Other, more recent projects are at various stages of decentralization, a process that takes time.

The challenge for entrepreneurs building blockchain networks under current rules is that although they are clear at the beginning and end, they aren't clear in the middle. What precisely does it mean to be sufficiently decentralized? The best guidelines come from regulations and court precedents from the pre-internet era. The most famous is a 1946 U.S. Supreme Court case that created what's called the Howey test for deciding what constitutes an "investment contract," another term for a security. The Howey test consists of three elements, or prongs. Applied to digital assets, the test looks at whether an offer or sale of digital assets involves (1) an investment of money, (2) in a common enterprise, (3) with a reasonable expectation of profit to be derived from the efforts of others. All three prongs must be met for the offer or sale of a digital asset to be considered a securities transaction.

As of this writing, the last time the Securities and Exchange Commission (SEC), the main regulator of the U.S. securities markets, gave substantive guidance on the topic was in 2019. The guidance suggested that blockchain networks that were sufficiently decentralized would fail the "efforts of others" portion of the third prong of the Howey test, and therefore that securities laws would not apply to their tokens. The agency has since brought several enforcement actions alleging that certain transactions of tokens were subject to securities laws, and it has done so without providing further clarification about the criteria by which it makes these determinations.

Applying pre-internet legal precedents to modern networks leaves gray areas that provide significant advantages to bad actors and non-U.S. companies that don't follow U.S. rules. Bad actors take shortcuts to decentralization. They are quick to launch tokens, which help them grow. Meanwhile, good faith actors spend heavily on lawyers to determine how "sufficient decentralization" applies to their projects, which creates a competitive disadvantage compared with those who don't bother to do so. The situation today is so complex that regulators themselves can't agree where to draw the line. For example, the SEC has suggested that Ethereum's token is a security, but the Commodity Futures Trading Commission, the primary U.S. regulator of commodities, has said that it is a commodity.

Ideally, policymakers and regulators would clarify the criteria that distinguish securities and commodities and provide a path for new projects to become sufficiently decentralized such that they are regulated as commodities. Today Bitcoin is the gold standard for decentralization, but it too started out centralized, as all inventions do. Had regulations without a path to decentralization been in place back in 2009, Bitcoin could never have been created. Without such a path, older technologies that developed before regulations were in place will be allowed, but new technologies will be blocked. In effect, this would arbitrarily outlaw future innovation.

It should be noted that there are various regulations that apply across the board to traded assets, whether they are securities or commodities. For example, for any traded asset, it's illegal to corner the market or manipulate prices. Consumer protection laws also prohibit false advertising and other misleading behavior. Everyone agrees these rules should apply to digital assets just as they do to traditional assets. The debate is focused on the narrower question of when digital assets should be subject to additional rules traditionally reserved for assets classified as securities.

Ownership and Markets Are Inextricable

Some policymakers have proposed rules that would effectively ban tokens and therefore, for all practical purposes, blockchains. If tokens were purely for speculation, these proposals might be justified. But, as I've argued here, speculation is just a side effect of tokens' true purpose as essential tools that enable community-owned networks.

Because tokens can, like all ownable things, be traded, it is easy to think of them as purely financial assets. Properly designed tokens have specific uses, including as native tokens that incentivize network development and power virtual economies. Tokens are not a sideshow of blockchain networks, a nuisance that can be stripped out and discarded. They are a necessary and central feature. Community ownership doesn't work unless communities have a way to own.

Sometimes people ask if it's possible to get the benefits of blockchains while removing any hint of the casino by making tokens impossible to trade, through either legal or technical means. If you remove the ability to buy or sell something, however, you remove ownership. Even intangibles, like copyrights and intellectual property, can be bought and sold at their owners' discretion. No trading means no ownership; you can't have one without the other.

Eliminating token trading also interferes with the productive uses of blockchains. Blockchains need token incentives to motivate validators to run network nodes, which cost money to operate. Whereas corporate networks fund their operations and development with fundraising, stock options, and revenues, blockchain networks fund their operations and development with tokens. If there aren't markets or prices associated with tokens, then users can't buy tokens to access the network. They also can't convert tokens into dollars or other currencies, making it hard, if not impossible, to use tokens as incentives for network participants, as discussed in "Building Networks with Token Incentives" and "Tokenomics." There are no known ways to design permissionless blockchains without tokens and token trading, and you should be skeptical of anyone who tells you otherwise.

One interesting question is whether hybrid approaches can tame the casino while still allowing the computer to be built. One proposal would prohibit token reselling after the debut of a new blockchain network, either for some fixed period or until specified milestones are met. Tokens could still be awarded as incentives to grow the network, but token holders might need to wait several years, or until the network hits certain thresholds, before trading restrictions are lifted.

Time horizons can be a very effective way to align people's incentives with broader, societal interests. Think of the hype cycle described earlier that technologies go through, with the early hype phase followed by a crash and then the "plateau of productivity." Long-term restrictions force token holders to weather the hype and its aftermath and to realize value by contributing to productive growth.

Some blockchain networks are self-imposing these kinds of restrictions, and there are legislative proposals in the United States and elsewhere to make temporary token restrictions mandatory. This would allow blockchain networks to use token incentives as a tool to compete with corporate networks, and it would encourage token holders to focus on creating long-term value as opposed to short-term hype. The milestones can also be tied to regulatory targets like "sufficient decentralization," satisfying the goals of securities and other regulatory regimes.

The industry needs further regulation, to be clear, and that regulation should focus on achieving policy objectives, like punishing bad actors, protecting consumers, providing stable markets, and encouraging responsible innovation. The stakes are high. As I've argued here, blockchain networks are the only known technology that can reestablish an open, democratic internet.

Limited Liability Corporations: A Regulatory Success Story

History shows that smart regulation can accelerate innovation. Until the mid-nineteenth century, the dominant corporate structure was a partnership. In a partnership, all the shareholders are partners and bear full liability for the actions of the business. If the company has a financial loss or causes nonfinancial harm, the liability pierces the corporate shield and falls on the shareholders. Imagine if shareholders of public companies like IBM and GE were personally liable, beyond any money invested, for mistakes the companies made. Very few people would buy stocks, making it much harder for companies to raise capital.

Limited liability corporations did exist back in the early nineteenth century, but were rare. Forming one required a special legislative act. As a result, almost all business ventures were close-knit partnerships among people who deeply trusted one another, like family members or close friends.

This changed during the railway boom of the 1830s and the period of industrialization that followed. Railroads and other heavy industries required significant up-front capital—more than could be provided by small groups, even when the groups were very wealthy. New and broadened sources of capital were needed to fund a transformation of the world economy.

As you might expect, the upheaval ignited controversy. Lawmakers faced pressure to make limited liability the new corporate standard. Meanwhile, skeptics argued that expanding limited liability would encourage reckless behavior, effectively transferring risk from shareholders to customers and society at large.

Eventually, the factions settled on a way forward. Industry and lawmakers crafted sensible compromises, arranged legal frameworks, and made limited liability the new norm. This led to the creation of public capital markets for stocks and bonds and all the wealth and wonders those innovations have generated since. Thus, technological innovation drove pragmatic changes to regulation.

The history of economic participation is one of increasing inclusion thanks to a combination of tech and legal advances. Partnerships had small groups of owners that counted in the tens. The limited liability structure expanded ownership dramatically, to the point that public companies today have millions of shareholders. Blockchain networks, through mechanisms such as airdrops, grants, and contributor rewards, expand the circle once more. Future networks could have billions of owners.

Just as industrial-era businesses had new organizational needs, so do network-era businesses today. Corporate networks bolt an old legal structure, C-corporations and LLCs and the like, onto a new network structure. This mismatch is the root cause of many of the problems with corporate networks, including their inexorable switchover from attract to extract mode and the exclusion of so many contributors from the upside of their networks. The world needs new, digitally native ways for people to coordinate, cooperate, collaborate, compete.

Blockchains provide a sensible organizational structure for networks. Tokens are the natural asset class. Policymakers and industry leaders can work together to find the right guardrails for blockchain networks, just as their forerunners did for limited liability corporations. The rules should permit and encourage decentralization, not default to centralization as corporate entities do. There are many things that can be done to rein in casino culture while allowing computer culture to develop. Hopefully, smart regulators will encourage innovation and let founders do what they do best—build the future.

The casino should not hold the computer down.

Part Five
What's Next

13. The iPhone Moment: From Incubation to Growth

The future is not to be forecast, but created.

—**Arthur C. Clarke**

It can takes years, decades even, for new computing platforms to go from prototype to mainstream adoption. This is true for hardware-based computers like PCs, mobile phones, and VR headsets, and it's also true for software-based virtual computers like blockchains and AI systems. After years of false starts, someone releases a breakthrough product that kicks off a period of exponential growth.

The PC industry followed this pattern. The Altair was one of the first PCs when it launched in 1974, but the launch of the IBM PC in 1981 kicked off the industry's growth phase. Even then, enthusiasts mostly used PCs to make games and hack around. Incumbent computer companies dismissed PCs as overpriced toys because they didn't solve problems for their existing customers who wanted higher-end machines. But then PC developers built applications like word processors and spreadsheets, and the market exploded.

The internet developed this way too. The incubation phase took place in the 1980s and early 1990s, when it was mostly a text-based tool used by academia and government. Then, with the release of the Mosaic web browser in 1993 and the wave of commercialization that followed, the growth phase kicked off and has continued ever since.

AI has had the longest gestation period of any computing movement to date. The researchers Warren McCulloch and Walter Pitts conceived of neural networks, the core models that underpin modern AI, in a 1943 paper. Seven years later, Alan Turing wrote his famous paper outlining what people now call the Turing test, the idea that truly intelligent AI could answer questions in a way that is indistinguishable from a human. After many so-called summer and winter cycles, when funding sources came and went, AI now appears to be going mainstream, eighty years from its inception. Advances in graphics processing units, or GPUs, the special computer chips that underpin the technology, are a major reason why. GPU performance has been improving along an exponential curve, enabling neural networks to scale to trillions of parameters, the key driver of the intelligence of AI systems.

When I was an entrepreneur and starting out as a part-time investor, around the time the iPhone debuted in 2007, everyone was talking about mobile computing. My friends and I were starting to explore potential mobile applications and everyone wanted to know what the "killer apps" might be. Recent history provided a clue. Some apps that were already popular on PCs would likely translate to mobile, it was safe to assume. Shopping and social networking would no doubt continue to be popular adaptations. These mobile apps would be the skeuomorphic uses, taking existing activities and making them better.

Another clue came from mobile's novel capabilities. Killer apps seemed likely to take advantage of these unique traits. The iPhone had many things that PCs didn't. The device was always with you.

It had GPS sensors and a built-in camera. These features enabled native uses, brand-new things you couldn't do before.

In retrospect, the biggest hits closely followed this pattern. Breakout apps exploited the unique capabilities of mobile phones while also reimagining popular activities. Instagram and TikTok were social networks that relied on the camera. Uber and Door-Dash were on-demand delivery services that relied on GPS. WhatsApp and Snapchat were messaging apps that relied on always being with you.

In 2007, the big question for mobile was, what kinds of mobile apps would matter? Today the big question for blockchains is, what kinds of blockchain networks will matter? Blockchain infrastructure only recently matured enough to support internet-scale applications. The industry is likely now nearing the end of its incubation phase and entering its growth phase. It is a good time to be asking what a killer blockchain network might look like.

Some blockchain networks will be skeuomorphic, doing what could have been done before, but better. Social networks are an obvious choice. They're where people spend the most time, they influence billions of users' ideas and behaviors, and they're the primary economic engine for creators. Blockchains can create social networks that eliminate the high take rates and capricious rules that characterize today's corporate networks.

Another important skeuomorphic category will likely be financial networks. Sending money should be as easy as sending text messages. Improving how payments work is mostly a collective action problem, something blockchains are well suited to solve. Blockchain-based payment systems could lower fees, reduce friction, and unlock new categories of applications.

There will also be important blockchain networks that are native, doing what couldn't be done before. I expect many of these will involve media and creative activities. Other native applications will intersect with emerging areas like AI and virtual worlds, as I discuss in the sections ahead.

Inevitably, there will be categories of applications not covered here that end up being important. Entrepreneurs and developers who build the future are always going to outsmart armchair predictions. Nevertheless, I will try to make some informed guesses about what popular blockchain networks we might see in the read-write-own era. The list is non-exhaustive. I hope it will get you thinking.

14. Some Promising Applications

Social Networks: Millions of Profitable Niches

In his classic 2008 essay, "1,000 True Fans," Kevin Kelly, the founder of *Wired,* predicted the internet would transform the economics of creative activities. He saw the internet as the ultimate matchmaker, enabling twenty-first-century patronage. No matter how niche, creators could discover their true fans, who would, in turn, support them:

> To be a successful creator you don't need millions. You don't need millions of dollars or millions of customers, millions of clients or millions of fans. To make a living as a crafts-person, photographer, musician, designer, author, animator, app maker, entrepreneur, or inventor you need only thousands of true fans.
>
> A true fan is defined as a fan that will buy anything you produce. These diehard fans will drive 200 miles to see you

sing; they will buy the hardback and paperback and audible versions of your book; they will purchase your next figurine sight unseen; they will pay for the "best-of" DVD version of your free YouTube channel; they will come to your chef's table once a month.

Kelly's vision hasn't exactly panned out. The reality is creators do, generally, need millions of fans, or at least hundreds of thousands, to support themselves today. Corporate networks got in the way, inserting themselves between creators and audiences, siphoning away value and becoming the dominant way for people to connect.

Social networks are probably the most important networks on the internet today. Besides their economic impact, they have a huge effect on people's lives. The average internet user spends almost two and a half hours a day on social networks. Next to text messaging, social networking is the most popular online activity.

The design of the dominant social networks explains what went wrong. Powerful network effects locked users into Big Tech's clutches, and that lock-in led to high take rates. It's hard to know precisely what take rates many major corporate networks charge, because their terms can be opaque and noncommittal, but it's reasonable to estimate they charge around 99 percent. With the combined revenue of the five biggest social networks—Facebook, Instagram, YouTube, TikTok, and Twitter—at about $150 billion per year, that means these networks pay out on the order of $20 billion to users, with the overwhelming majority of that share coming from YouTube alone.

Corporate networks won out because they made it easy for people to connect—more so than protocol networks like RSS did. But that doesn't mean corporate networks are the only, or even the best, way for people to connect. The alternative to today's world would be one where social networks are decentralized and community owned, meaning built with either protocol or blockchain architectures. This could have meaningful economic effects for users, creators, and developers and could revive Kelly's compelling vision for internet patronage.

To understand the effect of a different network design, let's do some back-of-the-envelope math. Protocol networks have take rates that are effectively zero. Sometimes companies build apps on top of these networks, providing easy access and other features. Substack does this for email newsletters, and it charges roughly 10 percent for the convenience. (Substack's take rates stay low, as in other markets that respect ownership, because users own their connections—that is, their email subscriber lists—which they can export and load into rival email access providers at any time.)

Let's pretend the top five social networks charged a similar amount. If they all had take rates of 10 percent, their share of the $150 billion in annual revenue would drop from $130 billion to $15 billion. That would put into the pockets of network participants such as creators an extra $115 billion per year. How many lives might that change? At the average U.S. salary of $59,000 per year, that extra $115 billion of redirected revenue could fund almost two million jobs. This is a rough estimate, but the numbers are clearly big.

Low take rates have a multiplier effect. More money to the edges of the network means more people reach an income level where they can pursue creative work full-time. The two-tier class system that divides creators and users on most social networks would become more permeable. Barriers to social mobility would ease as more users could build sustainable media enterprises of one. Meanwhile, full-time work would result in better-quality content for others to consume, attracting larger audiences and generating more income across the network.

Better economics for creators leads to a virtuous cycle. Millions of people working full-time on creative activities improves the quality of the internet for everyone. Social networking should be a place to chat and trade memes, but it should also supercharge longer-form activities: writing essays, creating games, making movies, composing music, recording podcasts, and more. These endeavors require time, money, and effort. For the internet to be an accelerator of deep creativity, it needs a better economic engine.

Creating new jobs isn't just nice; it's necessary. As new technologies like AI automate work, social networks can be a counterweight that provides people with fulfilling career opportunities.

Decentralized social networks would also be good for users and software developers. The high take rates, capricious rules, and platform risks of corporate networks are deterrents for developers. In contrast, decentralized networks encourage investment and building. With more tools being built, users can shop around for a greater variety of software and features. Choice drives competition, which leads to better user experiences. Don't like the way a client ranks posts, filters spam, or tracks your personal data? Switch. Nothing's holding you back, and you won't lose your connections.

This might all sound great in theory. The practical question is whether today, given where we are in the evolution of social networking, it's possible to build a decentralized social network that can actually succeed. Occasionally users awaken to the problems of today's platforms, and after an incident happens—a deplatforming, a rule change, a new corporate owner, a data privacy or legal scandal—people flee to some upstart social network. These anti-communities usually don't last. Durable social networks are built out of friendships and shared interests, not anger.

The value proposition needs to be full parity with corporate network user experiences, plus much better economics. Corporate social networks succeeded because they made it so easy for people to connect. It's not too late to design decentralized social networks that make connecting just as easy. Protocol social networks like

RSS were a good starting point, but they failed because they lacked the features and funding of corporate rivals. Blockchains can address both shortcomings. We can now, for the first time ever, build networks with the societal benefits of protocol networks and the competitive advantages to rival corporate networks. Indeed, the timing is right: blockchains have only recently become performant enough to support social networking.

Today, a cohort of blockchain projects is taking on the social networking establishment. Each project is designed in its own way, but the common thread is that each one overcomes the weaknesses that doomed RSS. The best designs fund software developers and subsidize username registrations and hosting fees through their token treasuries, analogous to corporate coffers. And in terms of features, blockchains have core infrastructure that provides a centralized global state to support basic services, making it easy to search and follow across the entire network, avoiding the user experience issues that the partitioning in protocol networks and federated networks creates (as covered in "Federated Networks").

The key marketing challenge is to kick-start a network effect. One tactic is to start on the supply side, where the pain of high take rates is greatest. Users may not realize how much value they're forgoing by participating in corporate networks, but creators and software developers care deeply about how much money they earn. Offering a predictable platform where they receive a greater share of the value they generate would be a compelling proposition. If the best content and software were available only on another platform, the demand side of the network—the users, many of whom are passive consumers—would likely seek it out. That users can participate in a blockchain network's economic upside and governance, privileges from which they were previously excluded, adds further motivation for them to switch.

Starting in narrow and deep niches could help a new social network get over the initial hump. Targeting a group with common interests, like people interested in new technologies or new media genres, is one way to plant the seeds of a community. The most valuable users will likely be up-and-comers who don't have big followings elsewhere. When YouTube started out, it didn't succeed by getting creators from TV and other forms of media. New stars rose along with the platform. That's the power of native over skeuomorphic thinking.

What we have today may feel like a golden age for creative people: creators can push a button and instantly publish to five billion people. They can find fans, critics, and collaborators just about anywhere on earth. But they're mostly forced to route everything through corporate networks that devour tens of billions of dollars that might otherwise have funded an immeasurably greater diversity of content. Imagine how much creativity we're missing out on because earlier attempts at decentralized social networks, while noble, like RSS, couldn't hold their own.

We can do better. The internet should be an accelerant for human creativity and authenticity, not an inhibitor. A market structure with millions of profitable niches, enabled by blockchain networks, makes this possible. With fairer revenue sharing, more users will find their true callings, and more creators will reach their true fans.

Games and the Metaverse: Who Will Own the Virtual World?

The plot of *Ready Player One,* the most popular recent book about the so-called metaverse, revolves around a contest to see who gets to control the OASIS, the book's 3-D virtual world. I won't spoil who wins the contest, but the real issue is not who wins—it's that one person can control that virtual world at all.

Ready Player One builds on a tradition of speculative fiction that owes much to Neal Stephenson, the sci-fi author who coined the term "metaverse" in his 1992 novel, *Snow Crash*. Back when Stephenson was writing, 3-D multiplayer games had simple graphics and supported interactions among only a few players. Obviously, the state of the art has come a long way since then. Today, game graphics rival Hollywood movies, hundreds or even thousands of players can interact in the same virtual world, and audiences for games number in the hundreds of millions of players. Video games like *Fortnite* and *Roblox* are the closest equivalents we have today to full-fledged virtual worlds like the OASIS.

You hardly have to squint to see where we're headed. Soon enough, digital worlds will have lifelike graphics and let many thousands if not millions of people play together. Audience sizes will continue to grow, and people will spend more time in game worlds. High-quality virtual reality headsets will be common. Haptic interfaces that provide physical feedback will make the experience even more realistic. Artificial intelligence will create an abundance of rich characters, worlds, and other content. The trends all point in this direction.

As the quality of virtual experiences improves, digital interactions will spill over into the physical world. You might make friends, meet a future spouse, or get a new job in "virtual" reality. As more of the economy moves online, more jobs will exist solely in online worlds. The distinction between work and play will blur. What happens in digital worlds will have consequences and meaning in the physical world, and vice versa. The same pattern unfolded in social networking. Twitter started off as a way to share what you had for lunch, and now it's at the center of global politics. Things that look like toys sometimes remain toys, but sometimes they become much more than that.

As the metaverse vision materializes, a central question is how these worlds will be designed and what architecture will underpin them. Today's most popular video games use the corporate network model. The players connect through shared virtual worlds that game development studios control. Many of these game economies have digital currencies and virtual goods, but they are centrally managed, with high take rates and limited opportunities for entrepreneurs.

The alternative to the corporate model is an open model based on either protocol networks or blockchain networks. Tim Sweeney, the founder of Epic, maker of *Fortnite* and the popular game engine Unreal, describes his vision of an open metaverse as a combination of the two:

> We need several things. We need a file format for representing 3D worlds. . . . These could be used as a standard for representing 3D content. You need a protocol for exchanging it, which could be HTTPS or something like the Interplanetary File System, which is decentralized and open to everyone. You need a means of performing secure commerce, which could be the blockchain, and you need a realtime protocol for sending and receiving positions of objects in the world and facial motion. . . .
>
> We're several iterations away from having the remaining components for the Metaverse. They're all similar enough that a common denominator could be identified and standardized, just like HTTP was standardized for the web.

Sweeney's vision is on the right track, but he could take the openness even further. Limiting blockchains to commerce is skeuomorphic thinking. Blockchains are computers, capable of running arbitrary software. The strongest form of an open metaverse would be a collection of composable blockchain networks, each of which meets one of the needs Sweeney describes, and which themselves interoperate, forming a meta-network. This could start from an initial core blockchain network and expand out to a fabric of interconnected networks, the whole composed from its parts, built from the bottom up.

It wouldn't take much to meet the technical specs. Fungible tokens representing virtual currencies and NFTs representing virtual goods would flow freely through the network. Some NFTs would be "soulbound," or nontransferable, representing a special achievement or an item forever tied to the person who attained it. Some NFTs would be tradable commodities, like virtual clothing, or "skins," that can be bought and sold. And other NFTs would be a combination, with some features that are tradable and some that are not. An avatar might acquire experience points that reset on transfer, for instance.

The game designers would have a rich design space to work in. They would build applications on top of an underlying blockchain network, but they would still have access to all the tools of today's game designers. They would also get new design elements like persistent, transferable ownership and economies that span across networks.

Fees paid back to the blockchain networks could cover development costs. The take rates would be low, as they should be in blockchain networks, but a larger total economy driven by entrepreneurship would compensate. Creators could set up shops to sell their wares, keeping most of their earnings for themselves. Investors would have an incentive to fund entrepreneurs building on top of the network, knowing upside wouldn't be capped. The interoperability and composability of blockchain networks would mean users could move between games and applications, migrating from one network to another, creating competition among networks. Digital property rights would be guaranteed by persistent, blockchain-enforced rules. Governance and moderation would be managed by the community.

In corporate networks, cross-network interoperability is often considered a liability. Blockchains reverse this logic and make in-

teroperability a tool for growth. If one network builds a community of token holders, another network can incentivize that same
community to become its own participants, such as by offering to
support the other network's tokens in its applications. So, the
sword and potion collection someone spent years building in one
game doesn't go to waste when that person stops playing. The
player can transfer it to a new game. Maybe the graphics and
gameplay are different, but the item and core properties persist.

To the extent that a protocol network like the web can help
build a metaverse, I welcome it. But as Sweeney points out, many
pieces will still need to be built that protocol networks like the
web don't provide. If open systems like protocol or blockchain networks don't step in to fill the void, corporate networks will, and
then the world will end up with the dystopia of *Ready Player One.*

NFTs: Scarce Value in an Era of Abundance

Copying is a core activity of the internet. When people write online, information gets copied from their machines to servers and
then back to readers. Almost every action a person takes, from
likes to posts to retweets, creates copies. Copies are free and frictionless, producing a flood of videos, memes, games, messages,
posts, and more.

Copying is both good and bad for creators. On the one hand,
it distributes creative work to a wide audience. On the other hand,
the abundance of media creates heated competition for attention.
Networks route and prune this information; nevertheless, far more
flows in than anyone could possibly consume. The good news is
you can instantly reach five billion people. The bad news is so can
everyone else.

Traditional media businesses rely on scarcity to make money.
In the pre-internet world, media, like books and CDs, were limited. Only so many were produced. People had to seek out and

acquire physical goods. In the digital world, where information flows freely by default, abundance is the norm. Many media businesses protect their interests by imposing restrictions, like paywalls and copyrights. You need to pay to read articles in *The New York Times* or listen to music on Spotify. (Pirating media is obviously illegal, and it has gotten less appealing as legal alternatives have sprouted up over time.)

Scarcity can convert attention into money, but scarcity also prevents media from benefiting from the supercharged copying machine that is the internet. Friction reduces the chance that content will survive in the struggle for attention. Restricted content can't be shared or remixed as easily as public content, for instance. This is what I call the attention-monetization dilemma—the trade-off media creators face between maximizing attention and maximizing money.

The video game industry is far ahead of other media businesses in navigating this dilemma. Games tend to have short lives and must adapt to changing technologies and trends. A few long-standing titles like *Madden* and *Call of Duty* are exceptions, but most other games come and go. As a result, the industry is fast moving, highly competitive, and open to experimentation. The enduring companies embrace new technologies and business models. The lessons video game studios have learned are applicable to other forms of media. Game makers just learned them sooner.

For many years, video game studios made money the same way just about all media businesses did. People would pay a onetime fee, typically around $50, to buy a game, whether as a physical CD or a digital download. With the advent of the internet, new genres of video games, such as massively multiplayer role-playing games and battle royal shooters, emerged and took advantage of the internet's native capabilities. New activities like streaming and new business models like sales of virtual goods became popular.

While experimenting, game studios made a discovery. They realized they could make even more money on free games. Taking their sole source of revenue and giving it away free of charge was a daring move, but it worked.

In the early days of the internet, game designers would offer a few levels for free and then charge for the full game. In the 2010s they took that idea further by giving away the full game and just charging for add-ons. Today, the most sophisticated games—including *Fortnite, League of Legends,* and *Clash Royale*—make all their money charging for virtual goods, which generally don't even make players better at the game. Mostly, the goods are cosmetic, like new outfits or animations for your character. (When people can "pay to win," players usually revolt.)

Video games solved the attention-monetization dilemma. Making the game free meant the game and all its derivative works—videos, memes, and so on—could spread freely across the internet. As a result, game-related content has become a consistently top-trending category across social media. The biggest game releases routinely have higher sales than the biggest movie releases (a trend amplified by the recent pandemic). In 2022, the gaming industry brought in around $180 billion in global revenues, seven times as much as global movie box office revenues. What was once a niche activity for enthusiasts is now a blockbuster pastime.

The gaming industry's savvy is also evident in its approach to streaming. On sites like Twitch users watch live videos of players who also chat with the audience—a mix between sports spectating and talk radio. Legally, it would be easy for the industry to crack down on streaming. When game streaming began in the late 2000s, some companies, notably Nintendo, pushed back. But today every game company encourages streaming because of an industry-wide realization that the attention gained more than offsets the monetization lost.

Game studios were smart. They looked at their products expansively, as bundles that included a game, but also streaming and virtual goods. Through experimentation they discovered the right blend of free and paid elements to optimize the trade-off between attention and monetization. In the process they created a new, scarce layer of value. Thus, the games themselves went from paid to free while adding new layers like streaming (free) and virtual goods (paid). Game studios shrank one part of the revenue balloon while finding other parts to inflate.

In contrast to video games, the music industry responded to the rise of the internet by squandering time filing lawsuits against innovators. Music companies focused far more on protecting existing business than on exploring new businesses. Only after a great deal of foot-dragging did record labels accept incremental change, such as allowing streaming services like Spotify to use their content in subscription bundles. And they weren't happy about it.

The kicking and screaming persists to this day. When music startups try to find new ways to navigate the attention-monetization dilemma, record labels usually threaten them with lawsuits. These threats chill experimentation. New music-related tech products, to the extent there are any, are generally just minor variations of previous products. Novel approaches are considered too risky and expensive.

The effects are palpable. Founders create hundreds of video game startups each year, but they found very few music-related startups. That's because entrepreneurs want to spend their time inventing new things, not getting sued. Investors have learned their lesson too. They rarely back startups related to music.

The outcome of these two approaches shouldn't be surprising. As the next graphs show, the revenues of the video game industry have far outpaced the revenues of the music industry over the past thirty years. The games industry grew by embracing each new wave of technology. The music industry's litigious approach stunted growth.

Industry Revenues, Inflation Adjusted

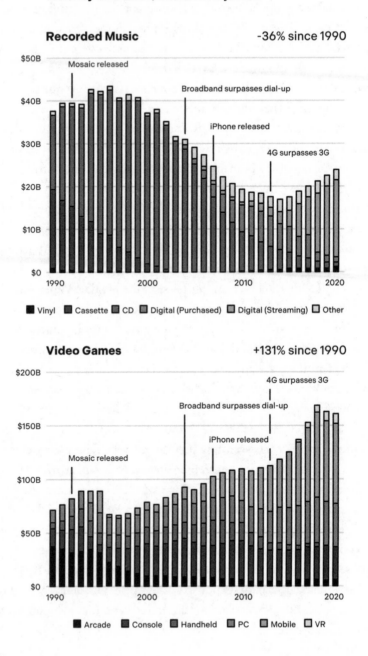

Recorded Music — -36% since 1990

- Mosaic released
- Broadband surpasses dial-up
- iPhone released
- 4G surpasses 3G

Legend: ■ Vinyl ■ Cassette ■ CD ■ Digital (Purchased) ■ Digital (Streaming) □ Other

Video Games — +131% since 1990

- 4G surpasses 3G
- Broadband surpasses dial-up
- iPhone released
- Mosaic released

Legend: ■ Arcade ■ Console ■ Handheld ■ PC ■ Mobile □ VR

There is nothing magical about video games that makes them more able to be monetized than other forms of media. People love video games, but people also love music, books, films, podcasts, and digital art. These other creative industries have simply experimented with fewer new business models. People make and listen to music as much as ever. The problem isn't supply and demand; it's the broken business models in between.

What virtual goods did for video games, NFTs can do for other forms of internet media. NFTs create a new layer of value—digital ownership—that didn't exist before.

Why would people pay for digital ownership? There are many reasons, but one is the same reason people buy art, collectible toys, and vintage handbags: an emotional connection to the ideas and stories behind the goods. Think of buying an NFT as buying an official product from a brand, or a copy of an artwork signed by an artist. The NFT connects you to the brand, artist, or creator as well as to a collector community through an immutable signature trail. The more you copy, remix, and share the art, the better known it becomes, and the more valuable the connections between the creator and the community may become.

But NFTs aren't just art. They're general-purpose containers for representing ownership. This means you can also design NFTs to have value that goes beyond buying an official or signed work. One popular NFT design gives owners behind-the-scenes access or memberships in private discussion groups. NFTs can also confer voting rights, enabling people to guide the creative direction of characters and stories in narrative worlds. (More on this in "Collaborative Storytelling: Unleashing Fantasy Hollywood.")

Skeptics sometimes suggest that NFTs will restrict the sharing of media. In fact, NFTs provide an incentive to loosen restrictions. Copying and remixing generally increase the value of NFTs, just as more players in video games increase the value of virtual goods. The same effect happens with physical art too. Both owner and artist can benefit from copying because, as the art is more widely shared, the original copies can grow in value. In the extreme case, a work of art, like the *Mona Lisa*, can become a widely reproduced cultural icon.

Art generally doesn't come with embedded copyrights. When you buy a painting, you typically aren't buying the copyright. Instead, you are buying the physical object and a license to use and display it. The value is more emotional and subjective. You can't analyze cash flows or use other objective valuation methods. NFTs that represent signed copies are similar.

Yet NFTs are flexible, so creators can embed copyrights if they so choose. The simplest example is an NFT-plus-copyright where the purchaser acquires a traditional copyright. Because NFTs can include code, however, you can create copyright variations that would be hard to implement in the offline world. For example, you can design an NFT where the purchaser is granted commercial rights but must share some revenue back with the original creator. You can also have different rules for remixes and derivative works. Taking advantage of the built-in audit trails of blockchains, you can encode rules that pass money back to different sets of owners and contributors. A remix of a remix might keep a third of the revenue for itself, pass a third back to the remix, and a third back to the original. It's software; you can design it any way you want.

NFTs can transform the economics of creators too. Consider the music business again. There are around nine million musicians on the streaming service Spotify, yet fewer than eighteen thousand musicians—less than 0.2 percent of them—made more than $50,000 in 2022. Most of the revenue generated went to streaming services and music labels. Tokens cut out layers of high take-rate intermediaries. With NFTs, musicians keep most of the revenue and can therefore support themselves with much smaller fan bases.

Musicians often sell physical merchandise, which also cuts out high take-rate intermediaries. But physical merchandise tends to be a much smaller market than digital merchandise. The music industry sold $3.5 billion in merchandise in 2018, whereas the video game industry sold $36 billion in virtual goods that same year—a figure that has nearly doubled for video games since. Digital goods are also higher margin, leave more room for product experimentation, and make it easier to maintain ongoing interactions with fans.

For those accustomed to the corporate network model, NFT-based businesses require a mindset shift. In the corporate approach, a company manages an entire service end to end. It builds the core service, the supporting apps and tools, and the business model around it. It's command and control from beginning to end.

With NFTs, creators start with core, minimal components, like a simple collection of NFTs, and independent third parties build applications from the bottom up around the network and tokens. A band might issue NFTs that attract patrons and hardcore fans. Third-party applications that provide experiences around the NFTs—like access to private events, forums, or exclusive merchandise—might come later.

Third-party developers have an incentive to build around these NFTs for two reasons. First, to accelerate adoption of their products and services by piggybacking on existing communities. A marketer could give NFT holders in a target demographic exclusive perks, like early or free access to new products. In the blockchain model, interoperability becomes a customer acquisition tactic.

Second, NFTs are credibly neutral. The users own the NFTs, and the creator who issued them can't change the rules (unless explicitly enabled by the code). The incentives are very different from those in corporate networks, where interoperating is risky because corporate owners almost always end up changing the rules in their favor.

Here again the analogy of theme parks and cities is useful. The corporate model is like a highly managed theme park that builds the whole experience end to end. The blockchain network is like a city that starts with core building blocks and encourages bottom-up entrepreneurship. NFTs with permissive copyrights encourage third-party innovation and so fit naturally in the city model.

NFTs are still evolving, but there are early signs of success. The NFT standard was formalized in 2018, and NFT sales began growing in 2020. From 2020 to early 2023, creators received about $9 billion in payments from NFT sales. YouTube, a much more established player, paid out about $47 billion during the same period. (That's the 55 percent paid to creators out of the $85 billion in revenue that YouTube brought in during the same period.) Instagram, TikTok, Twitter, and others paid out almost nothing to creators.

The trend toward abundant media will only accelerate with the rise of generative AI, which can already create impressive visual art, music, and text and is improving so rapidly it will likely, maybe even someday soon, surpass human abilities. Just as social networks democratized content distribution, generative AI will democratize content creation. This will make the model of restricting media—the copyright model—difficult to sustain. People won't be willing to pay as much for media when they can generate compelling substitutes with AI.

Fortunately, value doesn't disappear. As the balloon gets squeezed, value shifts to adjacent layers, as covered in "Take Rates." Chess-playing AI has trounced humans for two decades, yet playing and watching chess on websites like chess.com is more popular than ever. People crave human interaction despite the rise of machine intelligence. Post-AI artistic expression will focus less on the media itself and more on the curation, community, and culture around it.

NFTs add layers of scarce value onto a sea of abundant media.

They provide an elegant solution to the attention-monetization dilemma. Creators can make money through new business models, inspired by virtual goods in video games. The internet can keep doing what it does best, copying and remixing. It's a win-win.

Collaborative Storytelling: Unleashing Fantasy Hollywood

When the British writer Arthur Conan Doyle dispatched his best-known character, Sherlock Holmes, over a Swiss waterfall in an 1893 story, fans were dismayed. Thousands of Holmesians canceled their subscriptions to *The Strand Magazine,* the publication that had serialized his tales. They wore black in mourning and wrote a torrent of letters pleading for the detective's resurrection. (Doyle ignored them for years, until he finally caved and brought Holmes back.)

To this day, nothing excites people's passions quite like a good story. Internet forums are full of fans of narrative universes like *Harry Potter* and *Star Wars* who follow every update, dissect lore, and bicker over the significance of even minor plot points. Sometimes fans develop their own story lines and characters, even going so far as to write entire books on fan fiction sites like Wattpad. (*Fifty Shades of Grey* began as one such homage, to the *Twilight* series.)

People get so deeply invested in a franchise that it can become part of their identities. Yet the feeling of ownership is an illusion. Fans might, collectively, have some influence over a story's direction—because people hated the irritating alien Jar Jar Binks so much, many believe George Lucas cut the character's role in subsequent *Star Wars* films—but for the most part fans are just passive observers, with no formal voice and no financial stake.

Meanwhile, the media world is addicted to sequels and reboots because it's risky to market new intellectual property. Media companies need to spend tens of millions of dollars to promote new stories. It's safer just to recycle proven material.

But what if fans really could be owners, and media companies could harness their energy to help create and evangelize original stories? That's the idea behind a group of new blockchain projects that enable fans to collaboratively create narrative worlds.

When given the right tools, diverse groups of strangers can work together to create great things. That's a key lesson from the read-write era, of which Wikipedia is the most stunning example. The crowdsourced encyclopedia, founded in 2001, defied skeptics who viewed it as a digital graffiti wall run by utopian radicals. Today, most people barely remember Encarta, the Microsoft-owned knowledge compendium, written by paid experts, which was once considered the favorite to win the digital encyclopedia war. Wikipedia continues to face endless spam and defacement, but its community soldiers on, undaunted, editing and improving the site. Positive edits outnumber the negative, netting out to steady progress.

Today, Wikipedia is the internet's seventh most popular website. People accept it as a trusted reference. The site's success has inspired a wave of other collaborative knowledge projects, including the question-and-answers sites Quora and Stack Overflow.

Collaborative storytelling combines the lessons of Wikipedia with the power of credibly neutral, low take-rate blockchain networks that reward fans with ownership over their creations. The way this works most commonly in practice is that users receive tokens in proportion to their contribution to the narrative corpus. The resulting intellectual property is controlled by the community and can be licensed to third parties to make books, comics, games, TV shows, movies, and more. Licensing revenue is sent back to the blockchain network treasury, where it can be held to fund further development or be distributed back to token holders.

These projects give users a say in how the characters and stories develop. If they don't like the current narrative path, they can "fork" characters by copying them and changing them to versions they do like. They can even fork complete stories, creating alternative timelines and worlds—whole user-generated multiverses. Characters and stories become composable Lego bricks for people to mix and match, mod and remix.

The collaborative storytelling model has multiple benefits:

- **Widening the talent funnel.** Permissionless access removes gatekeepers and broadens who can contribute to the writing process. The traditional media model uses gate-keepers to green-light people and projects. Creative jobs often still depend on living in the right city and knowing the right people. It's a narrow funnel that likely overlooks a wide range of talent. Wikipedia brought the bazaar model to an encyclopedia industry dominated by cathedrals; collaborative storytelling can do the same for media.

- **Viral marketing of new IP.** Harnessing fandom is a powerful way to market new story universes without spending millions on advertising. Think of the viral marketing power of memecoins like Dogecoin, but imagine it focused on meaningful narratives instead of meaningless speculation. Enthusiastic fans go from passive consumers to active evangelists.

- **Increased creator income.** Token rewards can boost the income of creators. Blockchain networks have low take rates, which means most of the money earned goes back to creators. Removing layers of intermediaries transforms creator economics. A million dollars doesn't mean that much to a big studio, but it can mean a lot to groups of independent creators.

Wikipedia defied skeptics to become an essential resource. Blockchain networks can extend the model Wikipedia pioneered to collaborative creative work, letting creators own a stake in what they create. Cuy Sheffield, head of crypto at Visa, calls this idea "fantasy Hollywood," drawing an analogy to fantasy football. The model turns fans into active participants, and in this case they are actually in the game, not imagining it.

Making Financial Infrastructure a Public Good

When the commercial internet rose in the 1990s, it promised to modernize payments. But moving money online turned out to be difficult. Basic security measures like encrypted internet traffic were nascent and controversial. People didn't trust entering credit card information online. Some companies like Amazon managed to win customers' trust, but getting users to make electronic payments was a challenge for most.

So, many internet services flocked to advertising. Ads created a frictionless, closed loop that was effective from the start. The first banner ad, purchased by AT&T, appeared on the *Wired* site hotwired.com in 1994. A few years later advertising companies like DoubleClick held hotly anticipated IPOs. The ad gusher hasn't stopped flowing since—with all the cluttered experiences and user tracking that entails.

It wasn't until the 2010s that business models based on payments caught up to those based on advertising. E-commerce was the obvious beneficiary. People are now comfortable using debit and credit cards at miscellaneous merchants around the world.

Shopify, which provides services to smaller e-commerce merchants, became a credible Amazon rival by riding this trend.

Freemium and virtual goods are the other popular payment-based models. Freemium providers give away a free version of a service and upsell a premium version. This model is used by media companies like *The New York Times* and Spotify, social networks like LinkedIn and Tinder, and software providers like Dropbox and Zoom.

Video game studios pioneered the virtual goods model, as covered in "NFTs: Scarce Value in an Era of Abundance." As in the freemium model, providers gave away the basic product—in this case, a game—in hopes that a subset of users would buy add-ons. Some of these à la carte items might be useful in the game, like weapons, but many are purely cosmetic, like new outfits for players' avatars. This model has supported several megahits, such as *Candy Crush Saga, Clash of Clans,* and *Fortnite.*

Although internet payments are now common, they are still high friction. Users have to enter credit card information. Incidents of fraud and charge-backs are high. Credit card fees are between 2 and 3 percent, low by the standards of other internet take rates, but high enough to prohibit many possible uses. (As discussed earlier, mobile platforms charge much higher fees, up to 30 percent of app store transactions.)

It shouldn't be this hard to move money; sending money should be as easy and cheap as text messaging. The internet is the greatest tool the world has ever known for moving and managing information, but so far it has barely affected the mechanisms underlying how most payments work. The payments problem has proven far more stubborn than the problem of moving other kinds of information.

There are some things that make money harder to manage than other information. A typical consumer payment will pass through multiple layers of intermediaries on its way to a recipient. A patchwork of systems run by banks, merchants, card networks, and payment processors must all coordinate. There need to be systems for managing compliance, fraud, theft, and aiding law enforcement.

These are problems that have been successfully managed for a long time, but in redundant and sometimes inefficient ways, within individual financial organizations. They could be managed more efficiently within a unified, modern system. The challenge is getting these various organizations to align around a single system.

The way to solve collective action problems is by creating new networks. As I've argued throughout this book, there are three options: corporate, protocol, or blockchain networks.

A corporate payment network would have the same problem as all corporate networks. As long as the network has relatively low market share and weak network effects, it would be incentivized to attract users, merchants, banks, and other partners. But once its network effects become strong enough, it would inevitably use its power to extract higher fees from the network and put in place rules that limit competition. Banks and payment providers are savvy about platform risk and, being aware of the possible consequences, avoid handing power over to corporate networks if they can help it. (These companies did cede a lot of power to Visa and Mastercard, but that was back when Visa was a nonprofit and Mastercard was an alliance of banks; both payment-processing networks have since become independent, for-profit companies in moves reminiscent of Mozilla and OpenAI.)

A protocol payment network would present two challenges. The first would be recruiting people to build the network, since protocols have no inherent way to raise money and hire developers. The second problem would be feature limitations. Payment networks need to keep track of transactions, which means they need to maintain databases. Protocol networks have no core services and therefore no way to administer neutral, centralized data-bases.

Blockchain networks offer the benefits of corporate and protocol networks but without the limitations. Blockchain networks can raise money to fund developers, and they can store payment records in their core software, which acts as a shared ledger. They can run rules that ensure regulatory compliance. They have built-in audit trails to aid law enforcement. They also have low take rates and predictable rules that give developers incentives to build on top of them. All of these pros should be familiar by now.

By creating a neutral layer that can raise money, maintain shared data, and make strong commitments to users, a network like this would solve both technical and coordination problems that plague other payments networks. Blockchain networks can make payments a public good, analogous to a public highway system that spurs commerce and development in the physical world. Private companies would still play a role developing new financial products, but they would build these on top of credibly neutral blockchains. In any tech stack, the optimal design is a mix of private and public goods. In finance, it makes sense to have the payment layer be a neutral public good. (In the "squeezing the balloon" framework, the payment networks should be the thin part of the balloon.)

It's possible a system like this could be built on top of Bitcoin. Bitcoin is a neutral, permissionless system. The original Bitcoin white paper describes it as an "electronic payment system," but Bitcoin's success with payments has been held back by high transaction costs and volatile prices. The high costs are due to a limited supply of block space—that is, how many transactions can fit in a given block. A number of projects building on top of Bitcoin are trying to remove these limitations. The most prominent of these is Lightning, a transaction network layered on top of Bitcoin that has higher capacity and therefore lower costs. Price volatility might still be an issue, but faster settlement times can mitigate this.

Ethereum offers another option. Systems built on top of Ethereum, like so-called rollups, also lower transaction costs and improve latency. People can use a dollar-pegged stablecoin like USDC to avoid price volatility. Sending money with USDC on Ethereum is usually faster and cheaper than using bank wires. While the transaction fees are still too high to handle smaller, everyday payments, this should improve as more scaling solutions come online, boosted by Ethereum's platform-app feedback loop.

A global payments system would have multiple benefits. The first would be fixing problems with existing payments systems. Credit card payment fees are low relative to other internet fees, but still add unnecessary friction. The fees are even higher on international remittances, which can act as a regressive tax on lower-income people who send money to family members abroad. Any internet retailer will also tell you it is difficult to handle international payments, especially when they involve developing countries.

These problems are similar to ones that affected phone calls and text messages prior to smartphones. Users had to pay for calls by the minute and texts by the message, and international fees were high. The problems were fixed when applications like WhatsApp and FaceTime created new networks to replace older networks. A new global payment network could do the same for money.

The second benefit would be new applications that weren't possible before. If transaction fees were low enough, micropayments could become possible. Users could pay small fees to read news articles or access pieces of media. Music royalties could be paid to rights holders using easily audited, blockchain-based payment receipts. Computers could pay one another programmatically for data, computing time, API calls, and other resources.

Artificial intelligence systems could reward content creators who contribute to their training data sets, as we'll cover more ahead.

Micropayments have been discussed for decades, and even tried at times, but have never worked. The hurdle has mainly been transaction costs. Some industry practitioners also argue that they ask too much of users. Each of these obstacles is surmountable, though. More scalable blockchains could address the transaction costs, and rules-based automation could lower the cognitive overhead. One day users may even be able to set a budget with some simple rules and leave it to "smart" wallets to disburse the payments.

The third benefit would be composability. Consider the composability of digital photos stored in standard file formats such as GIFs and JPEGs. These files can be seamlessly integrated into almost any application, resulting in a wave of innovation around photos. Some innovations are creative, like filters and memes. Some are services, like Instagram and Pinterest. Okay, now imagine a fictional universe where every photo is controlled, via APIs, by corporate networks. In this world, photos can be used only in ways some companies allow. The API providers would be the gatekeepers, controlling what users and developers can do. They would have an incentive to lock down the photos and stifle competition. That's how money on the internet works today.

A blockchain-based system would make money remixable and composable, as digital photos are today. Or even better, it would turn money into open-source code. Making finance composable and open source is exactly the aim of DeFi networks, which perform the same functions as banks and other financial institutions but do so using blockchains. The most popular DeFi networks have handled tens of billions of dollars in transactions over the last few years. During recent market volatility, when many centralized organizations failed, DeFi networks stayed up and running. Users can inspect DeFi code to confirm their funds are safe. They can retrieve funds with a few clicks. These systems are simple, transparent, and credibly neutral—traits that also mitigate the risk of discriminatory practices.

Critics accuse DeFi of being overly self-referential, an internal micro-economy that doesn't touch the outside world. There is some truth to that criticism. DeFi can operate only on money that is composable, which today limits its scope to money held on blockchains and limits its appeal to a relatively small subset of internet users. If the internet had a composable money system, the concepts DeFi pioneered could be scaled from micro to macro.

Finance has always been centralized, run mostly by for-profit companies, but it doesn't have to be. Blockchain networks can make financial infrastructure a public good, upgrading the internet from handling bits to handling money.

Artificial Intelligence: A New Economic Covenant for Creators

The internet operates on an implicit economic covenant. Content creators, like writers, critics, bloggers, and designers, whether they are independent or part of organizations, publish work in the understanding that content distributors, like social networks and search engines, will reward them with attention. Creators bring supply; distributors bring demand. That's the deal.

Google search exemplifies the covenant. Google crawls the web, analyzes and indexes content, and shows snippets of its findings in search results. In return for indexing and excerpting content, Google sends traffic back to the content providers through its ranked links. This arrangement enables content providers, like news organizations, to make money through advertising, subscriptions, or whatever business model they've chosen.

When this relationship began in the 1990s, many content providers didn't foresee the stakes. Search engines took cover under fair-use exemptions in copyright law while content providers took a hands-off approach. Over time, as the internet grew, the balance of power between the two sides grew more lopsided. A surplus of content filtered through just a few distributors, giving distributors the upper hand. The end result: Google, as one example, now commands more than 80 percent of internet search. No content provider claims anywhere near that level of market share.

Some media businesses have tried to make up for their missteps. The media giant News Corp has been protesting Google's free riding and trying to get more money out of the arrangement, including by lodging formal antitrust complaints, for more than a decade. (The two reached an ad-revenue-sharing agreement in 2021.) For most of its existence, the review site Yelp has been campaigning to rein in Google's power, an effort that culminated in congressional testimony by Yelp's CEO, Jeremy Stoppelman:

> The problem with Big Tech is they control the distribution channels. Distribution is the key. If Google is the starting place for all of the people that are tapping into the web, to the extent they get in front of consumers and block them from finding the best information, it's really problematic, and that can stifle innovation.

With distributors in the way, content providers lost their leverage. Google grew so dominant in the 2000s that opting out of search results became unviable. If individual companies like Yelp and News Corp opt out, they lose traffic, and their competitors fill in the gaps.

If content providers had the foresight to see this coming in the 1990s, they might have preemptively coordinated to take collective action. If they had, they might be in a stronger position now. Today, content providers are too fragmented to wield any individual power, and they're not collectively organized. (A few savvy ones did see the endgame coming: the South African newspaper publisher Naspers became an internet powerhouse by pivoting its business from news production to internet investing.)

Distribution came out on top. Google made the bulk of the profits from the arrangement. The search giant knew its relationship with content providers was symbiotic, and also faced regulatory pressure, so it let enough money flow back to publishers to allow many to subsist. But the settlements and deals struck over the years are piddling compared with Google's windfall.

Occasionally, Google breaks the covenant. One of the worst things that can happen to a website is "one-boxing," when Google extracts a site's content and places a summary at the top of its search results so users no longer need to click to get an answer. Searches related to movies, lyrics, or restaurants are commonly one-boxed. For startups that are dependent on Google for traffic, one-boxing is a death sentence. Sadly, I've seen this happen to a few companies I've been involved with. Traffic evaporates overnight and, with it, revenue.

Artificial intelligence has the potential to take one-boxing to its logical conclusion. New AI tools are already generating and summarizing content, obviating the need for users to click through to the sites of content providers. OpenAI's release of its superpowered chatbot, ChatGPT, provides a preview of this future. You can ask the bot for a list of restaurants to visit, or to summarize a news event, and it will give you a self-contained answer—no clicking to other sites required. If this becomes the new way to search, AI could one-box the entire internet, thereby breaking the multidecade covenant between search engines and the content they index.

Recent AI products have produced incredible results. From large language model bots to generative art systems like Midjourney, AI is improving at a rapid and, perhaps, exponential rate. The next decade in AI should be exciting. New applications will increase economic productivity and improve people's lives. But advances in AI also mean we will need new economic models for content providers.

If AI systems can answer queries, this could replace most uses for search engines as well as the need to click through results to find content on websites. If an AI system can instantly generate an image, why go searching for images by human artists to cite or license? If AI can summarize news, why go read primary sources? AI systems will be a one-stop shop.

Most current AI systems have no economic model for creators. Consider AI image generation. Generative image systems like Midjourney feed hundreds of millions of captioned images into large neural networks to train them. The neural networks learn how to take captions as input and generate novel images that fit those captions. The results are often hard to distinguish from original human-made art. Despite learning from data from all over the internet, these systems generally neither compensate nor credit their sources. AI companies say these systems simply learn from the input images and the outputs do not infringe on copyrights. In their view, the AI is like a human artist who is inspired by other paintings to create an original work of art.

This might be a perfectly reasonable stance under existing copyright laws (there will likely be court cases and possibly legislation to sort that out). But, in the long run, we are still going to need an economic covenant between AI systems and content providers. AI will always need new data to stay up to date. The world evolves: tastes change, new genres emerge, things get invented. There will be new subjects to describe and represent. The people who create content that feeds AI systems will need to be compensated.

There are a few possible futures. One extends what current AI systems are already doing: "We will take your work, use it, and show the output to other people with no attribution or traffic back." This behavior will incentivize creators to remove their work from the internet or put it behind paywalls so AI can't train on it. We're already seeing many internet services curtail their API access and enter lockdowns in response.

Maybe AI systems could fill in the gaps by funding their own content. This is already happening today with "content farms"—buildings full of workers who are instructed to create specific content to supplement AI training data. This might work well for the AI systems, but it seems like a depressing outcome for the world at large. Machines direct progress, and humans toil like cogs.

A much better outcome would be a new covenant between AI systems and creators that encourages deep, authentic creativity over content farming. The best way to establish a new covenant is by designing new networks that mediate the economic relationship between AI systems and content creators.

Why do we need new networks? Couldn't a new covenant evolve organically through the choices individual creators make to opt in or out of AI training data?

We learned this lesson the hard way with search in the 1990s. Web standards groups provided a way for websites to exclude themselves from search engines through the "noindex" tag, part of the robots.txt standard. Content providers learned that when they opted out and others didn't, they lost traffic and gained nothing in return. Individually the websites had no power. The only way they would have power is if they organized and bargained as a group, which they never did.

An opt-out solution to AI would lead to the same outcome. Other content providers would fill the gaps, and whatever is left would be filled by content farms. Indeed, the problem is worse than with search because it's hard to restrict the flow of loosely inspired ideas and imagery. Elements of the opted-out content will seep into the opted-in content, which will likely be enough for the AI systems to get what they need. If creators act alone, the AI will get what it wants, one way or another.

Blockchain networks could be the foundation for a new covenant. Among other things, blockchains are collective bargaining machines. They are perfectly suited to solve large-scale economic coordination problems, especially when one side of the network has more power than the other side. Blockchains have fixed rules, low take rates, and incentives for builders. The network governance could be jointly managed by creators and AI providers to ensure the network stays true to its mission.

Creators could set terms and conditions for using their work, backed up by software-enforced rules and copyright restrictions focused on commercial uses, including AI training. The blockchain would enforce an attribution system that allocates portions of revenue generated by the AI systems back to the creators who contributed to their training. AI companies would face a binary choice—accept the terms of the collective group or not—instead of using their leverage against individual creators. It's the same reason labor unions bargain collectively with employers. There's strength in numbers.

Could someone design a system like this using a corporate network? Yes, and someone probably will. But this will lead to the usual problems with corporate networks, including the attract-extract cycle. The corporate owner will eventually use its leverage to extract fees and implement self-serving rules.

The internet I would like to see is one where people are encouraged to be creative and can make a living that way. If people create things and put them on the open internet, they make the internet better. AI puts human creators at the beginning of the creative pipeline instead of the end of it. Shouldn't creators get paid for being part of the process regardless of where they fit in? Plenty of money flows through search engines and social networks, more than enough to send some back to the people who created the content that makes search and social tools useful in the first place.

Everyone using the internet should ask themselves, if I'm doing something valuable, am I getting paid for it? Often, the answer is no. A few large companies have concentrated bargaining power thanks to the corporate network model. They dictate the economic terms for everyone else. It's harder to shift the balance of power in mature categories like search and social where the lock-in is strong. For new categories, like networks that mediate the economics of AI, there's an opportunity to start from scratch.

The time to address this is now, before the market structure is settled. Will content farms feed AI? Or will machines and creators happily coexist? Do machines serve the people, or will people serve the machines? These are key questions in the age of AI.

Deepfakes: Moving Beyond the Turing Test

In the 1968 novel *Do Androids Dream of Electric Sheep?*, a bounty hunter named Rick Deckard hunts robots. A major plot point of the book, which would inspire the classic sci-fi film *Blade Runner,* involves Deckard's attempts to tell "replicants," or rogue AI, from humans.

If life imitates art, then art is now imitating life. Androids walk among us, virtually: AI makes it easy to create "deepfakes," media that looks and sounds real but is actually generated by machines. A deepfake video might show politicians, celebrities, or even ordinary people saying something they didn't say, or a fabricated version of news events that feed conspiracy theories. Video often serves as a ground truth on an internet already awash with conflicting interpretations of events. Deepfakes make video no longer trustworthy.

One proposal to fight deepfakes is to try to contain AI through regulation. Some proposals call for a government certification process so only approved organizations can offer AI services. A number of AI and tech leaders, including Elon Musk and Yoshua Bengio, a pioneer of modern AI, signed a petition calling for a six-month pause on all AI research. The United States and the EU are in the process of developing comprehensive AI regulatory frameworks.

But regulation isn't the answer. No one can put the generative genie back in the bottle. Neural networks, the core technology behind modern AI, are an application of mathematical ideas that cannot be unlearned; linear algebra is here to stay, whether government officials like it or not. Open-source systems can already create convincing deepfakes, and these will continue to improve. Other countries will continue to pursue the technology too.

Regulatory restrictions will just entrench power in big companies that already have advanced AI. They will anoint haves and exclude have-nots. Burdensome rules will hold back innovation, and users will suffer as Big Tech tightens its grip even further, exacerbating the problem of internet consolidation.

Regulation also won't solve the real problem: the internet's lack of an effective reputation system. Instead of holding technology back, a better solution is to push it forward. We should build systems that allow users and applications to verify the authenticity of media. One idea is to allow "attestations"—claims backed up by cryptographic digital signatures—on blockchains where users and organizations can vouch for individual pieces of media.

Here's how that might work. The author of a video, photo, or audio track could digitally sign a media identifier, called a hash, saying, "I created this content." Another organization, like a media company, could add to that attestation by signing a transaction that says, "I attest that this content is authentic." Users could identify themselves in the signatures by cryptographically proving control of domain names (for example, nytimes.com), newer identifiers tied to blockchain-based naming services like Ethereum Name Service (nytimes.eth), or usernames on older identity systems like Facebook and Twitter (@nytimes).

The advantages of storing media attestations on blockchains are threefold. *Transparent and immutable audit trails:* Anyone can examine the full content and attestation history, and no one can alter it. *Credible neutrality:* If a company controlled the attestation database, it could leverage this control to restrict or charge for access. A credibly neutral database de-risks the platform and ensures a widely accessible public good. *Composability:* Social networks could integrate the attestations, displaying verification check marks on media that trusted sources have authenticated. Third parties could build reputation systems that evaluate the track records of attesters, assigning trust scores. An ecosystem of apps and services could develop around the database, helping users differentiate between real and fabricated content.

Attestations can also address the proliferation of bots and "counterfeit persons." AI is going to make bots so sophisticated that users can't distinguish between real and fake people. (We're already beginning to see this happen.) In this case, the answer is to attach attestations to social network identifiers instead of pieces of media. For example, *The New York Times* could attest that the @nytimes handle on a new social network is controlled by the same organization that controls the website www.nytimes.com. Users could examine the blockchain, or rely on third-party services that do, to verify the authenticity of these attestations.

Such authentication systems would help defeat spam and impersonators. Social media services could display verification check marks for usernames that have credible attestations. They could offer settings that let users filter out bots ("only show me people who have signed attestation from credible sources"). Verification check marks shouldn't be bought, doled out through favors, or subject to the biases of corporate employees. They should be objectively verified and auditable.

One of the lessons from the last era of the internet is that if a service needs to be built, it will probably get built—if not as a public good, then as a private good. When users needed a reputation system to sift through websites, Google ended up building that system, originally called PageRank and today a set of proprietary rankings. Had blockchains been around, a reputation system like this could have been built as a public good, owned by everyone instead of one company. Website rankings would be publicly verifiable, and third parties could build services on top of them.

Turing tests no longer distinguish real people from bots, and people can no longer tell real from fake media. The right approach is a credibly neutral, community-owned network—a blockchain network—that makes authenticity a trusted internet primitive.

Conclusion

If you want to build a ship, don't drum up the men and women to gather wood, divide the work, and give orders. Instead, teach them to yearn for the vast and endless sea.
—Antoine de Saint-Exupéry

In one version of the future, networks are owned by a handful of companies that stifle innovation while users, developers, creators, and entrepreneurs compete for leftovers. The internet becomes another mass medium, favoring content and experiences that are broad and shallow. Users become no better than serfs, toiling in the fields for the benefit of a corporate overlord.

This is neither the internet I want to see nor the world I wish to live in. The issue goes beyond "the future of the internet," which sounds tame and esoteric. The future of the internet is us—you and me. The internet is, increasingly, where we live our lives, and it overlaps more and more with the so-called real world. Think about how much of your life you live online, how much of your identity resides there, how much you interact with friends whom you've developed relationships with through the medium of the internet.

Whom do you want in control of that world?

Reinventing the Internet

The way to set the internet back on course is by creating new networks with better architectures. There are only two known network architectures that preserve the democratic and egalitarian spirit of the early internet: protocol networks and blockchain networks. If new protocol networks could succeed, I would be the first to support them. But after decades of disappointment, I'm skeptical. Email and the web developed at a time when there wasn't serious competition from corporate networks. Since then, protocol networks haven't been able to compete because of their core architectural limitations.

Blockchains are the only credible, known architecture for building networks with the societal benefits of protocol networks and the competitive advantages of corporate networks.

Google's motto was once "Don't be evil." In corporate networks, you need to trust company management to behave. This works for a while when networks are growing, but it inevitably breaks down. Blockchains offer a much stronger assurance: "Can't be evil." The rules are baked into immutable code. Developers and creators get low take rates and predictable incentives. Users get transparent rules and participation in the governance and financial upside of networks. In this way, blockchain networks extend the best features of protocol networks.

At the same time, blockchain networks adopt the best aspects of corporate networks. They can attract and accrue capital to invest in hiring and growth, allowing them to compete on a level playing field with well-financed internet companies. They also enable the development of software experiences that match what users have come to expect from modern internet services. With blockchains, it's possible to build social networks, video games, marketplaces, and financial services, as covered in part 5, as well as whatever else entrepreneurs dream up next.

If the next wave of networks adopts blockchain architectures, the world can reverse the trend toward internet consolidation and restore communities, rather than a handful of companies, to their rightful place as stewards of the future.

I'm optimistic about this and I hope, after everything I've shared, that you are too.

Cause for Optimism

What gives me hope is that the technology is working; it's attracting users; and it's getting better all the time. Multiple compounding feedback loops are driving the growth of blockchain networks, and another computing cycle appears to be under way:

- **The platform-app feedback loop.** The infrastructure is good enough now to support internet-scale apps. The growth of apps feeds back into investment in infrastructure. The same compounding feedback loop that drove PCs, the internet, and mobile is now driving blockchains.

- **The inherent network effect of social technologies.** Blockchain networks are massively multiplayer social technologies, just as protocol and corporate networks were before them. They become more useful as they attract more users, creators, and developers.

- **Composability.** Blockchain network code is open source, so it needs to be written only once. Open-source software can combine into bigger constructions, like Lego bricks. This grows the global knowledge store at a compounding rate.

Another tailwind driving blockchain networks forward is a wave of new talent entering the tech industry as the next generation looks to put its mark on the internet. In every generational change, there are people who want to do more than just work on technology for its own sake. They want to set out on their own and shake things up and challenge incumbents. I see this firsthand at my firm. Every year, thousands of students and others early in their careers come to me and my partners to collaborate on blockchain projects. When we ask why, they tell us they don't want to spend their careers helping Google or Meta sell more ads. They want to work on the frontier.

The opportunity ahead is to build the great networks of the future: the economic, social, and cultural substrate of the digital world. Networks are the internet's killer app. While protocol networks democratize access to information, their weaknesses limit their viability for the future. Corporate networks improve and extend the internet's capabilities, but they stifle growth in pursuit of controlled, theme-park-like experiences.

Outside blockchains, all of today's major technology movements involve sustaining technologies that look set to reinforce existing industry structures. Artificial intelligence favors big companies with stockpiles of capital and data. New devices like virtual reality headsets and self-driving cars require multibillion-dollar capital investments. Blockchains are the only credible counterweight to these centralizing forces.

Blockchain networks are like cities, built from the bottom up by the people who inhabit them. Entrepreneurs build businesses, creators cultivate audiences, and users have meaningful choices, rights, and agency. Networks operate transparently, governed by communities. People who contribute are rewarded financially. It's an internet built by everybody, for everybody.

The promise of the read-write-own era of the internet is to

maintain a healthy civic life in the digital world. Civic life thrives through a balance of private and community ownership. The public sidewalk allows passersby to discover new restaurants, bookstores, and shops. A homeowner spends weekends remodeling, in turn improving a neighborhood. A world without both private and community ownership is a world that stifles creativity and human flourishing.

I have presented what I think are some of the best ideas for developing blockchain networks today, but entrepreneurs are better at building the future than people like me are at predicting it. Most likely, the best ideas either seem strange today or are yet unimagined. If you are used to participating in blockchain networks, you are used to people looking at you funny or thinking what you do is silly or a scam. Often there aren't names for what you're working on. Inside-out technologies arrive nicely packaged, ready for the market. Outside-in technologies arrive messy, mysterious, disguised as something else. Grasping their potential takes work.

Blockchains are at the computing frontier, as PCs were in the 1980s, the internet was in the 1990s, and mobile phones were in the 2010s. People look back today on classic moments in computing and wonder what it was like to be there. Noyce and Moore. Jobs and Wozniak. Page and Brin. Hobbyists dabbling, debating, driving forward. Tinkerers hacking away on nights and weekends.

What seems late is actually early. Now is the time to reimagine what networks can be and what they can do. Software is an unbeatable playground for ingenuity. You don't have to accept the internet as you found it. You can make something better . . . as a builder, as a creator, as a user, and, most important, as an *owner*.

You are here now. These are the good old days.

Acknowledgments

This book is the product of many years of blogging, thinking, writing, and participating in the internet industry and the crypto community, so there are countless inspirations behind the ideas presented here. I am especially grateful to the colleagues and founders I've worked with. The best part of my job is talking to and learning from you. I'd also like to acknowledge some specific people who helped shape the book and make it possible.

First and foremost, I want to thank Robert Hackett, who was an extremely valuable editing and thought partner throughout the writing process. He contributed so much time, attention, and care to the project. He also taught me how to be a better writer.

Thanks to Kim Milosevich and Sonal Chokshi, my longtime partners in all things creative, who nurtured the project from the start and guided me through the publishing process.

Thank you to my agent, Chris Parris-Lamb, and my editor, Ben Greenberg—and the broader Random House team, including

Greg Kubie and Windy Dorresteyn—who made publishing this book far easier than I thought it could be. I am also grateful to Rodrigo and Anna Corral, who created the cover art and interior graphics.

There were many people who reviewed the book and gave insightful comments at various phases, but I especially want to thank Tim Roughgarden, Sep Kamvar, Miles Jennings, Elena Burger, Arianna Simpson, Porter Smith, Bill Hinman, Ali Yahya, Brian Quintenz, Andy Hall, Collin McCune, Tim Sullivan, Eddy Lazzarin, and Scott Kominers for their detailed feedback. Thanks also to Daren Matsuoka for data sourcing and analysis, Michael Blau for his NFT design, and Maura Fox for research and fact checking.

I'd also like to thank Marc Andreessen and Ben Horowitz for being great business partners and providing unwavering support for all my various endeavors over the years.

I dedicated this book to Elena, my wife and best friend, who has always stood by me and believed in me. I am so thankful for your patience and support while I worked on this book day and night (and countless weekends and holidays); it takes a remarkable, confident person who allows space for that while also pursuing her own passions and interests. I am so grateful to you, and thankful for meeting you all those years ago in NYC. You're my partner in everything, and this book is as much yours as it is mine.

Finally, this book is for my son. You are the future; I hope it shines bright for you.

Notes

Introduction

vii **When the great innovation appears:** Freeman Dyson quotation is from Kenneth Brower, *The Starship and the Canoe* (New York: Holt, Rinehart and Winston, 1978).

xiv **Today the top 1 percent of social networks:** Similarweb: Website traffic—check and analyze any website, Feb. 15, 2023, www.similarweb.com/.

xiv **The top 1 percent of search engines:** Apptopia: App Competitive Intelligence Market Leader, Feb. 15, 2023, apptopia.com/.

xiv **Nearly 50 percent of the market capitalization of the Nasdaq-100:** Truman Du, "Charted: Companies in the Nasdaq 100, by Weight," *Visual Capitalist,* June 26, 2023, www.visualcapitalist.com/cp/nasdaq-100-companies-by-weight/.

xiv **Meta, Google, and other ad-based companies run elaborate tracking systems:** Adam Tanner, "How Ads Follow You from Phone to Desktop to Tablet," *MIT Technology Review,* July 1, 2015, www.technologyreview.com/2015/07/01/167251/how-ads-follow-you-from-phone-to-desktop-to-tablet/; Kate Cox, "Facebook and Google Have Ad Trackers on Your Streaming TV, Studies Find," *Ars Technica,* Sept. 19, 2019, arstechnica.com/tech-policy/2019/09/studies-google-netflix-and-others-are-watching-how-you-watch-your-tv/.

xv   **An estimated 40 percent of internet users use ad blockers:** Stephen Shank-land, "Ad Blocking Surges as Millions More Seek Privacy, Security, and Less Annoyance," *CNET,* May 3, 2021, www.cnet.com/news/privacy/ad-blocking-surges-as-millions-more-seek-privacy-security-and-less-annoyance/.

xv   **Apple . . . expanding its own advertising network:** Chris Stokel-Walker, "Apple Is an Ad Company Now," *Wired,* Oct. 20, 2022, www.wired.com/story/apple-is-an-ad-company-now/.

xv   **The most visible example of this is deplatforming:** Merrill Perlman, "The Rise of 'Deplatform,'" *Columbia Journalism Review,* Feb. 4, 2021, www.cjr.org/language_corner/deplatform.php.

xv   **People may get silenced and not even know it:** Gabriel Nicholas, "Shadow-banning Is Big Tech's Big Problem," *Atlantic,* April 28, 2022, www.theatlantic.com/technology/archive/2022/04/social-media-shadowbans-tiktok-twitter/629702/.

xvi   **People spend about seven hours per day on internet-connected devices:** Simon Kemp, "Digital 2022: Time Spent Using Connected Tech Continues to Rise," DataReportal, Jan. 26, 2022, datareportal.com/reports/digital-2022-time-spent-with-connected-tech.

xvi   **About half that time they spend using phones:** Yoram Wurmser, "The Majority of Americans' Mobile Time Spent Takes Place in Apps," *Insider Intelligence,* July 9, 2020, www.insiderintelligence.com/content/the-majority-of-americans-mobile-time-spent-takes-place-in-apps.

xvi   **These companies charge up to 30 percent for payments:** Ian Carlos Campbell and Julia Alexander, "A Guide to Platform Fees," *Verge,* Aug. 24, 2021, www.theverge.com/21445923/platform-fees-apps-games-business-marketplace-apple-google/.

xvii **Facebook itself pointed out:** "Lawsuits Filed by the FTC and the State Attorneys General Are Revisionist History," Meta, Dec. 9, 2020, about.fb.com/news/2020/12/lawsuits-filed-by-the-ftc-and-state-attorneys-general-are-revisionist-history/.

xvii **Amazon learns which products in its marketplaces are top sellers:** Aditya Kalra and Steve Stecklow, "Amazon Copied Products and Rigged Search Results to Promote Its Own Brands, Documents Show," *Reuters,* Oct. 13, 2021, www.reuters.com/investigates/special-report/amazon-india-rigging/.

xviii **Google faces scrutiny:** Jack Nicas, "Google Uses Its Search Engine to Hawk Its Products," *Wall Street Journal,* Jan. 9, 2017, www.wsj.com/articles/google-uses-its-search-engine-to-hawk-its-products-1484827203.

xviii **Ranking its own products above others:** Adrianne Jeffries and Leon Yin, "Amazon Puts Its Own 'Brands' First Above Better-Rated Products,"

Markup, Oct. 14, 2021, www.themarkup.org/amazons-advantage/2021/10/14/amazon-puts-its-own-brands-first-above-better-rated-products/.

xviii **$38 billion ad business:** Hope King, "Amazon Sees Huge Potential in Ads Business as AWS Growth Flattens," *Axios,* April 27, 2023, www.axios.com/2023/04/28/amazon-earnings-aws-retail-ads/.

xviii **Google's ($225 billion):** Ashley Belanger, "Google's Ad Tech Dominance Spurs More Antitrust Charges, Report Says," *Ars Technica,* June 12, 2023, www.arstechnica.com/tech-policy/2023/06/googles-ad-tech-dominance-spurs-more-antitrust-charges-report-says/.

xviii **Meta's ($114 billion):** Ryan Heath and Sara Fischer, "Meta's Big AI Play: Shoring Up Its Ad Business," *Axios,* Aug. 7, 2023, www.axios.com/2023/08/07/meta-ai-ad-business/.

xviii **Filed similar complaints over Apple's high fees and anticompetitive rules:** James Vincent, "EU Says Apple Breached Antitrust Law in Spotify Case, but Final Ruling Yet to Come," *Verge,* Feb. 28, 2023, www.theverge.com/2023/2/28/23618264/eu-antitrust-case-apple-music-streaming-spotify-updated-statement-objections; Aditya Kalra, "EXCLUSIVE Tinder-Owner Match Ups Antitrust Pressure on Apple in India with New Case," *Reuters,* Aug. 24, 2022, www.reuters.com/technology/exclusive-tinder-owner-match-ups-antitrust-pressure-apple-india-with-new-case-2022-08-24/; Cat Zakrzewski, "Tile Will Accuse Apple of Worsening Tactics It Alleges Are Bullying, a Day After iPhone Giant Unveiled a Competing Product," *Washington Post,* April 21, 2021, www.washingtonpost.com/technology/2021/04/21/tile-will-accuse-apple-tactics-it-alleges-are-bullying-day-after-iphone-giant-unveiled-competing-product/.

xx **This is why Steve Jobs once described the computer as:** Jeff Goodell, "Steve Jobs in 1994: The Rolling Stone Interview," *Rolling Stone,* Jan. 17, 2011, www.rollingstone.com/culture/culture-news/steve-jobs-in-1994-the-rolling-stone-interview-231132/.

xxv **The 1990s were full of spectacular failures:** Robert McMillan, "Turns Out the Dot-Com Bust's Worst Flops Were Actually Fantastic Ideas," *Wired,* Dec. 8, 2014, www.wired.com/2014/12/da-bom/.

xxviii **There's an urgency to that conviction:** "U.S. Share of Blockchain Developers Is Shrinking," Electric Capital Developer Report, March 2023, www.developerreport.com/developer-report-geography.

1. Why Networks Matter

3 **I am thinking about something much more:** John von Neumann quotation is from Ananyo Bhattacharya, *The Man from the Future* (New York: W. W. Norton, 2022), 130.

3   **Critics who knock the tech startup industry:** Derek Thompson, "The Real Trouble with Silicon Valley," *Atlantic,* Jan./Feb. 2020, www.theatlantic .com/magazine/archive/2020/01/wheres-my-flying-car/603025/; Josh Hawley, "Big Tech's 'Innovations' That Aren't," *Wall Street Journal,* Aug. 28, 2019, www.wsj.com/articles/big-techs-innovations-that-arent -11567033288.

3   **Even pro-tech investors play up the idea:** Bruce Gibney, "What Happened to the Future?," Founders Fund, accessed March 1, 2023, foundersfund .com/the-future/; Pascal-Emmanuel Gobry, "Facebook Investor Wants Flying Cars, Not 140 Characters," *Business Insider,* July 30, 2011, www .businessinsider.com/founders-fund-the-future-2011-7.

5   **So yes, networks matter:** Kevin Kelly, "New Rules for the New Economy," *Wired,* Sept. 1, 1997, www.wired.com/1997/09/newrules/.

6   **The law takes its name from Robert Metcalfe:** "Robert M. Metcalfe," IEEE Computer Society, accessed March 1, 2023, www.computer.org/profiles /robert-metcalfe.

6   **Some argue for variations to the law:** Antonio Scala and Marco Delmastro, "The Explosive Value of the Networks," *Scientific Reports* 13, no. 1037 (2023), www.ncbi.nlm.nih.gov/pmc/articles/PMC9852569/.

6   **In 1999, David Reed, another computer scientist:** David P. Reed, "The Law of the Pack," *Harvard Business Review,* Feb. 2001, hbr.org/2001/02/the -law-of-the-pack.

6   **Facebook has nearly 3 billion monthly active users:** "Meta Reports First Quarter 2023 Results," Meta, April 26, 2023, investor.fb.com/investor -news/press-release-details/2023/Meta-Reports-First-Quarter-2023 -Results/default.aspx.

7   **Defang the largest internet companies with regulation:** "FTC Seeks to Block Microsoft Corp.'s Acquisition of Activision Blizzard, Inc.," Federal Trade Commission, Dec. 8, 2022, www.ftc.gov/news-events/news/press -releases/2022/12/ftc-seeks-block-microsoft-corps-acquisition-activision -blizzard-inc; Federal Trade Commission, "FTC Seeks to Block Vir- tual Reality Giant Meta's Acquisition of Popular App Creator Within," July 27, 2022, www.ftc.gov/news-events/news/press-releases/2022/07 /ftc-seeks-block-virtual-reality-giant-metas-acquisition-popular-app -creator-within.

7   **Other regulatory proposals require companies to interoperate:** Augmenting Compatibility and Competition by Enabling Service Switching Act, H.R. 3849, 117th Cong. (2021).

7   **Open and permissionless protocol networks that characterized the early internet:** Joichi Ito, "In an Open-Source Society, Innovating by the Seat of Our Pants," *New York Times,* Dec. 5, 2011, www.nytimes

.com/2011/12/06/science/joichi-ito-innovating-by-the-seat-of-our -pants.html.

2. Protocol Networks

8   **What was often difficult for people to understand:** Tim Berners-Lee with Mark Fischetti, *Weaving the Web: The Original Design and Ultimate Destiny of the World Wide Web by Its Inventor* (New York: Harper, 1999), 36.

8   **The earliest version of the internet:** "Advancing National Security Through Fundamental Research," accessed Sept. 1, 2023, Defense Advanced Research Projects Agency.

9   **Poet-activist and sometime lyricist for the Grateful Dead:** John Perry Barlow, "A Declaration of the Independence of Cyberspace," Electronic Frontier Foundation, 1996, www.eff.org/cyberspace-independence.

9   **Protocols layer on top of one another:** Henrik Frystyk, "The Internet Protocol Stack," World Wide Web Consortium, July 1994, www.w3.org /People/Frystyk/thesis/TcpIp.html.

10   **Above the physical layer is the networking layer:** Kevin Meynell, "Final Report on TCP/IP Migration in 1983," Internet Society, Sept. 15, 2016, www.internetsociety.org/blog/2016/09/final-report-on-tcpip-migration -in-1983/.

10   **Helped invent futuristic technologies:** "Sea Shadow," DARPA, www.darpa .mil/about-us/timeline/sea-shadow/; Catherine Alexandrow, "The Story of GPS," *50 Years of Bridging the Gap,* DARPA, 2008, www.darpa.mil /attachments/(2O1O)%20Global%20Nav%20-%20About%20Us%20-%20 History%20-%20Resources%20-%2050th%20-%20GPS%20(Approved) .pdf.

11   **The protocol behind email:** Jonathan B. Postel, "Simple Mail Transfer Protocol," Request for Comments: 788, Nov. 1981, www.ietf.org/rfc/rfc788 .txt.pdf.

11   **History of the internet:** Katie Hafner and Matthew Lyon, *Where Wizards Stay Up Late* (New York: Simon & Schuster, 1999).

11   **The web started going mainstream:** "Mosaic Launches an Internet Revolution," National Science Foundation, April 8, 2004, new.nsf.gov/news /mosaic-launches-internet-revolution.

13   **One organization maintained the official internet directory:** "Domain Names and the Network Information Center," SRI International, Sept. 1, 2023, www.sri.com/hoi/domain-names-the-network-information -center/.

13   **Enter domain name system, or DNS:** "Brief History of the Domain Name System," Berkman Klein Center for Internet & Society at Harvard Uni-

versity, 2000, cyber.harvard.edu/icann/pressingissues2000/briefingbook
/dnshistory.html.

13   **Paul Mockapetris, an American computer scientist:** Cade Metz, "Why Does the Net Still Work on Christmas? Paul Mockapetris," *Wired,* July 23, 2012, www.wired.com/2012/07/paul-mockapetris-dns/.

13   **Postel administered DNS at the University of Southern California:** Cade Metz, "Remembering Jon Postel—and the Day He Hijacked the Internet," *Wired,* Oct. 15, 2012, www.wired.com/2012/10/joe-postel/.

13   **Summed up the significance of his role:** "Jonathan B. Postel: 1943–1998," *USC News,* Feb. 1, 1999, www.news.usc.edu/9329/Jonathan-B-Postel -1943-1998/.

14   **ICANN became independent:** Maria Farrell, "Quietly, Symbolically, US Control of the Internet Was Just Ended," *Guardian,* March 14, 2016, www.theguardian.com/technology/2016/mar/14/icann-internet-control -domain-names-iana.

19   **Email, namely newsletter writing, is having a renaissance:** Molly Fischer, "The Sound of My Inbox," *Cut,* July 7, 2021, www.thecut.com/2021/07 /email-newsletters-new-literary-style.html.

19   **Issues between content creators and corporate networks:** Sarah Frier, "Musk's Volatility Is Alienating Twitter's Top Content Creators," *Bloomberg,* Dec. 18, 2022, www.bloomberg.com/news/articles/2022-12-19/musk-s -volatility-is-alienating-twitter-s-top-content-creators.; Taylor Lorenz, "Inside the Secret Meeting That Changed the Fate of Vine Forever," *Mic,* Oct. 29, 2016, www.mic.com/articles/157977/inside-the-secret -meeting-that-changed-the-fate-of-vine-forever; Krystal Scanlon, "In the Platforms' Arms Race for Creators, YouTube Shorts Splashes the Cash," *Digiday,* Feb. 1, 2023, www.digiday.com/marketing/in-the -platforms-arms-race-for-creators-youtube-shorts-splashes-the-cash/.

20   **Zuckerberg gave the nod to shut down Vine's access:** Adi Robertson, "Mark Zuckerberg Personally Approved Cutting Off Vine's Friend-Finding Feature," *Verge,* Dec. 5, 2018, www.theverge.com/2018/12/5 /18127202/mark-zuckerberg-facebook-vine-friends-api-block-parliament -documents.; Jane Lytvynenko and Craig Silverman, "The Fake Newsletter: Did Facebook Help Kill Vine?," *BuzzFeed News,* Feb. 20, 2019, www.buzzfeednews.com/article/janelytvynenko/the-fake-newsletter-did -facebook-help-kill-vine.

20   **Facebook's crackdowns on apps like BranchOut (job hunting):** Gerry Shih, "On Facebook, App Makers Face a Treacherous Path," *Reuters,* March 10, 2013, www.reuters.com/article/uk-facebook-developers/insight -on-facebook-app-makers-face-a-treacherous-path-idUKBRE92A02T 20130311.

20   **MessageMe (messaging):** Kim-Mai Cutler, "Facebook Brings Down the Hammer Again: Cuts Off MessageMe's Access to Its Social Graph," *TechCrunch,* March 15, 2013, techcrunch.com/2013/03/15/facebook -messageme/.

20   **Path (social networking):** Josh Constine and Mike Butcher, "Facebook Blocks Path's 'Find Friends' Access Following Spam Controversy," *Tech-Crunch,* May 4, 2013, techcrunch.com/2013/05/04/path-blocked/.

20   **Phhhoto (GIF making):** Isobel Asher Hamilton, "Mark Zuckerberg Downloaded and Used a Photo App That Facebook Later Cloned and Crushed, Antitrust Lawsuit Claims," *Business Insider,* Nov. 5, 2021, www .businessinsider.com/facebook-antitrust-lawsuit-cloned-crushed-phhhoto -photo-app-2021-11.

20   **Voxer (voice chat):** Kim-Mai Cutler, "Facebook Brings Down the Hammer Again: Cuts Off MessageMe's Access to Its Social Graph," *TechCrunch,* March 15, 2013, techcrunch.com/2013/03/15/facebook -messageme/.

20   **When spam became a serious issue in the late 1990s:** Justin M. Rao and David H. Reiley, "The Economics of Spam," *Journal of Economic Perspectives* 26, no. 3 (2012): 87–110, pubs.aeaweb.org/doi/pdf/10.1257/jep .26.3.87; Gordon V. Cormack, Joshua Goodman, and David Heckerman, "Spam and the Ongoing Battle for the Inbox," *Communications of the Association for Computing Machinery* 50, no. 2 (2007): 24–33, dl.acm .org/doi/10.1145/1216016.1216017.

20   **Notoriously insecure version of Microsoft's web browser:** Emma Bowman, "Internet Explorer, the Love-to-Hate-It Web Browser, Has Died at 26," NPR, June 15, 2022, www.npr.org/2021/05/22/999343673/internet -explorer-the-love-to-hate-it-web-browser-will-die-next-year.

21   **Jabber, an open-source instant messaging protocol:** Ellis Hamburger, "You Have Too Many Chat Apps. Can Layer Connect Them?," *Verge,* Dec. 4, 2013, www.theverge.com/2013/12/4/5173726/you-have-too-many-chat -apps-can-layer-connect-them.

21   **OpenSocial . . . tried to challenge Facebook and Twitter:** Erick Schonfeld, "OpenSocial Still 'Not Open for Business,'" *TechCrunch,* Dec. 6, 2007, techcrunch.com/2007/12/06/opensocial-still-not-open-for-business/.

21   **Diaspora, a decentralized social network:** Will Oremus, "The Search for the Anti-Facebook," *Slate,* Oct. 28, 2014, slate.com/technology/2014/10 /ello-diaspora-and-the-anti-facebook-why-alternative-social-networks -cant-win.html.

23   **Google shut down Google Reader:** Christina Bonnington, "Why Google Reader Really Got the Axe," *Wired,* June 6, 2013, www.wired.com /2013/06/why-google-reader-got-the-ax/.

23   **Consolidation of network power among a few internet giants:** Ryan Holmes, "From Inside Walled Gardens, Social Networks Are Suffocating the Internet As We Know It," *Fast Company,* Aug. 9, 2013, www.fastcompany.com /3015418/from-inside-walled-gardens-social-networks-are-suffocating -the-internet-as-we-know-it.

23   **"That little tangerine bubble":** Sinclair Target, "The Rise and Demise of RSS," *Two-Bit History,* Sept. 16, 2018, twobithistory.org/2018/09/16 /the-rise-and-demise-of-rss.html.

24   **Its bid to build a social network:** Scott Gilbertson, "Slap in the Facebook: It's Time for Social Networks to Open Up," *Wired,* Aug. 6, 2007, www .wired.com/2007/08/open-social-net/.

24   **Database of social graphs run by nonprofit organizations:** Brad Fitzpatrick, "Thoughts on the Social Graph," bradfitz.com, Aug. 17, 2007, bradfitz .com/social-graph-problem/.

25   **The bug, dubbed Heartbleed:** Robert McMillan, "How Heartbleed Broke the Internet—and Why It Can Happen Again," *Wired,* April 11, 2014, www.wired.com/2014/04/heartbleedslesson/.

26   **The nonprofit responsible for maintaining the internet protocol:** Steve Marquess, "Of Money, Responsibility, and Pride," *Speeds and Feeds,* April 12, 2014, veridicalsystems.com/blog/of-money-responsibility-and -pride/.

26   **Companies that benefit from the proliferation of open-source operating systems:** Klint Finley, "Linux Took Over the Web. Now, It's Taking Over the World," *Wired,* Aug. 25, 2016, www.wired.com/2016/08/linux-took -web-now-taking-world/.

3. Corporate Networks

27   **When I was in college, I remember thinking:** Mark Zuckerberg quoted in Mathias Döpfner, "Mark Zuckerberg Talks about the Future of Facebook, Virtual Reality and Artificial Intelligence," *Business Insider,* Feb. 28, 2016, www.businessinsider.com/mark-zuckerberg-interview-with-axel-springer -ceo-mathias-doepfner-2016-2.

28   **Apple popularized the idea:** Nick Wingfield and Nick Bilton, Apple Shake-Up Could Lead to Design Shift," *New York Times,* Oct. 31, 2012, www.nytimes.com/2012/11/01/technology/apple-shake-up-could-mean -end-to-real-world-images-in-software.html.

29   **Internet of the 1990s and early 2000s:** Lee Rainie and John B. Horrigan, "Getting Serious Online: As Americans Gain Experience, They Pursue More Serious Activities," Pew Research Center: Internet, Science & Tech, March 3, 2002, www.pewresearch.org/internet/2002/03/03/getting

-serious-online-as-americans-gain-experience-they-pursue-more-serious
-activities/.

29 **List of greatest engineering achievements of the twentieth century:** William A. Wulf, "Great Achievements and Grand Challenges," National Academy of Engineering, *The Bridge* (vol. 30, issue 3/4), Sept. 1, 2000, www .nae.edu/7461/GreatAchievementsandGrandChallenges/.

29 **Amazon's share price hit an all-time low:** "Market Capitalization of Amazon," CompaniesMarketCap.com, accessed Sept. 1, 2023, companies marketcap.com/amazon/marketcap/.

29 **If they would adopt broadband:** John B. Horrigan, "Broadband Adoption at Home," Pew Research Center: Internet, Science & Tech, May 18, 2003, www.pewresearch.org/internet/2003/05/18/broadband-adoption -at-home/.

30 **Richard MacManus put it best:** Richard MacManus, "The Read/Write Web," *ReadWriteWeb*, April 20, 2003, web.archive.org/web/20100111 030848/http:/www.readwriteweb.com/archives/the_readwrite_w.php.

32 **eBay showed the way:** Adam Cohen, *The Perfect Store: Inside eBay* (Boston: Little, Brown, 2022).

32 **Quickly became a stock market darling:** Jennifer Sullivan, "Investor Frenzy over eBay IPO," *Wired*, Sept. 24, 1998, www.wired.com/1998/09 /investor-frenzy-over-ebay-ipo/.

32 **The company was more profitable than Amazon:** Erick Schonfeld, "How Much Are Your Eyeballs Worth? Placing a Value on a Website's Customers May Be the Best Way to Judge a Net Stock. It's Not Perfect, but on the Net, What Is?," *CNN Money*, Feb. 21, 2000, money.cnn .com/magazines/fortune/fortune_archive/2000/02/21/273860/index .htm.

32 **In the mid-2000s, broadband home internet started going mainstream:** John H. Horrigan, "Home Broadband Adoption 2006," Pew Research Center: Internet, Science & Tech, May 28, 2006, www.pewresearch.org /internet/2006/05/28/home-broadband-adoption-2006/.

32 **The service started as a video-dating site:** Jason Koebler, "10 Years Ago Today, YouTube Launched as a Dating Website," *Vice*, April 23, 2015, www.vice.com/en/article/78xqjx/10-years-ago-today-youtube-launched -as-a-dating-website.

32 **A tactic I call "come for the tool, stay for the network":** Chris Dixon, "Come for the Tool, Stay for the Network," cdixon.org, Jan. 31, 2015, cdixon .org/2015/01/31/come-for-the-tool-stay-for-the-network.

33 **Instagram made it easy to share touched-up photos on existing networks:** Avery Hartmans, "The Rise of Kevin Systrom, Who Founded Instagram 10 Years Ago and Built It into One of the Most Popular Apps in the

World," *Business Insider,* Oct. 6, 2020, www.businessinsider.com/kevin
-systrom-instagram-ceo-life-rise-2018-9.

33 **YouTube also faced existential legal challenges:** James Montgomery,
"YouTube Slapped with First Copyright Lawsuit for Video Posted
Without Permission," MTV, July 19, 2006, www.mtv.com/news/dtyii2
/youtube-slapped-with-first-copyright-lawsuit-for-video-posted-without
-permission.

34 **YouTube contributes more than $160 billion to Google's market cap:** Doug
Anmuth, Dae K. Lee, and Katy Ansel, "Alphabet Inc.: Updated Sum-of-
the-Parts Valuation Suggests Potential Market Cap of Almost $2T; Re-
iterate OW & Raising PT to $2,575," North America Equity Research,
J. P. Morgan, April 19, 2021.

36 **Microsoft provided a high-profile demonstration:** John Heilemann, "The
Truth, the Whole Truth, and Nothing but the Truth," *Wired,* Nov. 1,
2000, www.wired.com/2000/11/microsoft-7/.

36 **The U.S. Department of Justice accused the company of antitrust violations
in 1998:** Adi Robertson, "How the Antitrust Battles of the '90s Set the
Stage for Today's Tech Giants," *Verge,* Sept. 6, 2018, www.theverge.com
/2018/9/6/17827042/antitrust-1990s-microsoft-google-aol-monopoly
-lawsuits-history.

37 **Marketing costs for most are rising:** Brad Rosenfeld, "How Marketers Are
Fighting Rising Ad Costs," *Forbes,* Nov. 14, 2022, www.forbes.com
/sites/forbescommunicationscouncil/2022/11/14/how-marketers-are
-fighting-rising-ad-costs/.

37 **Social networks often encourage the growth of third-party apps at first:** Dean
Takahashi, "MySpace Says It Welcomes Social Games to Its Platform,"
VentureBeat, May 21, 2010, venturebeat.com/games/myspace-says-it
-welcomes-social-games-to-its-platform/; Miguel Helft, "The Class
That Built Apps, and Fortunes," *New York Times,* May 7, 2011, www
.nytimes.com/2011/05/08/technology/08class.html.

38 **Rebranded version of Tweetie:** Mike Schramm, "Breaking: Twitter Acquires Tweetie, Will Make It Official and Free," *Engadget,* April 9, 2010,
www.engadget.com/2010-04-09-breaking-twitter-acquires-tweetie-will
-make-it-official-and-fr.html.

38 **Twitter deprecated features available to other third-party apps:** Mitchell
Clark, "The Third-Party Apps Twitter Just Killed Made the Site What It
Is Today," *Verge,* Jan. 22, 2023, www.theverge.com/2023/1/22/23564460
/twitter-third-party-apps-history-contributions.

38 **Developers felt betrayed:** Ben Popper, "Twitter Follows Facebook Down
the Walled Garden Path," *Verge,* July 9, 2012, www.theverge.com
/2012/7/9/3135406/twitter-api-open-closed-facebook-walled-garden.

38   **RockYou (ad network):** Eric Eldon, "Q&A with RockYou—Three Hit Apps on Facebook, and Counting," *VentureBeat,* June 11, 2007, venturebeat.com/business/q-a-with-rockyou-three-hit-apps-on-facebook-and -counting/.

38   **Slide (social app maker):** Claire Cain Miller, "Google Acquires Slide, Maker of Social Apps," *New York Times,* Aug. 4, 2010, archive.nytimes .com/bits.blogs.nytimes.com/2010/08/04/google-acquires-slide-maker -of-social-apps/.

38   **StockTwits (stock market tracker):** Ben Popper, "Life After Twitter: Stock-Twits Builds Out Its Own Ecosystem," *Verge,* Sept. 18, 2012, www.the verge.com/2012/9/18/3351412/life-after-twitter-stocktwits-builds-out -its-own-ecosystem.

38   **UberMedia (another social app maker):** Mark Milian, "Leading App Maker Said to Be Planning Twitter Competitor," CNN, April 13, 2011, www.cnn.com/2011/TECH/social.media/04/13/ubermedia.twitter/index .html.

38   **Netflix introduced an API in 2008:** Adam Duvander, "Netflix API Brings Movie Catalog to Your App," *Wired,* Oct. 1, 2008, www.wired.com /2008/10/netflix-api-brings-movie-catalog-to-your-app/.

38   **The company changed its policies:** Sarah Mitroff, "Twitter's New Rules of the Road Mean Some Apps Are Roadkill," *Wired,* Sept. 6, 2012, www .wired.com/2012/09/twitters-new-rules-of-the-road-means-some-apps -are-roadkill/.

38   **Startups depending too much on Twitter:** Chris Dixon, "The Inevitable Showdown Between Twitter and Twitter Apps," *Business Insider,* Sept. 16, 2009, www.businessinsider.com/the-coming-showdown-between-twitter -and-twitter-apps-2009-9.

39   **Google started warning users:** Elspeth Reeve, "In War with Facebook, Google Gets Snarky," *Atlantic,* Nov. 11, 2010, www.theatlantic.com /technology/archive/2010/11/in-war-with-facebook-google-gets-snarky /339626/.

40   **Bill Joy, the co-founder of Sun Microsystems:** Brent Schlender, "Whose Internet Is It, Anyway?" *Fortune,* Dec. 11, 1995.

42   **Zynga's first major breakout game, FarmVille:** Dave Thier, "These Games Are So Much Work," *New York,* Dec. 9, 2011, www.nymag.com/news /intelligencer/zynga-2011-12/.

42   **Double-digit percentages of Facebook's revenue:** Jennifer Booten, "Facebook Served Disappointing Analyst Note in Wake of Zynga Warning," Fox Business, March 3, 2016, www.foxbusiness.com/features/facebook -served-disappointing-analyst-note-in-wake-of-zynga-warning.

42   **Facebook diversified its revenue:** Tomio Geran, "Facebook's Dependence

on Zynga Drops, Zynga's Revenue to Facebook Flat," *Forbes,* July 31, 2012, www.forbes.com/sites/tomiogeron/2012/07/31/facebooks-dependence -on-zynga-drops-zyngas-revenue-to-facebook-flat/.

42 **Ripped up its partnership with Zynga:** Harrison Weber, "Facebook Kicked Zynga to the Curb, Publishers Are Next," *VentureBeat,* June 30, 2016, www .venturebeat.com/mobile/facebook-kicked-zynga-to-the-curb-publishers -are-next/; Josh Constine, "Why Zynga Failed," *TechCrunch,* Oct. 5, 2012, www.techcrunch.com/2012/10/05/more-competitors-smarter-gamers -expensive-ads-less-virality-mobile/.

42 **Bought it for $12.7 billion:** Aisha Malik, "Take-Two Completes $12.7B Acquisition of Mobile Games Giant Zynga," *TechCrunch,* May 23, 2022, www.techcrunch.com/2022/05/23/take-two-completes-acquisition-of -mobile-games-giant-zynga/.

44 **Five billion internet users:** Simon Kemp, "Digital 2022 October Global Statshot Report," DataReportal, Oct. 20, 2022, datareportal.com/reports /digital-2022-october-global-statshot.

4. Blockchains

49 **Whereas most technologies tend to automate:** Vitalik Buterin quoted in "Genius Gala," Liberty Science Center, Feb. 26, 2021, www.lsc.org/gala /vitalik-buterin-1.

49 **The rate that describes this process is known as Moore's law:** David Rotman, "We're not prepared for the end of Moore's Law," *MIT Technology Review,* Feb. 24, 2020, www.technologyreview.com/2020/02/24/905789 /were-not-prepared-for-the-end-of-moores-law/.

51 **Major computing cycles:** Chris Dixon, "What's Next in Computing?," *Software Is Eating the World,* Feb. 21, 2016, medium.com/software-is -eating-the-world/what-s-next-in-computing-e54b870b80cc.

51–52 **Significant investments in these areas:** Filipe Espósito, "Apple Bought More AI Companies Than Anyone Else Between 2016 and 2020," *9to5Mac,* March 25, 2021, 9to5mac.com/2021/03/25/apple-bought- more-ai-companies-than-anyone-else-between-2016-and-2020/; Tristan Bove, "Big Tech Is Making Big AI Promises in Earnings Calls as Chat- GPT Disrupts the Industry: 'You're Going to See a Lot from Us in the Coming Few Months,'" *Fortune,* Feb. 3, 2023, fortune.com/2023/02/03 /google-meta-apple-ai-promises-chatgpt-earnings/; Lauren Feiner, "Al- phabet's Self-Driving Car Company Waymo Announces $2.5 Billion Investment Round," CNBC, June 16, 2021, www.cnbc.com/2021/06/16 /alphabets-waymo-raises-2point5-billion-in-new-investment-round.html.

52 **New technologies follow one of two paths:** Chris Dixon, "Inside-out vs.

Outside-in: The Adoption of New Technologies," Andreessen Horo-witz, Jan. 17, 2020, www.a16z.com/2020/01/17/inside-out-vs-outside-in-technology/; cdixon.org, Jan. 17, 2020, www.cdixon.org/2020/01/17/inside-out-vs-outside-in/.

53 **Attending the Homebrew Computer Club:** Lily Rothman, "More Proof That Steve Jobs Was Always a Business Genius," *Time,* March 5, 2015, www.time.com/3726660/steve-jobs-homebrew/.

53 **Linus Torvalds as a student:** Michael Calore, "Aug. 25, 1991: Kid from Helsinki Foments Linux Revolution," *Wired,* Aug. 25, 2009, www.wired.com/2009/08/0825-torvalds-starts-linux/.

53 **Web-link-cataloging project:** John Battelle, "The Birth of Google," *Wired,* Aug. 1, 2005, www.wired.com/2005/08/battelle/.

54 **Back-end web services to scale:** Ron Miller, "How AWS Came to Be," *TechCrunch,* July 2, 2016, techcrunch.com/2016/07/02/andy-jassys-brief-history-of-the-genesis-of-aws/.

55 **Introduced the world's first blockchain:** Satoshi Nakamoto, "Bitcoin: A Peer-to-Peer Electronic Cash System," Oct. 31, 2008, bitcoin.org/bitcoin.pdf.

55 **Computers are an abstraction:** Trevor Timpson, "The Vocabularist: What's the Root of the Word Computer?," BBC, Feb. 2, 2016, www.bbc.com/news/blogs-magazine-monitor-35428300.

55 **Rigorous foundation in a famous 1936 paper:** Alan Turing, "On Comput-able Numbers, with an Application to the Entscheidungsproblem," *Proceedings of the London Mathematical Society* 42, no. 2 (1937): 230–65, londmathsoc.onlinelibrary.wiley.com/doi/10.1112/plms/s2-42.1.230.

56 **IBM developed the first one:** "IBM VM 50th Anniversary," IBM, Aug. 2, 2022, www.vm.ibm.com/history/50th/index.html.

56 **Blockchains are resilient:** Alex Pruden and Sonal Chokshi, "Crypto Glos-sary: Cryptocurrencies and Blockchain," a16z crypto, Nov. 8, 2019, www.a16zcrypto.com/posts/article/crypto-glossary/.

58 **Made its debut in 2015:** Daniel Kuhn, "CoinDesk Turns 10: 2015—Vitalik Buterin and the Birth of Ethereum," *CoinDesk,* June 2, 2023, www.coindesk.com/consensus-magazine/2023/06/02/coindesk-turns-10-2015-vitalik-buterin-and-the-birth-of-ethereum/.

60 **Less energy-intensive systems:** Gian M. Volpicelli, "Ethereum's 'Merge' Is a Big Deal for Crypto—and the Planet," *Wired,* Aug. 18, 2022, www.wired.com/story/ethereum-merge-big-deal-crypto-environment/.

61 **Annualized energy consumption (TWh) comparison to PoS Ethereum:** "Ethereum Energy Consumption," Ethereum.org, accessed Sept. 23, 2023, ethereum.org/en/energy-consumption/; George Kamiya and Oskar Kvarnström, "Data Centres and Energy—From Global Head-

lines to Local Headaches?" International Energy Agency, Dec. 20, 2019, iea.org/commentaries/data-centres-and-energy-from-global-headlines -to-local-headaches; "Cambridge Bitcoin Energy Consumption Index: Comparisons," Cambridge Centre for Alternative Finance, accessed July 2023, ccaf.io/cbnsi/cbeci/comparisons; Evan Mills et al., "Toward Greener Gaming: Estimating National Energy Use and Energy Efficiency Potential," *The Computer Games Journal,* vol. 8(2), Dec. 1, 2019, researchgate.net/publication/336909520_Toward_Greener_Gaming _Estimating_National_Energy_Use_and_Energy_Efficiency_Potential; "Cambridge Blockchain Network Sustainability Index: Ethereum Network Power Demand," Cambridge Centre for Alternative Finance, accessed July 2023, ccaf.io/cbnsi/ethereum/1; "Google Environmental Report 2022," Google, June 2022, gstatic.com/gumdrop/sustainability /google-2022-environmental-report.pdf; "Netflix Environmental Social Governance Report 2021," Netflix, March 2022, assets.ctfassets.net/4cd 45et68cgf/7B2bKCqkXDfHLadrjrNWD8/e44583e5b288bdf61e8bf3 d7f8562884/2021_US_EN_Netflix_EnvironmentalSocialGovernance Report-2021_Final.pdf; "PayPal Inc. Holdings—Climate Change 2022," Carbon Disclosure Project, May 2023, s202.q4cdn.com/805890769/files /doc_downloads/global-impact/CDP_Climate_Change_PayPal-(1) .pdf; "An Update on Environmental, Social, and Governance (ESG) at Airbnb," Airbnb, Dec. 2021, s26.q4cdn.com/656283129/files/doc _downloads/governance_doc_updated/Airbnb-ESG-Factsheet-(Final) .pdf; "The Merge—Implications on the Electricity Consumption and Carbon Footprint of the Ethereum Network," Crypto Carbon Ratings Institute, accessed Sept. 2022, carbon-ratings.com/eth-report-2022; Rachel Rybarczyk et al., "On Bitcoin's Energy Consumption: A Quantitative Approach to a Subjective Question," Galaxy Digital Mining, May 2021, docsend.com/view/adwmdeeyfvqwecj2.

61   **Straightforward for law enforcement:** Andy Greenberg, "Inside the Bitcoin Bust That Took Down the Web's Biggest Child Abuse Site," *Wired,* April 7, 2022, www.wired.com/story/tracers-in-the-dark-welcome-to -video-crypto-anonymity-myth/.

62   **Innovations like "zero knowledge proofs":** Lily Hay Newman, "Hacker Lexicon: What Are Zero-Knowledge Proofs?," *Wired,* Sept. 14, 2019, www.wired.com/story/zero-knowledge-proofs/; Elena Burger et al., "Zero Knowledge Canon, part 1 & 2," a16z crypto, Sept. 16, 2022, www .a16zcrypto.com/posts/article/zero-knowledge-canon/.

62   **That can mitigate the risk of illegal activities:** Joseph Burlseon et al., "Privacy-Protecting Regulatory Solutions Using Zero-Knowledge Proofs:

Full Paper," a16z crypto, Nov. 16, 2022, a16zcrypto.com/posts/article/privacy-protecting-regulatory-solutions-using-zero-knowledge-proofs-full-paper/; Shlomit Azgad-Tromer et al., "We Can Finally Reconcile Privacy and Compliance in Crypto. Here Are the New Technologies That Will Protect User Data and Stop Illicit Transactions," *Fortune*, Oct. 28, 2022, fortune.com/2022/10/28/finally-reconcile-privacy-compliance-crypto-new-technology-celsius-user-data-leak-illicit-transactions-crypto-tromer-ramaswamy/.

62 **Mathematical breakthrough from the 1970s:** Steven Levy, "The Open Secret," *Wired*, April 1, 1999, www.wired.com/1999/04/crypto/.

64 **Keep your private data private:** Vitalik Buterin, "Visions, Part 1: The Value of Blockchain Technology," Ethereum Foundation Blog, April 13, 2015, www.blog.ethereum.org/2015/04/13/visions-part-1-the-value-of-blockchain-technology.

65 **Attacks are known as 51 percent attacks:** Osato Avan-Nomayo, "Bitcoin SV Rocked by Three 51% Attacks in as Many Months," *CoinTelegraph*, Aug. 7, 2021, cointelegraph.com/news/bitcoin-sv-rocked-by-three-51-attacks-in-as-many-months; Osato Avan-Nomayo, "Privacy-Focused Firo Cryptocurrency Suffers 51% Attack," *CoinTelegraph*, Jan. 20, 2021, cointelegraph.com/news/privacy-focused-firo-cryptocurrency-suffers-51-attack.

68 **As it has done to nearly three hundred products to date:** Killed by Google, accessed Sept. 1, 2023, killedbygoogle.com/.

5. Tokens

70 **Technologies that change society:** César Hidalgo quoted in Denise Fung Cheng, "Reading Between the Lines: Blueprints for a Worker Support Infrastructure in the Emerging Peer Economy," MIT master of science thesis, June 2014, wiki.p2pfoundation.net/Worker_Support_Infrastructure_in_the_Emerging_Peer_Economy.

73 **Billions of dollars per year selling virtual goods:** Field Level Media, "Report: League of Legends Produced $1.75 Billion in Revenue in 2020," *Reuters*, Jan. 11, 2021, www.reuters.com/article/esports-lol-revenue-idUSFLM2vzDZL.; Jay Peters, "Epic Is Going to Give 40 Percent of Fortnite's Net Revenues Back to Creators," *Verge*, March 22, 2023, www.theverge.com/2023/3/22/23645633/fortnite-creator-economy-2-0-epic-games-editor-state-of-unreal-2023-gdc.

73 **Revoked the Instagram handle of an artist:** Maddison Connaughton, "Her Instagram Handle Was 'Metaverse.' Last Month, It Vanished," *New*

York Times, Dec. 13, 2021, www.nytimes.com/2021/12/13/technology/instagram-handle-metaverse.html.

73   **When Twitter rebranded itself X in 2023:** Jon Brodkin, "Twitter Commandeers @X Username from Man Who Had It Since 2007," *Ars Technica,* July 26, 2023, arstechnica.com/tech-policy/2023/07/twitter-took-x-handle-from-longtime-user-and-only-offered-him-some-merch/.

73   **Suspended by corporate networks:** Veronica Irwin, "Facebook Account Randomly Deactivated? You're Not Alone," *Protocol,* April 1, 2022, www.protocol.com/bulletins/facebook-account-deactivated-glitch; Rachael Myrow, "Facebook Deleted Your Account? Good Luck Retrieving Your Data," KQED, Dec. 21, 2020, www.kqed.org/news/11851695/facebook-deleted-your-account-good-luck-retrieving-your-data.

74   **That comes in two overarching types:** Anshika Bhalla, "A Quick Guide to Fungible vs. Non-fungible Tokens," Blockchain Council, Dec. 9, 2022, www.blockchain-council.org/blockchain/a-quick-guide-to-fungible-vs-non-fungible-tokens/.

75   **People call currency-pegged tokens:** Garth Baughman et al., "The Stable in Stablecoins," Federal Reserve FEDS Notes, Dec. 16, 2022, www.federalreserve.gov/econres/notes/feds-notes/the-stable-in-stablecoins-20221216.html.

75   **U.S. Congressman Ritchie Torres (D-NY) . . . has argued:** "Are Democrats Against Crypto? Rep. Ritchie Torres Answers," *Bankless,* May 11, 2023, video, www.youtube.com/watch?v=ZbUHWwrplxE&ab_channel=Bankless.

75   **People's Bank of China mints a digital renminbi:** Amitoj Singh, "China Includes Digital Yuan in Cash Circulation Data for First Time," *CoinDesk,* Jan. 11, 2023, www.coindesk.com/policy/2023/01/11/china-includes-digital-yuan-in-cash-circulation-data-for-first-time/.

75   **USD Coin (USDC) is a popular fiat-backed stablecoin:** Brian Armstrong and Jeremy Allaire, "Ushering in the Next Chapter for USDC," Coinbase, Aug. 21, 2023, www.coinbase.com/blog/ushering-in-the-next-chapter-for-usdc.

76   **Terra, an infamous bust that crashed in 2022:** Lawrence Wintermeyer, "From Hero to Zero: How Terra Was Toppled in Crypto's Darkest Hour," *Forbes,* May 25, 2022, www.forbes.com/sites/lawrencewintermeyer/2022/05/25/from-hero-to-zero-how-terra-was-toppled-in-cryptos-darkest-hour/.

77   **Tiffany & Co. and Louis Vuitton created NFTs:** Eileen Cartter, "Tiffany & Co. Is Making a Very Tangible Entrance into the World of NFTs," *GQ,*

Aug. 1, 2022, www.gq.com/story/tiffany-and-co-cryptopunks-nft-jewelry-collaboration.

78   **Collection where the NFTs represent digital artworks:** Paul Dylan-Ennis, "Damien Hirst's 'The Currency': What We'll Discover When This NFT Art Project Is Over," *Conversation*, July 19, 2021, theconversation.com/damien-hirsts-the-currency-what-well-discover-when-this-nft-art-project-is-over-164724.

78   **NFTs that represent digital sneakers:** Andrew Hayward, "Nike Launches .Swoosh Web3 Platform, with Polygon NFTs Due in 2023," *Decrypt*, Nov. 14, 2022, decrypt.co/114494/nike-swoosh-web3-platform-polygon-nfts.

79   **"Chat group with a bank account":** Max Read, "Why Your Group Chat Could Be Worth Millions," *New York*, Oct. 24, 2021, nymag.com/intelligencer/2021/10/whats-a-dao-why-your-group-chat-could-be-worth-millions.html.

79   **That movie you bought from Apple's iTunes store:** Geoffrey Morrison, "You Don't Really Own the Digital Movies You Buy," *Wirecutter, New York Times*, Aug. 4, 2021, www.nytimes.com/wirecutter/blog/you-dont-own-your-digital-movies/.

81   **Homeowners are known to invest:** John Harding, Thomas J. Miceli, and C. F. Sirmans, "Do Owners Take Better Care of Their Housing Than Renters?," *Real Estate Economics* 28, no. 4 (2000): 663–81; "Social Benefits of Homeownership and Stable Housing," National Association of Realtors, April 2012, www.nar.realtor/sites/default/files/migration_files/social-benefits-of-stable-housing-2012-04.pdf.

81   **How often tech giants miss major new trends:** Alison Beard, "Can Big Tech Be Disrupted? A Conversation with Columbia Business School Professor Jonathan Knee," *Harvard Business Review*, Jan.–Feb. 2022, hbr.org/2022/01/can-big-tech-be-disrupted.

82   **The reason incumbents whiff:** Chris Dixon, "The Next Big Thing Will Start out Looking Like a Toy," cdixon.org, Jan. 3, 2010, www.cdixon.org/2010/01/03/the-next-big-thing-will-start-out-looking-like-a-toy.

82   **This is one of the main insights of the late business academic:** Clayton Christensen, "Disruptive Innovation," claytonchristensen.com, Oct. 23, 2012, claytonchristensen.com/key-concepts/.

82   **The leading telco of the time, Western Union:** "The Telephone Patent Follies: How the Invention of the Phone was Bell's and not Gray's, or . . . ," The Telecommunications History Group, Feb. 22, 2018, www.telcomhistory.org/the-telephone-patent-follies-how-the-invention-of-the-hone-was-bells-and-not-grays-or/.

83   **The same thing happened a century later:** Brenda Barron, "The Tragic Tale of DEC. The Computing Giant That Died Too Soon," Digital.com, June 15, 2023, digital.com/digital-equipment-corporation/; Joshua Hyatt, "The Business That Time Forgot: Data General Is Gone. But Does That Make Its Founder a Failure?" *Forbes,* April 1, 2023, money .cnn.com/magazines/fsb/fsb_archive/2003/04/01/341000/.

83   **Missed out on smartphones:** Charles Arthur, "How the Smartphone Is Killing the PC," *Guardian,* June 5, 2011, www.theguardian.com/technology /2011/jun/05/smartphones-killing-pc.

84   **OpenAI has reportedly raised $13 billion:** Jordan Novet, "Microsoft's $13 Billion Bet on OpenAI Carries Huge Potential Along with Plenty of Uncertainty," CNBC, April 8, 2023, www.cnbc.com/2023/04/08/micro softs-complex-bet-on-openai-brings-potential-and-uncertainty.html.

84   **He famously misread the iPhone:** Ben Thompson, "What Clayton Christensen Got Wrong," *Stratechery,* Sept. 22, 2013, stratechery.com/2013 /clayton-christensen-got-wrong/.

85   **Shut down its related digital wallet product:** Olga Kharif, "Meta to Shut Down Novi Service in September in Crypto Winter," *Bloomberg,* July 1, 2022, www.bloomberg.com/news/articles/2022-07-01/meta-to-shut -down-novi-service-in-september-in-crypto-winter#xj4y7vzkg.

6. Blockchain Networks

86   **Cities have the capability of providing something for everybody:** Jane Jacobs, *The Death and Life of Great American Cities* (New York, N.Y.: Random House, 1961).

7. Community-Created Software

101   **Think Zen:** Linus Torvalds, *Just for Fun: The Story of an Accidental Revolutionary* (New York: Harper, 2001).

101   **A contrarian idea:** David Bunnell, "The Man Behind the Machine?," *PC Magazine,* Feb.–March 1982, www.pcmag.com/news/heres-what-bill -gates-told-pcmag-about-the-ibm-pc-in-1982.

102   **IBM agreed to license Microsoft's early crown jewel:** Dylan Love, "A Quick Look at the 30-Year History of MS DOS," *Business Insider,* July 27, 2011, www.businessinsider.com/history-of-dos-2011-7; Jeffrey Young, "Gary Kildall: The DOS That Wasn't," *Forbes,* July 7, 1997, www.forbes .com/forbes/1997/0707/6001336a.html?sh=16952ca9140e.

102   **Described the situation in his 1998 blog post:** Tim O'Reilly, "Freeware: The Heart & Soul of the Internet," *O'Reilly,* March 1, 1998, www .oreilly.com/pub/a/tim/articles/freeware_0398.html.

103 **Spirit of interoperability:** Alexis C. Madrigal, "The Weird Thing About Today's Internet," *Atlantic,* May 16, 2017, www.theatlantic.com /technology/archive/2017/05/a-very-brief-history-of-the-last-10-years -in-technology/526767/.

103 **The rise of smartphones:** "Smart Device Users Spend as Much Time on Facebook as on the Mobile Web," Marketing Charts, April 5, 2013, www.marketingcharts.com/industries/media-and-entertainment-28422.

104 **Perhaps the most famous example:** Paul C. Schuytema, "The Lighter Side of Doom," *Computer Gaming World,* Aug. 1994, 140, www.cgwmuseum .org/galleries/issues/cgw_121.pdf.

104 **The popular PC game store Steam:** Alden Kroll, "Introducing New Ways to Support Workshop Creators," Steam, April 23, 2015, steamcommunity.com /games/SteamWorkshop/announcements/detail/208632365237576574.

105 **Mods of other games:** Brian Crecente, "League of Legends Is Now 10 Years Old. This Is the Story of Its Birth," *Washington Post,* Oct. 27, 2019, www.washingtonpost.com/video-games/2019/10/27/league-legends-is -now-years-old-this-is-story-its-birth/; Joakim Henningson, "The History of Counter-strike," Red Bull, June 8, 2020, www.redbull.com/se-en /history-of-counterstrike.

105 **Open source began as a radical idea:** "History of the OSI," Open Source Initiative, last modified Oct. 2018, opensource.org/history/.

105 **Part of a fringe political movement:** Richard Stallman, "Why Open Source Misses the Point of Free Software," GNU Operating System, last modified Feb. 3, 2022, www.gnu.org/philosophy/open-source-misses-the -point.en.html; Steve Lohr, "Code Name: Mainstream," *New York Times,* Aug. 28, 2000, archive.nytimes.com/www.nytimes.com/library/tech/00/08 /biztech/articles/28code.html.

106 **Proof of open source's mainstream arrival:** Frederic Lardinois, "Four Years After Being Acquired by Microsoft, GitHub Keeps Doing Its Thing," *TechCrunch,* Oct. 26, 2022, www.techcrunch.com/2022/10/26/four-years -after-being-acquired-by-microsoft-github-keeps-doing-its-thing/.

107 **Albert Einstein once purportedly said:** James Forson, "The Eighth Wonder of the World—Compounding Interest," Regenesys Business School, April 13, 2022, www.regenesys.net/reginsights/the-eighth-wonder-of -the-world-compounding-interest/.

107 **He probably didn't:** "Compound Interest Is Man's Greatest Invention," Quote Investigator, Oct. 31, 2011, quoteinvestigator.com/2011/10/31 /compound-interest/.

110 **Eric Raymond contrasts two models of software development:** Eric Raymond, *The Cathedral and the Bazaar: Musings on Linux and Open Source by an Accidental Revolutionary* (Sebastopol, Calif.: O'Reilly Media, 1999).

112   **Your margin is my opportunity:** Adam Lashinsky, "Amazon's Jeff Bezos: The Ultimate Disrupter," *Fortune,* Nov. 16, 2012, fortune.com/2012/11/16/amazons-jeff-bezos-the-ultimate-disrupter/.

113   **Craigslist absorbed newspaper classifieds businesses:** Alicia Shepard, "Craig Newmark and Craigslist Didn't Destroy Newspapers, They Outsmarted Them," *USA Today,* June 17, 2018, www.usatoday.com/story/opinion/2018/06/18/craig-newmark-craigslist-didnt-kill-newspapers-outsmarted-them-column/702590002/.

113   **Google and Facebook swallowed advertising-based media:** Julia Kollewe, "Google and Facebook Bring in One-Fifth of Global Ad Revenue," *Guardian,* May 1, 2017, www.theguardian.com/media/2017/may/02/google-and-facebook-bring-in-one-fifth-of-global-ad-revenue.

113   **TripAdvisor and Airbnb tackled the travel industry:** Linda Kinstler, "How TripAdvisor Changed Travel," *Guardian,* Aug. 17, 2018, www.theguardian.com/news/2018/aug/17/how-tripadvisor-changed-travel.

114   **It has stuck to it ever since:** Peter Kafka, "Facebook Wants Creators, but YouTube Is Paying Creators Much, Much More," *Vox,* July 15, 2021, www.vox.com/recode/22577734/facebook-1-billion-youtube-creators-zuckerberg-mr-beast.

114   **These networks have all recently created cash-based programs:** Matt Binder, "Musk Says Twitter Will Share Ad Revenue with Creators . . . Who Give Him Money First," *Mashable,* Feb. 3, 2023, mashable.com/article/twitter-ad-revenue-share-creators.

114   **Time-bound "creator funds":** Zach Vallese, "In the Three-way Battle Between YouTube, Reels and Tiktok, Creators Aren't Counting on a Big Payday," CNBC, February 27, 2023, www.cnbc.com/2023/02/27/in-youtube-tiktok-reels-battle-creators-dont-expect-a-big-payday.html.

114   **It forces people to fight over limited resources:** Hank Green, "So . . . TikTok Sucks," hankschannel, Jan. 20, 2022, video, www.youtube.com/watch?v=jAZapFzpP64&ab_channel=hankschannel.

114   **Apple has extraordinary pricing power:** "Five Fast Facts," Time to Play Fair, Oct. 25, 2022, timetoplayfair.com/facts/.

114   **Apple exercises this power:** Geoffrey A. Fowler, "iTrapped: All the Things Apple Won't Let You Do with Your iPhone," *Washington Post,* May 27, 2021, www.washingtonpost.com/technology/2021/05/27/apple-iphone-monopoly/.

114   **Ever try to subscribe to Spotify:** "Why Can't I Get Premium in the App?," Spotify, support.spotify.com/us/article/why-cant-i-get-premium-in-the-app/.

114 **Or buy an Amazon Kindle book:** "Buy Books for Your Kindle App," Help & Customer Service, Amazon, www.amazon.com/gp/help/customer /display.html?nodeId=GDZF9S2BRW5NWJCW.

115 **Some companies would rather go to war:** *Epic Games Inc. v. Apple Inc.,* U.S. District Court for the Northern District of California, Sept. 10, 2021; Bobby Allyn, "What the Ruling in the Epic Games v. Apple Lawsuit Means for iPhone Users," *All Things Considered,* NPR, Sept. 10, 2021, www.npr.org/2021/09/10/1036043886/apple-fortnite-epic-games-ruling -explained.

115 **Banded together to sue Apple:** Foo Yun Chee, "Apple Faces $1 Billion UK Lawsuit by App Developers over App Store Fees," *Reuters,* July 24, 2023, www.reuters.com/technology/apple-faces-1-bln-uk-lawsuit-by-apps -developers-over-app-store-fees-2023-07-24/.

115 **eBay (mostly secondhand goods):** "Understanding Selling Fees," eBay, accessed Sept. 1, 2023, www.ebay.com/sellercenter/selling/seller-fees.

115 **Etsy (handmade items):** "Fees & Payments Policy," Etsy, accessed Sept. 1, 2023, www.etsy.com/legal/fees/.

115 **StockX (sneakers):** Sam Aprile, "How to Lower Seller Fees on StockX," StockX, Aug. 25, 2021, stockx.com/news/how-to-lower-seller-fees-on -stockx/.

116 **Yields an ever-increasing number of sponsored results:** Jefferson Graham, "There's a Reason So Many Amazon Searches Show You Sponsored Ads," *USA Today,* Nov. 9, 2018, www.usatoday.com/story/tech/talking tech/2018/11/09/why-so-many-amazon-searches-show-you-sponsored -ads/1858553002/.

117 **They're charged additional fees:** Jason Del Rey, "Basically Everything on Amazon Has Become an Ad," *Vox,* Nov. 10, 2022, www.vox.com/recode /2022/11/10/23450349/amazon-advertising-everywhere-prime-sponsored -products.

117 **Meta has gross margins of over 70 percent:** "Meta Platforms Gross Profit Margin (Quarterly)," YCharts, last modified Dec. 2022, ycharts.com /companies/META/gross_profit_margin.

118 **Compare the take rates:** "Fees," Uniswap Docs, accessed Sept. 1, 2023, docs.uniswap.org/contracts/v2/concepts/advanced-topics/fees; Coin Metrics data to calculate Ethereum take rate, accessed July 2023, charts.coin metrics.io/crypto-data/.

119 **One critique of blockchain networks:** Moxie Marlinspike, "My First Impressions of Web3," moxie.org, Jan. 7, 2022, moxie.org/2022/01/07 /web3-first-impressions.html.

121 **Exploited the low switching costs of NFT platforms:** Callan Quinn, "What Blur's Success Reveals About NFT Marketplaces," *Forbes,* March 17,

2023, www.forbes.com/sites/digital-assets/2023/03/17/what-blurs
-success-reveals-about-nft-marketplaces/.

122 **His "law of conservation of attractive profits":** Clayton M. Christensen and
Michael E. Raynor, *The Innovator's Solution: Creating and Sustaining Successful Growth* (Brighton, Mass.: Harvard Business Review Press, 2013).

123 **The company can charge Google:** Daisuke Wakabayashi and Jack Nicas,
"Apple, Google, and a Deal That Controls the Internet," *New York Times,*
Oct. 25, 2020, www.nytimes.com/2020/10/25/technology/apple-google
-search-antitrust.html.

123 **Apple is using the popularity of the iPhone:** Alioto Law Firm, "Class Action Lawsuit Filed in California Alleging Google Is Paying Apple to
Stay out of the Search Engine Business," PRNewswire, Jan. 3, 2022, www
.prnewswire.com/news-releases/class-action-lawsuit-filed-in-california
-alleging-google-is-paying-apple-to-stay-out-of-the-search-engine
-business-301453098.html.

124 **Classic tech strategy known as "commoditize your complement":** Lisa
Eadicicco, "Google's Promise to Simplify Tech Puts Its Devices Everywhere," *CNET,* May 12, 2022, www.cnet.com/tech/mobile/googles
-promise-to-simplify-tech-puts-its-devices-everywhere/; Chris Dixon,
"What's Strategic for Google?," cdixon.org, Dec. 30, 2009, cdixon.org
/2009/12/30/whats-strategic-for-google.

124 **Coined the phrase in 2002:** Joel Spolsky, "Strategy Letter V," *Joel on
Software,* June 12, 2002, www.joelonsoftware.com/2002/06/12/strategy
-letter-v/.

9. Building Networks with Token Incentives

128 **Show me the incentives:** Quote widely attributed to Charlie Munger as
in Joshua Brown, "Show me the incentives and I will show you the
outcomes," *Reformed Broker,* Aug. 26, 2018, thereformedbroker
.com/2018/08/26/show-me-the-incentives-and-i-will-show-you-the
-outcome/.

128 **To quote *The Cluetrain Manifesto:*** David Weinberger, David Searls, and
Christopher Locke, *The Cluetrain Manifesto: The End of Business as Usual*
(New York: Basic Books, 2000).

131 **Grants can be distributed:** Uniswap Foundation, "Uniswap Grants Program
Retrospective," June 20, 2022, mirror.xyz/kennethng.eth/0WHWvyE4
Fzz50aORNg3ixZMlvFjZ7frkqxnY4UIfZxo; Brian Newar, "Uniswap
Foundation Proposal Gets Mixed Reaction over $74M Price Tag," *Coin-Telegraph,* Aug. 5, 2022, cointelegraph.com/news/uniswap-foundation
-proposal-gets-mixed-reaction-over-74m-price-tag.

133 **DeFi networks like Compound pioneered:** "What Is Compound in 5 Minutes," *Cryptopedia,* Gemini, June 28, 2022, www.gemini.com/en-US /cryptopedia/what-is-compound-and-how-does-it-work.

134 **Took a crack at the challenge:** Daniel Aguayo et al., "MIT Roofnet: Construction of a Community Wireless Network," MIT Computer Science and Artificial Intelligence Laboratory, Oct. 2003, pdos.csail.mit.edu /~biswas/sosp-poster/roofnet-abstract.pdf; Marguerite Reardon, "Taking Wi-Fi Power to the People," *CNET,* Oct. 27, 2006, www.cnet.com /home/internet/taking-wi-fi-power-to-the-people/; Bliss Broyard, "'Welcome to the Mesh, Brother': Guerrilla Wi-Fi Comes to New York," *New York Times,* July 16, 2021, www.nytimes.com/2021/07/16 /nyregion/nyc-mesh-community-internet.html.

134 **An experimental blockchain project:** Ali Yahya, Guy Wuollet, and Eddy Lazzarin, "Investing in Helium," a16z crypto, Aug. 10, 2021, a16zcrypto .com/content/announcement/investing-in-helium/.

134 **Other projects are using similar methods:** C+Charge, "C+Charge Launch Revolutionary Utility Token for EV Charging Station Management and Payments That Help Organize and Earn Carbon Credits for Holders," press release, April 22, 2022, www.globenewswire.com/news-release /2022/04/22/2427642/0/en/C-Charge-Launch-Revolutionary-Utility -Token-for-EV-Charging-Station-Management-and-Payments-That -Help-Organize-and-Earn-Carbon-Credits-for-Holders.html; Swarm, "Swarm, Ethereum's Storage Network, Announces Mainnet Storage Incentives and Web3PC Inception," Dec. 21, 2022, news.bitcoin .com/swarm-ethereums-storage-network-announces-mainnet-storage -incentives-and-web3pc-inception/; Shashi Raj Pandey, Lam Duc Nguyen, and Petar Popovski, "FedToken: Tokenized Incentives for Data Contribution in Federated Learning," last modified Nov. 3, 2022, arxiv .org/abs/2209.09775.

135 **Hotmail added a default footer to emails:** Adam L. Penenberg, "PS: I Love You. Get Your Free Email at Hotmail," *TechCrunch,* Oct. 18, 2009, tech crunch.com/2009/10/18/ps-i-love-you-get-your-free-email-at-hotmail/.

135 **Top apps in the Apple or Google mobile stores:** Juli Clover, "Apple Reveals the Most Downloaded iOS Apps and Games of 2021," *MacRumors,* Dec. 1, 2021, www.macrumors.com/2021/12/02/apple-most-downloaded -apps-2021.

135 **Even the parent company of TikTok:** Rita Liao and Catherine Shu, "TikTok's Epic Rise and Stumble," *TechCrunch,* Nov. 16, 2020, techcrunch .com/2020/11/26/tiktok-timeline/.

136 **Startups justify the increased marketing expenses:** Andrew Chen, "How Startups Die from Their Addiction to Paid Marketing," andrewchen.com,

accessed March 1, 2023 (originally tweeted May 7, 2018), andrewchen .com/paid-marketing-addiction/.

136 **Marginal profitability of advertising declines:** Abdo Riani, "Are Paid Ads a Good Idea for Early-Stage Startups?," *Forbes*, April 2, 2021, www.forbes .com/sites/abdoriani/2021/04/02/are-paid-ads-a-good-idea-for-early -stage-startups/; Willy Braun, "You Need to Lose Money, but a Negative Gross Margin Is a Really Bad Idea," *daphni chronicles*, Medium, Feb. 28, 2016, medium.com/daphni-chronicles/you-need-to-lose -money-but-a-negative-gross-margin-is-a-really-bad-idea-82ad12cd6d96; Anirudh Damani, "Negative Gross Margins Can Bury Your Startup," *ShowMeDamani*, Aug. 25, 2020, www.showmedamani.com/post/negative -gross-margins-can-bury-your-startup.

137 **Purest example of the self-marketing phenomenon:** Grace Kay, "The History of Dogecoin, the Cryptocurrency That Surged After Elon Musk Tweeted About It but Started as a Joke on Reddit Years Ago," *Business Insider*, Feb. 9, 2021, www.businessinsider.com/what-is-dogecoin -2013-12.

137 **More than two million users subscribe to the Dogecoin Reddit discussion forum:** "Dogecoin," Reddit, Dec. 8, 2013, www.reddit.com/r/dogecoin/.

137 **Some people have even gotten married:** Julia Glum, "To Have and to HODL: Welcome to Love in the Age of Cryptocurrency," *Money*, Oct. 20, 2021, money.com/cryptocurrency-nft-bitcoin-love-relationships/.

138 **Uniswap combines a useful product:** "Introducing Uniswap V3," Uniswap, March 23, 2021, uniswap.org/blog/uniswap-v3.

138 **More than $1 trillion in assets:** Cam Thompson, "DeFi Trading Hub Uniswap Surpasses $1T in Lifetime Volume," *CoinDesk*, May 25, 2022, www.coindesk.com/business/2022/05/24/defi-trading-hub-uniswap -surpasses-1t-in-lifetime-volume/.

139 **"Airdrop" worth thousands of dollars per user:** Brady Dale, "Uniswap's Retroactive Airdrop Vote Put Free Money on the Campaign Trail," *CoinDesk*, Nov. 3, 2020, www.coindesk.com/business/2020/11/03 /uniswaps-retroactive-airdrop-vote-put-free-money-on-the-campaign -trail/.

140 **Set aside equity for users:** Ari Levy and Salvador Rodriguez, "These Airbnb Hosts Earned More Than $15,000 on Thursday After the Company Let Them Buy IPO Shares," CNBC, Dec. 10, 2020, www.cnbc .com/2020/12/10/airbnb-hosts-profit-from-ipo-pop-spreading-wealth -beyond-investors.html; Chaim Gartenberg, "Uber and Lyft Reportedly Giving Some Drivers Cash Bonuses to Use Towards Buying IPO Stock," *Verge*, Feb. 28, 2019, www.theverge.com/2019/2/28/18244479/uber -lyft-drivers-cash-bonus-stock-ipo-sec-rules.

140 **Community receives more than 50 percent of the total tokens:** Andrew Hayward, "Flow Blockchain Now 'Controlled by Community,' Says Dapper Labs," *Decrypt,* Oct. 20, 2021, decrypt.co/83957/flow-blockchain -controlled-community-dapper-labs; Lauren Stephanian and Cooper Turley, "Optimizing Your Token Distribution," Jan. 4, 2022, lstephanian .mirror.xyz/kB9Jz_5joqbY0ePO8rU1NNDKhiqvzU6OWyYsbSA-Kcc.

10. Tokenomics

141 **Prices are important not because money is considered paramount:** Thomas Sowell quoted in Mark J. Perry, "Quotations of the Day from Thomas Sowell," American Enterprise Institute, April 1, 2014, www.aei.org /carpe-diem/quotations-of-the-day-from-thomas-sowell-2/.

141 **Arcades started swapping out:** Laura June, "For Amusement Only: The Life and Death of the American Arcade," *Verge,* Jan. 16, 2013, www .theverge.com/2013/1/16/3740422/the-life-and-death-of-the-american -arcade-for-amusement-only.

142 *Eve* **has millions of players who trade and battle:** Kyle Orland, "How EVE Online Builds Emotion out of Its Strict In-Game Economy," *Ars Technica,* Feb. 5, 2014, arstechnica.com/gaming/2014/02/how-eve-online -builds-emotion-out-of-its-strict-in-game-economy/.

142 **It made headlines in 2007:** Scott Hillis, "Virtual World Hires Real Economist," *Reuters,* Aug. 16, 2007, www.reuters.com/article/us-videogames -economist-life/virtual-world-hires-real-economist-idUSN09256192 20070816.

142 **"Incentive structures work":** Steve Jobs quoted in Brent Schlender, "The Lost Steve Jobs Tapes," *Fast Company,* April 17, 2012, www.fastcompany .com/1826869/lost-steve-jobs-tapes.

147 **Warren Buffett branded them "rat poison":** Sujha Sundararajan, "Billionaire Warren Buffett Calls Bitcoin 'Rat Poison Squared,'" *CoinDesk,* Sept. 13, 2021, www.coindesk.com/markets/2018/05/07/billionaire-warren-buffett -calls-bitcoin-rat-poison-squared/.

147 **Labeled them "magic beans":** Theron Mohamed, "'Big Short' Investor Michael Burry Slams NFTs with a Quote Warning 'Crypto Grifters' Are Selling Them as 'Magic Beans,'" Markets, *Business Insider,* March 16, 2021, markets.businessinsider.com/currencies/news/big-short-michael -burry-slams-nft-crypto-grifters-magic-beans-2021-3-1030214014.

150 **Tech-driven economic revolutions follow predictable cycles:** Carlota Perez, *Technological Revolutions and Financial Capital: The Dynamics of Bubbles and Golden Ages* (Northampton, Mass.: Edward Elgar, 2014).

150 **Another way of looking at the course of tech innovation:** "Gartner Hype

Cycle Research Methodology," Gartner, accessed Sept. 1, 2023, www
.gartner.com/en/research/methodologies/gartner-hype-cycle. (Gartner
and Hype Cycle are registered trademarks of Gartner, Inc. and/or its affiliates in the U.S. and internationally and are used herein with permission. All rights reserved.)

150 **Gartner's model builds on the work of other thinkers:** Doug Henton and
Kim Held, "The Dynamics of Silicon Valley: Creative Destruction and the
Evolution of the Innovation Habitat," *Social Science Information* 52(4):
539–57, 2013, https://journals.sagepub.com/doi/10.1177/0539018413
497542.

153 **Wall Street adage attributed to Benjamin Graham:** David Mazor, "Lessons
from Warren Buffett: In the Short Run the Market Is a Voting Machine,
in the Long Run a Weighing Machine," *Mazor's Edge,* Jan. 7, 2023,
mazorsedge.com/lessons-from-warren-buffett-in-the-short-run-the
-market-is-a-voting-machine-in-the-long-run-a-weighing-machine/.

11. Network Governance

154 **Democracy is the worst form of government:** Winston Churchill, House of
Commons speech, Nov. 11, 1947, quoted in Richard Langworth,
Churchill By Himself: The Definitive Collection of Quotations (New York,
N.Y.: PublicAffairs, 2008), 574.

154 **Provides a forum for hundreds of member organizations:** "Current Members
and Testimonials," World Wide Web Consortium, accessed March 2,
2023, www.w3.org/Consortium/Member/List.

155 **Maintains standards for internet protocols like email:** "Introduction to the
IETF," Internet Engineering Task Force, accessed March 2, 2023, www
.ietf.org/.

155 **Best captured the spirit of protocol network governance:** A. L. Russell, "'Rough
Consensus and Running Code' and the Internet-OSI Standards War,"
*Institute of Electrical and Electronics Engineers Annals of the History of Com-
puting* 28, no. 3 (2006), https://ieeexplore.ieee.org/document/1677461.

157 **Wikipedia is a special case:** Richard Cooke, "Wikipedia Is the Last Best
Place on the Internet," *Wired,* Feb. 17, 2020, www.wired.com/story
/wikipedia-online-encyclopedia-best-place-internet/.

158 **The first is Mozilla:** "History of the Mozilla Project," Mozilla, accessed
Sept. 1, 2023, www.mozilla.org/en-US/about/history/.

158 **Multi-hundred-million-dollar deal with Google:** Steven Vaughan-Nichols,
"Firefox Hits the Jackpot with Almost Billion Dollar Google Deal,"
ZDNET, Dec. 22, 2011, www.zdnet.com/article/firefox-hits-the
-jackpot-with-almost-billion-dollar-google-deal/.

158 **Acquiring smaller companies:** Jordan Novet, "Mozilla Acquires Read-It-Later App Pocket, Will Open-Source the Code," *VentureBeat*, Feb. 27, 2017, venturebeat.com/mobile/mozilla-acquires-read-it-later-app-pocket-will-open-source-the-code/; Paul Sawers, "Mozilla Acquires the Team Behind Pulse, an Automated Status Updater for Slack," *TechCrunch*, Dec. 1, 2022, techcrunch.com/2022/12/01/mozilla-acquires-the-team-behind-pulse-an-automated-status-update-tool-for-slack/.

158 **OpenAI originally started as a nonprofit:** Devin Coldewey, "OpenAI Shifts from Nonprofit to 'Capped-Profit' to Attract Capital," *TechCrunch*, March 11, 2019, techcrunch.com/2019/03/11/openai-shifts-from-nonprofit-to-capped-profit-to-attract-capital/.

158 **Advocated for this approach:** Elizabeth Dwoskin, "Elon Musk Wants a Free Speech Utopia. Technologists Clap Back," *Washington Post*, April 18, 2022, www.washingtonpost.com/technology/2022/04/18/musk-twitter-free-speech/.

159 **"The biggest issue and my biggest regret":** Taylor Hatmaker, "Jack Dorsey Says His Biggest Regret Is That Twitter Was a Company At All," *TechCrunch*, Aug. 26, 2022, techcrunch.com/2022/08/26/jack-dorsey-biggest-regret/.

159 **Friend of a Friend:** "The Friend of a Friend (FOAF) Project," FOAF Project, 2008, web.archive.org/web/20080904205214/http://www.foaf-project.org/projects; Sinclair Target, "Friend of a Friend: The Facebook That Could Have Been," *Two-Bit History*, Jan. 5, 2020, twobithistory.org/2020/01/05/foaf.html#fn:1.

159 **A distributed open-source social network:** Erick Schonfeld, "StatusNet (of Identi.ca Fame) Raises $875,000 to Become the WordPress of Micro-blogging," *TechCrunch*, Oct. 27, 2009, techcrunch.com/2009/10/27/statusnet-of-identi-ca-fame-raises-875000-to-become-the-wordpress-of-microblogging/.

159 **Scuttlebutt, a self-hosted social networking project:** George Anadiotis, "Manyverse and Scuttlebutt: A Human-Centric Technology Stack for Social Applications," *ZDNET*, Oct. 25, 2018, www.zdnet.com/article/manyverse-and-scuttlebutt-a-human-centric-technology-stack-for-social-applications/.

159 **The web creator Tim Berners-Lee's Solid:** Harry McCracken, "Tim Berners-Lee Is Building the Web's 'Third Layer.' Don't Call It Web3," *Fast Company*, Nov. 8, 2022, www.fastcompany.com/90807852/tim-berners-lee-inrupt-solid-pods.

159 **Bluesky, a Dorsey-backed Twitter alternative:** Barbara Ortutay, "Bluesky, Championed by Jack Dorsey, Was Supposed to Be Twitter 2.0. Can It

Succeed?" *AP,* June 6, 2023, apnews.com/article/bluesky-twitter-jack
-dorsey-elon-musk-invite-f2b4fb2fefd34f0149cec2d87857c766.

159 **Interoperate with ActivityPub:** Gregory Barber, "Meta's Threads Could
Make—or Break—the Fediverse," *Wired,* July 18, 2023, www.wired
.com/story/metas-threads-could-make-or-break-the-fediverse/.

160 **Two main weaknesses:** Stephen Shankland, "I Want to Like Mastodon.
The Decentralized Network Isn't Making That Easy," *CNET,* Nov. 14,
2022,www.cnet.com/news/social-media/i-want-to-like-mastodon-the
-decentralized-network-isnt-making-that-easy/.

162 **Aware of the risks:** Sarah Jamie Lewis, "Federation Is the Worst of All
Worlds," *Field Notes,* July 10, 2018, fieldnotes.resistant.tech/federation
-is-the-worst-of-all-worlds/.

162 **Twitter pivoted and removed support for RSS:** Steve Gillmor, "Rest in
Peace, RSS," *TechCrunch,* May 5, 2009, techcrunch.com/2009/05/05
/rest-in-peace-rss/; Erick Schonfeld, "Twitter's Internal Strategy Laid
Bare: To Be 'the Pulse of the Planet,'" *TechCrunch,* July 16, 2009,
techcrunch.com/2009/07/16/twitters-internal-strategy-laid-bare-to-be
-the-pulse-of-the-planet-2/.

163 **Gives Google an outsized number of "votes":** "HTTPS as a Ranking
Signal," *Google Search Central,* Aug. 7, 2014, developers.google.com
/search/blog/2014/08/https-as-ranking-signal; Julia Love, "Google De-
lays Phasing Out Ad Cookies on Chrome Until 2024," *Bloomberg,*
July 27, 2022, www.bloomberg.com/news/articles/2022-07-27/google
-delays-phasing-out-ad-cookies-on-chrome-until-2024?leadSource
=uverify%20wall; Daisuke Wakabayashi, "Google Dominates Thanks
to an Unrivaled View of the Web," *New York Times,* Dec. 14, 2020,
www.nytimes.com/2020/12/14/technology/how-google-dominates
.html.

167 **In her 1972 essay of the same name:** Jo Freeman, "The Tyranny of Structurelessness," 1972, www.jofreeman.com/joreen/tyranny.htm.

12. The Computer versus the Casino

171 **Technology happens. It's not good, it's not bad:** Andy Grove quoted in
Walter Isaacson, "Andrew Grove: Man of the Year," *Time,* Dec. 29, 1997,
time.com/4267448/andrew-grove-man-of-the-year/.

172 **Bankruptcy of the Bahamas-based exchange FTX:** Andrew R. Chow, "After
FTX Implosion, Bahamian Tech Entrepreneurs Try to Pick Up the
Pieces," *Time,* March 30, 2023, time.com/6266711/ftx-bahamas-crypto/;
Sen. Pat Toomey (R-Pa.), "Toomey: Misconduct, Not Crypto, to Blame
for FTX Collapse," U.S. Senate Committee on Banking, Housing, and

Urban Affairs, Dec. 14, 2022, www.banking.senate.gov/newsroom /minority/toomey-misconduct-not-crypto-to-blame-for-ftx-collapse.

172 **Reactions from regulators and policymakers:** Jason Brett, "In 2021, Congress Has Introduced 35 Bills Focused on U.S. Crypto Policy," *Forbes,* Dec. 27, 2021, www.forbes.com/sites/jasonbrett/2021/12/27/in-2021 -congress-has-introduced-35-bills-focused-on-us-crypto-policy/.

172 **Focused on the nearest and easiest targets:** U.S. Securities and Exchange Commission, "Kraken to Discontinue Unregistered Offer and Sale of Crypto Asset Staking-as-a-Service Program and Pay $30 Million to Settle SEC Charges," press release, Feb. 9, 2023, www.sec.gov/news /press-release/2023-25; Sam Sutton, "Treasury: It's Time for a Crypto Crackdown," *Politico,* Sept. 16, 2022, www.politico.com/newsletters /morning-money/2022/09/16/treasury-its-time-for-a-crypto-crack down-00057144; Jonathan Yerushalmy and Alex Hern, "SEC Crypto Crackdown: US Regulator Sues Binance and Coinbase," *Guardian,* June 6, 2023, www.theguardian.com/technology/2023/jun/06/sec -crypto-crackdown-us-regulator-sues-binance-and-coinbase; Sidhartha Shukla, "The Cryptocurrencies Getting Hit Hardest Under the SEC Crackdown," *Bloomberg,* June 13, 2023, www.bloomberg.com/news /articles/2023-06-13/these-are-the-19-cryptocurrencies-are-securities -the-sec-says.

172 **Ethical entrepreneurs are afraid to build products:** Paxos, "Paxos Will Halt Minting New BUSD Tokens," Feb. 13, 2023, paxos.com/2023/02/13 /paxos-will-halt-minting-new-busd-tokens/; "New Report Shows 1 Million Tech Jobs at Stake in US Due to Regulatory Uncertainty," Coinbase, March 29, 2023, www.coinbase.com/blog/new-report-shows-1m -tech-jobs-at-stake-in-us-crypto-policy.

172 **Development is increasingly moving abroad:** Ashley Belanger, "America's Slow-Moving, Confused Crypto Regulation Is Driving Industry out of US," *Ars Technica,* Nov. 8, 2022, arstechnica.com/tech-policy/2022/11 /Americas-slow-moving-confused-crypto-regulation-is-driving-industry -out-of-us/; Jeff Wilser, "US Crypto Firms Eye Overseas Move Amid Regulatory Uncertainty," *Coindesk,* May 27, 2023, www.coindesk.com /consensus-magazine/2023/03/27/crypto-leaving-us/.

175 **Tokens that power "sufficiently decentralized" blockchain networks should be classified as commodities, not securities:** "Framework for 'Investment Contract' Analysis of Digital Assets," U.S. Securities and Exchange Commission, 2019, www.sec.gov/corpfin/framework-investment -contract-analysis-digital-assets.

175 **Decentralization, a process that takes time:** Miles Jennings, "Decentralization for Web3 Builders: Principles, Models, How," a16z crypto,

April 7, 2022, a16zcrypto.com/posts/article/web3-decentralization
-models-framework-principles-how-to/.

176 **They aren't clear in the middle:** "Watch GOP Senator and SEC Chair Spar
Over Definition of Bitcoin," *CNET* highlights, Sept. 16, 2022, www
.youtube.com/watch?v=3H19OF3lbnA; Miles Jennings and Brian
Quintenz, "It's Time to Move Crypto from Chaos to Order," *Fortune,*
July 15, 2023, fortune.com/crypto/2023/07/15/its-time-to-move
-crypto-from-chaos-to-order/; Andrew St. Laurent, "Despite Ripple,
Crypto Projects Still Face Uncertainty and Risks," *Bloomberg Law,* July 31,
2023, news.bloomberglaw.com/us-law-week/despite-ripple-crypto-projects
-still-face-uncertainty-and-risks; "Changing Tides or a Ripple in Still
Water? Examining the SEC v. Ripple Ruling," Ropes & Gray, July
25, 2023, www.ropesgray.com/en/newsroom/alerts/2023/07/changing
-tides-or-a-ripple-in-still-water-examining-the-sec-v-ripple-ruling; Jack
Solowey and Jennifer J. Schulp, "We Need Regulatory Clarity to Keep
Crypto Exchanges Onshore and DeFi Permissionless," Cato Institute,
May 10, 2023, www.cato.org/commentary/we-need-regulatory-clarity
-keep-crypto-exchanges-onshore-defi-permissionless.

176 **U.S. Supreme Court case that created what's called the Howey test:** *U.S. Securities and Exchange Commission v. W. J. Howey Co. et al.,* 328 U.S. 293
(1946).

176 **Substantive guidance on the topic:** "Framework for 'Investment Contract'
Analysis of Digital Assets," U.S. Securities and Exchange Commission, 2019, www.sec.gov/corpfin/framework-investment-contract-analysis
-digital-assets.

176 **Brought several enforcement actions:** Maria Gracia Santillana Linares,
"How the SEC's Charge That Cryptos Are Securities Could Face an
Uphill Battle," *Forbes,* Aug. 14, 2023, www.forbes.com/sites/digital
-assets/2023/08/14/how-the-secs-charge-that-cryptos-are-securities
-could-face-an-uphill-battle/; Jesse Coghlan, "SEC Lawsuits: 68 Cryptocurrencies Are Now Seen as Securities by the SEC," *Cointelegraph,* June 6,
2023, cointelegraph.com/news/sec-labels-61-cryptocurrencies-securities
-after-binance-suit/.

177 **SEC has suggested that Ethereum's token is a security:** David Pan, "SEC's
Gensler Reiterates 'Proof-of-Stake' Crypto Tokens May Be Securities,"
Bloomberg, March 15, 2023, www.bloomberg.com/news/articles/2023
-03-15/sec-s-gary-gensler-signals-tokens-like-ether-are-securities.

177 **Has said that it is a commodity:** Jesse Hamilton, "U.S. CFTC Chief
Behnam Reinforces View of Ether as Commodity," *CoinDesk,* March
28, 2023, www.coindesk.com/policy/2023/03/28/us-cftc-chief-behnam
-reinforces-view-of-ether-as-commodity/; Sandali Handagama, "U.S.

Court Calls ETH a Commodity While Tossing Investor Suit Against Uniswap," *CoinDesk,* Aug. 31, 2023, www.coindesk.com/policy/2023 /08/31/us-court-calls-eth-a-commodity-while-tossing-investor-suit -against-uniswap/.

177 **Ideally, policymakers and regulators would clarify:** Faryar Shirzad, "The Crypto Securities Market is Waiting to be Unlocked. But First We Need Workable Rules," Coinbase, July 21, 2022, www.coinbase.com/blog/the -crypto-securities-market-is-waiting-to-be-unlocked-but-first-we-need -workable-rules; Securities Clarity Act, H.R. 4451, 117th Cong. (2021); Token Taxonomy Act, H.R. 1628, 117th Cong. (2021).

177 **Rules that would effectively ban tokens:** Allyson Versprille, "House Stablecoin Bill Would Put Two-Year Ban on Terra-Like Coins," *Bloomberg,* Sept. 20, 2022, www.bloomberg.com/news/articles/2022-09-20/house-stablecoin-bill-would-put-two-year-ban-on-terra-like-coins; Andrew Asmakov, "New York Signs Two-Year Crypto Mining Moratorium into Law," *Decrypt,* Nov. 23, 2022, decrypt.co/115416/new-york-signs-2-year -crypto-mining-moratorium-law.

179 **Dominant corporate structure was a partnership:** John Micklethwait and Adrian Wooldridge, *The Company: A Short History of a Revolutionary Idea* (New York: Modern Library, 2005); Tyler Halloran, "A Brief History of the Corporate Form and Why It Matters," *Fordham Journal of Corporate and Financial Law,* Nov. 18, 2018, news.law.fordham .edu/jcfl/2018/11/18/a-brief-history-of-the-corporate-form-and-why-it -matters/.

180 **Limited liability corporations did exist back in the early nineteenth century:** Ron Harris, "A New Understanding of the History of Limited Liability: An Invitation for Theoretical Reframing," *Journal of Institutional Economics* 16, no. 5 (2020): 643–64, doi:10.1017/S1744137420000181.

180 **Technological innovation drove pragmatic changes:** William W. Cook, "'Watered Stock'—Commissions—'Blue Sky Laws'—Stock Without Par Value," *Michigan Law Review* 19, no. 6 (1921): 583–98, doi .org/10.2307/1276746.

13. The iPhone Moment: From Incubation to Growth

185 **The future is not to be forecast, but created:** Arthur C. Clarke, foreword to Ervin Laszlo, *Macroshift: Navigating the Transformation to a Sustainable World* (Oakland, Calif.: Berrett-Koehler, 2001).

185 **The Altair was one of the first PCs:** Randy Alfred, "Dec. 19, 1974: Build Your Own Computer at Home!," *Wired,* Dec. 19, 2011, www.wired .com/2011/12/1219altair-8800-computer-kit-goes-on-sale/.

185 **The launch of the IBM PC:** Michael J. Miller, "Project Chess: The Story Behind the Original IBM PC," *PCMag,* Aug. 12, 2021, www.pcmag .com/news/project-chess-the-story-behind-the-original-ibm-pc.

185 **Applications like word processors and spreadsheets:** David Shedden, "Today in Media History: Lotus 1-2-3 Was the Killer App of 1983," *Poynter,* Jan. 26, 2015, www.poynter.org/reporting-editing/2015/today-in-media -history-lotus-1-2-3-was-the-killer-app-of-1983/.

185 **The incubation phase took place:** "Celebrating the NSFNET," NSFNET, Feb. 2, 2017, nsfnet-legacy.org/.

186 **The release of the Mosaic web browser in 1993:** Michael Calore, "April 22, 1993: Mosaic Browser Lights Up Web with Color, Creativity," *Wired,* April 22, 2010, www.wired.com/2010/04/0422mosaic-web-browser/.

186 **The researchers Warren McCulloch and Walter Pitts:** Warren McCulloch and Walter Pitts, "A Logical Calculus of the Ideas Immanent in Nervous Activity," *Bulletin of Mathematical Biophysics* 5 (1943): 115–33.

186 **Paper outlining what people now call the Turing test:** Alan Turing, "Computing Machinery and Intelligence," *Mind,* n.s., 59, no. 236 (Oct. 1950): 433–60, phil415.pbworks.com/f/TuringComputing.pdf.

186 **Advances in graphics processing units:** Rashan Dixon, "Unleashing the Power of GPUs for Deep Learning: A Game-Changing Advancement in AI," *DevX,* July 6, 2023, www.devx.com/news/unleashing-the-power -of-gpus-for-deep-learning-a-game-changing-advancement-in-ai/.

14. Some Promising Applications

189 **In his classic 2008 essay:** Kevin Kelly, "1,000 True Fans," *The Technium,* March 4, 2008, kk.org/thetechnium/1000-true-fans/.

190 **The average internet user:** "How Much Time Do People Spend on Social Media and Why?," *Forbes India,* Sept. 3, 2022, www.forbesindia.com /article/lifes/how-much-time-do-people-spend-on-social-media-and -why/79477/1.

191 **At the average U.S. salary of $59,000 per year:** Belle Wong and Cassie Bottorff, "Average Salary by State in 2023," *Forbes,* Aug. 23, 2023, www .forbes.com/advisor/business/average-salary-by-state/.

195 **The sci-fi author who coined the term "metaverse":** Neal Stephenson, *Snow Crash* (New York: Bantam Spectra, 1992).

196 **His vision of an open metaverse:** Dean Takahashi, "Epic's Tim Sweeney: Be Patient. The Metaverse Will Come. And It Will Be Open," *Venture-Beat,* Dec. 16, 2016, venturebeat.com/business/epics-tim-sweeney-be -patient-the-metaverse-will-come-and-it-will-be-open/.

200 **More money on free games:** Daniel Tack, "The Subscription Transition:

MMORPGs and Free-to-Play," *Forbes,* Oct. 9, 2013, www.forbes.com /sites/danieltack/2013/10/09/the-subscription-transition-mmorpgs-and -free-to-play/.

200 **Few levels for free and then charge for the full game:** Kyle Orland, "The Return of the $70 Video Game Has Been a Long Time Coming," *Ars Technica,* July 9, 2020, arstechnica.com/gaming/2020/07/the-return-of -the-70-video-game-has-been-a-long-time-coming/.

200 **Charging for virtual goods:** Mitchell Clark, "Fortnite Made More Than $9 Billion in Revenue in Its First Two Years," *Verge,* May 3, 2021, www .theverge.com/2021/5/3/22417447/fortnite-revenue-9-billion-epic-games -apple-antitrust-case; Ian Thomas, "How Free-to-Play and In-Game Purchases Took Over the Video Game Industry," CNBC, Oct. 6, 2022, www.cnbc.com/2022/10/06/how-free-to-play-and-in-game-purchases -took-over-video-games.html.

200 **Players usually revolt:** Vlad Savov, "Valve Is Letting Money Spoil the Fun of Dota 2," *Verge,* Feb. 16, 2015, www.theverge.com/2015/2/16/8045369 /valve-dota-2-in-game-augmentation-pay-to-win.

200 **Higher sales than the biggest movie releases:** Felix Richter, "Video Games Beat Blockbuster Movies out of the Gate," *Statista,* Nov. 6, 2018, www .statista.com/chart/16000/video-game-launch-sales-vs-movie-openings/.

200 **Trend amplified by the recent pandemic:** Wallace Witkowski, "Video-games Are a Bigger Industry Than Movies and North American Sports Combined, Thanks to the Pandemic," *MarketWatch,* Dec. 22, 2020, www .marketwatch.com/story/videogames-are-a-bigger-industry-than-sports -and-movies-combined-thanks-to-the-pandemic-11608654990.

200 **Gaming industry brought in:** Jeffrey Rousseau, "Newzoo: Revenue Across All Video Game Market Segments Fell in 2022," *GamesIndustry.biz,* May 30, 2023, www.gamesindustry.biz/newzoo-revenue-across-all-video -game-market-segments-fell-in-2022.

200 **Some companies, notably Nintendo, pushed back:** Jacob Wolf, "Evo: An Oral History of Super Smash Bros. Melee," ESPN, July 12, 2017, www .espn.com/esports/story/_/id/19973997/evolution-championship-series -melee-oral-history-evo.

201 **Squandering time filing lawsuits against innovators:** Andy Maxwell, "How Big Music Threatened Startups and Killed Innovation," *Torrent Freak,* July 9, 2012, torrentfreak.com/how-big-music-threatened-startups-and -killed-innovation-120709/.

201 **Focused far more on protecting existing business:** David Kravets, "Dec. 7, 1999: RIAA Sues Napster," *Wired,* Dec. 7, 2009, www.wired.com /2009/12/1207riaa-sues-napster/; Michael A. Carrier, "Copyright and Innovation: The Untold Story," *Wisconsin Law Review* (2012): 891–962,

www.researchgate.net/publication/256023174_Copyright_and_Innovation
_The_Untold_Story.

201 **They rarely back startups:** *Pitchbook* data. accessed September 1, 2023.

201 **The revenues of the video game industry:** Yuji Nakamura, "Peak Video
Game? Top Analyst Sees Industry Slumping in 2019," *Bloomberg,*
Jan. 23, 2019, www.bloomberg.com/news/articles/2019-01-23/peak
-video-game-top-analyst-sees-industry-slumping-in-2019.

201 **The revenues of the music industry:** The Recording Industry Association of
America, "U.S. Music Revenue Database," Sept. 1, 2023, www.riaa.com
/u-s-sales-database/. (Note: Chart extrapolates global music revenue figures based on U.S. data.)

204 **NFTs can transform the economics of creators too:** "The State of Music/
Web3 Tools for Artists," *Water & Music,* Dec. 15, 2021, www.waterand
music.com/the-state-of-music-web3-tools-for-artists/; Marc Hogan,
"How NFTs Are Shaping the Way Music Sounds," *Pitchfork,* May 23,
2022, pitchfork.com/features/article/how-nfts-are-shaping-the-way-music
-sounds/.

204 **Consider the music business again:** Alyssa Meyers, "A Music Artist Says
Apple Music Pays Her 4 Times What Spotify Does per Stream, and
It Shows How Wildly Royalty Payments Can Vary Between Services,"
Business Insider, Jan. 10, 2020, www.businessinsider.com/how-apple
-music-and-spotify-pay-music-artist-streaming-royalties-2020-1; "Ex-
pressing the sense of Congress that it is the duty of the Federal Government to establish a new royalty program to provide income to
featured and non-featured performing artists whose music or audio
content is listened to on streaming music services, like Spotify," H Con.
Res. 102, 177th Cong. (2022), www.congress.gov/bill/117th-congress
/house-concurrent-resolution/102/text.

204 **Nine million musicians on the streaming service Spotify:** "Top 10 Take-
aways," *Loud & Clear,* Spotify, loudandclear.byspotify.com/.

205 **The music industry sold $3.5 billion:** Jon Chapple, "Music Merch Sales
Boom Amid Bundling Controversy," *IQ,* July 4, 2019, www.iq-mag
.net/2019/07/music-merch-sales-boom-amid-bundling-controversy/.

205 **Sold $36 billion in virtual goods:** "U.S. Video Game Sales Reach Record-
Breaking $43.3 Billion in 2018," Entertainment Software Association,
Jan.23,2019,www.theesa.com/news/u-s-video-game-sales-reach-record
-breaking-43-4-billion-in-2018/.

206 **There are early signs of success:** Andrew R. Chow, "Independent Musicians Are Making Big Money from NFTs. Can They Challenge the
Music Industry?" *Time,* Dec. 2, 2021, time.com/6124814/music
-industry-nft/.

206 **The NFT standard was formalized:** William Entriken et al., "ERC-721: Non-Fungible Token Standard," Ethereum.org, Jan. 24, 2018, eips .ethereum.org/EIPS/eip-721/.

206 **From 2020 to early 2023, creators received about $9 billion:** Nansen Query data, accessed Sept. 21, 2023, nansen.ai/query/; Flipside data, accessed Sept. 21, 2023, flipsidecrypto.xyz/.

206 **YouTube . . . paid out about $47 billion:** "Worldwide Advertising Revenues of YouTube as of 1st Quarter 2023," *Statista*, accessed Sept. 21, 2023, statista .com/statistics/289657/youtube-global-quarterly-advertising-revenues/.

207 **When the British writer Arthur Conan Doyle:** Jennifer Keishin Armstrong, "How Sherlock Holmes Changed the World," BBC, Jan. 6, 2016, www .bbc.com/culture/article/20160106-how-sherlock-holmes-changed-the -world.

207 **People hated the irritating alien Jar Jar Binks so much:** "Why Has Jar Jar Binks Been Banished from the Star Wars Universe?," *Guardian*, Dec. 7, 2015, www.theguardian.com/film/shortcuts/2015/dec/07/jar-jar-binks -banished-from-star-wars-the-force-awakens.

208 **Most people barely remember Encarta:** "Victim of Wikipedia: Microsoft to Shut Down Encarta," *Forbes*, March 30, 2009, www.forbes.com /2009/03/30/microsoft-encarta-wikipedia-technology-paidcontent.html.

208 **Today, Wikipedia is the internet's seventh most popular website:** "Top Website Rankings," Similarweb, accessed Sept. 1, 2023, www.similarweb .com/top-websites/.

208 **The question-and-answers sites:** Alexia Tsotsis, "Inspired By Wikipedia, Quora Aims for Relevancy With Topic Groups and Reorganized Topic Pages," *TechCrunch*, June 24, 2011, techcrunch.com/2011/06/24 /inspired-by-wikipedia-quora-aims-for-relevancy-with-topic-groups -and-reorganized-topic-pages/.

210 **Calls this idea "fantasy Hollywood":** Cuy Sheffield, "'Fantasy Hollywood'— Crypto and Community-Owned Characters," a16z crypto, June 15, 2021, a16zcrypto.com/posts/article/crypto-and-community-owned -characters/.

210 **Basic security measures:** Steve Bodow, "The Money Shot," *Wired*, Sept. 1, 2001, www.wired.com/2001/09/paypal/.

210 **The first banner ad:** Joe McCambley, "The First Ever Banner Ad: Why Did It Work So Well?," *Guardian*, Dec. 12, 2013, www.theguardian.com /media-network/media-network-blog/2013/dec/12/first-ever-banner -ad-advertising.

212 **These companies did cede a lot of power:** Alex Rampell, Twitter post, Sept. 2018, twitter.com/arampell/status/1042226753253437440.

214 **Dollar-pegged stablecoin like USDC to avoid price volatility:** Abubakar

Idris and Tawanda Karombo, "Stablecoins Find a Use Case in Africa's Most Volatile Markets," *Rest of World,* Aug. 19, 2021, restofworld.org /2021/stablecoins-find-a-use-case-in-africas-most-volatile-markets/.

215   **DeFi networks stayed up and running:** Jacquelyn Melinek, "Investors Focus on DeFi as It Remains Resilient to Crypto Market Volatility," *Tech-Crunch,* July 26, 2022, techcrunch.com/2022/07/26/investors-focus-on -defi-as-it-remains-resilient-to-crypto-market-volatility/.

216   **Google search exemplifies the covenant:** Jennifer Elias, "Google 'Over-whelmingly' Dominates Search Market, Antitrust Committee States," CNBC, Oct. 6, 2020, www.cnbc.com/2020/10/06/google-overwhelmingly -dominates-search-market-house-committee-finds.html.

217   **Commands more than 80 percent of internet search:** Paresh Dave, "United States vs Google Vindicates Old Antitrust Gripes from Microsoft," *Reuters,* Oct. 21, 2020, www.reuters.com/article/us-tech-antitrust-google -microsoft-idCAKBN27625B.

217   **News Corp has been protesting Google's free riding:** Lauren Feiner, "Google Will Pay News Corp for the Right to Showcase Its News Articles," CNBC, Feb. 17, 2021, www.cnbc.com/2021/02/17/google -and-news-corp-strike-deal-as-australia-pushes-platforms-to-pay-for -news.html.

217   **Yelp has been campaigning to rein in Google's power:** Mat Honan, "Jeremy Stoppelman's Long Battle with Google Is Finally Paying Off," *BuzzFeed News,* Nov. 5, 2019, www.buzzfeednews.com/article/mathonan/jeremy -stoppelman-yelp.

218   **Naspers became an internet powerhouse:** John McDuling, "The Former Mouthpiece of Apartheid Is Now One of the World's Most Successful Tech Investors," *Quartz,* Jan. 9, 2014, qz.com/161792/naspers-africas -most-fascinating-company.

218   **Occasionally, Google breaks the covenant:** Scott Cleland, "Google's 'In-fringenovation' Secrets," *Forbes,* Oct. 3, 2011, www.forbes.com/sites /scottcleland/2011/10/03/googles-infringenovation-secrets/.

219   **The AI is like a human artist:** Blake Brittain, "AI Companies Ask U.S. Court to Dismiss Artists' Copyright Lawsuit," *Reuters,* April 19, 2023, www.reuters.com/legal/ai-companies-ask-us-court-dismiss-artists -copyright-lawsuit-2023-04-19/.

220   **Internet services curtail their API access:** Umar Shakir, "Reddit's Upcom-ing API Changes Will Make AI Companies Pony Up," *Verge,* April 18, 2023, www.theverge.com/2023/4/18/23688463/reddit-developer-api -terms-change-monetization-ai.

220   **Happening today with "content farms":** Sheera Frenkel and Stuart A. Thompson, "'Not for Machines to Harvest': Data Revolts Break Out

Against A.I.," *New York Times,* July 15, 2023, www.nytimes.com/2023 /07/15/technology/artificial-intelligence-models-chat-data.html.

220 **Content to supplement AI training data:** Tate Ryan-Mosley, "Junk Websites Filled with AI-Generated Text Are Pulling in Money from Programmatic Ads," *MIT Technology Review,* June 26, 2023, www .technologyreview.com/2023/06/26/1075504/junk-websites-filled-with -ai-generated-text-are-pulling-in-money-from-programmatic-ads/.

221 **Shouldn't creators get paid:** Gregory Barber, "AI Needs Your Data—and You Should Get Paid for It," *Wired,* Aug. 8, 2019, www.wired.com /story/ai-needs-data-you-should-get-paid/; Jazmine Ulloa, "Newsom Wants Companies Collecting Personal Data to Share the Wealth with Californians," *Los Angeles Times,* May 5, 2019, www.latimes.com/politics /la-pol-ca-gavin-newsom-california-data-dividend-20190505-story.html.

222 **Try to contain AI through regulation:** Sue Halpern, "Congress Really Wants to Regulate A.I., but No One Seems to Know How," *New Yorker,* May 20, 2023, www.newyorker.com/news/daily-comment/congress -really-wants-to-regulate-ai-but-no-one-seems-to-know-how.

223 **Government certification process:** Brian Fung, "Microsoft Leaps into the AI Regulation Debate, Calling for a New US Agency and Executive Order," CNN, May 25, 2023, www.cnn.com/2023/05/25/tech/microsoft -ai-regulation-calls/index.html.

223 **Calling for a six-month pause on all AI research:** Kari Paul, "Letter Signed by Elon Musk Demanding AI Research Pause Sparks Controversy," *Guardian,* April 1, 2023, www.theguardian.com/technology/2023/mar /31/ai-research-pause-elon-musk-chatgpt.

223 **Developing comprehensive AI regulatory frameworks:** "Blueprint for an AI Bill of Rights," White House, Oct. 2022, www.whitehouse.gov/wp -content/uploads/2022/10/Blueprint-for-an-AI-Bill-of-Rights.pdf; Billy Perrigo and Anna Gordon, "E.U. Takes a Step Closer to Passing the World's Most Comprehensive AI Regulation," *Time,* June 14, 2023, time.com/6287136/eu-ai-regulation/; European Commission, "Proposal for a Regulation Laying Down Harmonised Rules on Artificial Intelligence," Shaping Europe's Digital Future, April 21, 2021, digital -strategy.ec.europa.eu/en/library/proposal-regulation-laying-down -harmonised-rules-artificial-intelligence.

Conclusion

226 **If you want to build a ship:** Paraphrase of a quote widely attributed to Antoine de Saint-Exupéry, Quote Investigator, Aug. 25, 2015, quote investigator.com/2015/08/25/sea/.

Index

ActivityPub, 159, 160
Advanced Research Projects
    Agency (ARPA), 8, 10
advertising on internet, xv, 210
Airbnb, 140
algorithmic stablecoins, 76
Alphabet. *See* Google
Amazon
  abuses of power by, xviii
  as anticompetitive, xvii–xviii
  cost structure of, 112–13
  eBay's advantages over, 32
  take rate of, 117
anonymity on blockchains, 61–62
anticompetitiveness, ix, xvii–xviii
Apple, xviii, 44, 114–15, 118. *See*
    also iPhone
application layer "stack," 11
application programming
    interface (API)
  described, 20

internet payments built on
    blockchain networks and, 215
Netflix and, 38
RSS and, 25
successful providers, 109
Twitter's open, 22
two-way use of web and, 30
apps and smartphones, xvi–xvii,
    50, 135, 186–87
App Store, xviii, 44
Aptos, transactions per second, 90
ARPANET, 8, 9
art
  AI and, 206, 219
  modding and, 104
  NFTs and, 72, 77, 203–4
  software as, xx, 53, 106
artificial intelligence (AI)
  art and, 206, 219
  content creators and, 219–21
  funding, 84, 229

artificial intelligence (AI) (*cont'd*)
  gestation period of, 186
  growth of, 51
  one-boxing and, 218
  regulation of, 222–25
"attack surface," 64–65
attention-monetization dilemma, 198–99, 200, 201
"attestations," 223–24
attract-extract cycle, 42–43, 104
Auction Web, 32
authentication, described, 62
automation, 4

bait-and-switch, 37, 43
Barlow, John Perry, 8–9
Bengio, Yoshua, 223
Berners-Lee, Tim, 11, 53, 159
Bezos, Jeff, 112
Big Tech. *See also* specific companies
  blockchains and, 52, 54, 85
  growth of, xiv
  innovation and, xv
  startups and, xv, xvii, 84, 135–36
  treatment of users by, xiv–xv, 139
  virtual reality and, 51
Bitcoin
  commitments made by, 68
  creation of, 151
  decentralization of, 161, 175, 177
  energy consumption by, 60
  as first blockchain network, 87
  as fungible token, 74
  internet payment system built on top of, 213–14
  invention of blockchain and, 55
  miners, 57
  parody of, 137–38
  programming language of, 58

security, 65
  transactions per second, 90
blockchain networks. *See also* tokenomics; tokens
  advantages of, over earlier network architectures, xxiii–xxiv
  AI content payments using, 221
  American share of software developers, xxviii
  anonymity on, 61–62
  arguments against, 147–48
  benefit of building on, 91–92
  blockchains as core of, 87
  centralization of, 92, 94
  comparison to cities, 95, 97
  composability and, 110, 228
  content creators and, 210, 221
  control of supply of and demand for tokens, 144–47
  core services, 92, 94
  decentralization of, 94–95, 97–98
  development of, 91
  Dogecoin, 137–38
  downward price competition among, 121
  economic winners in, 132
  financial core, 95
  first, 87
  funding, 59, 109–10, 136, 153, 178
  future of, 187–88
  game theory and, 91
  as in "Goldilocks zone," 92
  governance of, 118–19, 165–67
  hardware-software power relationship in, xxiii
  as having architecture for building future networks, 227–29

importance of tokens, 79
importance of "treasuries" on, 79
internet payments using, 213–16, 221
internet scale operation of, 90
media coverage of, 171–72
metaverse and, 196–98
names and, 119
open-source software, 119
ownership and, 87, 140
platform-app feedback loops can be supported by, 228
risk of recentralization and, 120–21, 174
service commitments made by, 109
social networks and, 187, 193–94
software development by, 129, 130–31
software-hardware power relationship in, 87–88
storage of "attestations" on, 223–25
strengths and weaknesses of architecture, 93
take rates of, 92, 113, 118–22, 124–25, 126
treatment of users by, 140
blockchains. *See also* tokenomics; tokens
accessibility ethos of, 66
"attack surface" in, 64–65
Big Tech and, 52, 54, 85
blocks in state transitions, 58
as outside-in technology, 54–55
commitments about future behavior, 66–67
as computers, xxiii, 56
consensus processes in, 57–58, 63

as core of blockchain networks, 87
crypto and, 61–62
cryptography and, 57
development of, 55
digital signatures in, 62–63
effect on environment of, 60, 61
"enterprise," 70
federated networks and, 161
manipulability of software of, 67
multiplayer nature of, 70–71
as network constitutions, 164
operation of, 57
ownership on, 73, 79
participation in, 59
physical computers in, 56–57
potential applications of, 68
programming languages of, 58
properties of, 66–67
punishment for dishonesty, 63
security of, 56–57, 62–65
as software abstraction on top of physical devices, 56
software-hardware power relationship in, xxiii
transactions per second, 90
transparency of, 61–62, 66
as "trustless," 63, 64
Bluesky, 159
bootstrap problem, 132–34, 144
bots, 20
Brin, Sergey, 53
Buffett, Warren, 147

casino culture, xxv, 171, 172
"The Cathedral and the Bazaar" (Raymond), 110–11
CCP Games, 142
centralization. *See also* decentralization
of blockchain networks, 92, 94

centralization (*cont'd*)
  innovation and, xix
  of internet, xix, 6–7
  risk of recentralization of
    blockchain networks, 120–21,
    174
  RSS as symbol of defiance
    against, 23
Cerf, Vint, 10
ChatGPT, 158, 218
Christensen, Clayton, 82–84, 122
Circle, 75
Clark, David, 155
clients, 11–12, 17
Cloud technology, 54
The Cluetrain Manifesto, 128
collaborative storytelling, 208–10
commodities, 174, 175, 177
commoditization, 122–24
Commodity Futures Trading
  Commission (CFTC), 177
complements
  business use definition of, 34–35
  commoditization and, 124
  corporate networks and, 35–36,
    38–42
  as frenemies, 35
  network growth and, 40–42
  of social networks, 36–38
composability
  in blockchain metaverse, 197
  of blockchain networks, 228
  described, 83
  internet payments built on
    blockchain networks and, 215
  open-source software and, 106–10
  reusability and, 85, 107–8
  of software, 83, 85, 106–10
  storage of "attestations" on
    blockchain networks and, 224
  wisdom of crowds and, 108

computer chips, transistors on, 49,
  50
computer culture, characteristics
  of, xxv, 171
computers
  as ability accelerators, xx
  blockchains as, xxiii, 56
  changes in definition of, 56
  consensus in next advancements
    in, 51–52
  defining, 55–56
  history of, 185
  physical, in blockchains, 56–57
  software-hardware power
    relationship in, xxiii, 87–88
content creators
  AI and, 219–21
  attention-monetization dilemma
    and, 198–99
  "attestations" by, 223–25
  blockchain networks and, 210
  collaborative, 208–10
  corporate networks and, 38–40,
    190
  email use by, 19
  low take rates for, 114, 191–92
  micropayments and, 214–15
  NFTs and, 203–5, 207
  ownership and, xiii
  as primary complement of social
    networks, 36, 37
  revenue maximization of social
    networks and, 36–37
  tokens and, 130
"content farms," 220
content moderation, 17
control
  of anticompetitiveness, xix
  in blockchains, 56–57, 62–65,
    118–19
  of names and naming, 14–16

ownership and, 72
of supply of and demand for
    tokens, 144–47
corporate networks. *See also* social
    networks; specific networks
  access of software developers to,
    19–20
  access to capital of, 25, 31
  attract-extract cycle and, 42–43,
    104
  bait-and-switch strategy, 43
  basic facts about, xxi
  bootstrap problem and, 133
  commitments made by, 68–69
  competition to RSS from, 22–24
  complements and, 35–36, 38–42
  composability and, 110
  content creators and, 38–40, 190
  core services, 92
  described, xxi
  economic winners in, 132
  effect of old legal structure on,
    181
  federated networks evolution
    into, 162–63
  functionality of, 92
  games and, 195–96
  governance of, 156, 166
  growth of internet and, 44, 229
  internet payments using, 212
  interoperability and, 16, 41–42,
    108–9
  investment and, 19, 21
  lack of transparency of, 43
  logical and organizational
    centralization of, 94
  mapping control in, 15–16
  mobile phones and, 104
  new product development for,
    39–40
  ownership on, 79–80

platform-app feedback loop and,
    50–51
  protocol networks failure
    against, xxvi–xxvii
  security and, 64, 65
  services of, 30–31, 44
  social networks as, 192
  software development by, 128–30
  software-hardware power
    relationship in, 88
  startups and, 43
  strengths and weaknesses of
    architecture, 20, 93
  structure of, 30–31
  take rates of, xvi, 19, 116–17,
    118, 124, 125, 126
  treatment of users by, 139–40
  use of tool as hook for growth,
    32–33
  users' experience on, 160
crypto, xxv, 61–62
cryptocurrency, 75
cryptography, xxii, 57, 62

DARPA, 8, 10
Data General, 83
"data protectionism," 39
decentralization. *See also*
    centralization
  of Bitcoin, 175, 177
  decentralized finance (DeFi)
    networks, 89
  organizational, of blockchain
    networks, 94–95, 97–98
  RSS database need and, 24, 25
  of social networks, 190–92
decentralized autonomous
    organizations (DAOs), 79, 95,
    97
"Declaration of the Independence
    of Cyberspace" (Barlow), 9

deepfakes, 222–23, 224
DeFi networks
  bootstrap problem and, 133
  gas and sink fees charged by, 144–45
  in internet "stack," 89
  monetary transactions and, 215–16
  rules of, 121
  scaling limits and, 90
  take rates of, 126
  token supply and, 145
  as well-designed network for control of supply and demand for tokens, 148–49
deplatforming, defined, xv
Diaspora, 21–22
Diem, 85
Digital Equipment Corporation, 83
digital signatures, 62–63
digital world, fusion of physical world with, 4–5
disruptive technologies, 82–84, 85
DNS lookups, 14
Dogecoin, 137–38, 140
domain name system (DNS), 13–16, 19, 24, 155
Doom, 104
Dorsey, Jack, 158–59, 161
DOS operating system, 102

eBay, 32
Einstein, Albert, 107
email
  clients, 12
  content creators and, 19
  Gmail, 163

governance of, 155
  network effect accrues to community, 17–18
  platform-app feedback loop and, 50
  success of, as protocol network, 26
  transparency of, 43–44
encapsulation, 71–72, 107
encryption, described, 62
"enterprise blockchains," 70
environment and blockchains, 60, 61
Epic, xviii
Ethereum
  combining of security sinks and access sinks by, 146
  creation of, 151
  fungible token use in, 76
  gas and sink fees charged by, 144–45
  internet payment system built on top of, 214
  in internet "stack," 88–89
  programming languages, 58
  proof of stake energy consumption by, 60, 61
  punishment for dishonesty and, 63
  "rollups" "layer two" system, 91
  security, 65
  take rate of, 118
  transactions per second, 90
  "treasury" applications on, 79
  validators, 109
  as well-designed network for control of supply and demand for tokens, 148
Ethereum Name Service (ENS), 119, 121
Eve Online, 142

Facebook. *See also* Meta
access of software developers to, 19–20
as competition to RSS, 24
crackdown on third-party companies, xvii
exporting of Google Contacts to, 39
rebranded, 73
take rate of, 113–14, 118
value of, according to Reed's law, 6
Vine and, 20, 38
Zynga and, 42
fans and ownership, 207, 208, 209
"fantasy Hollywood," 210
FarmVille, 42
federated networks, 158–64
"Federation Is the Worst of All Worlds" (blog), 162
51 percent attacks, 65
financial networks, 126, 187
Fitzpatrick, Brad, 24–25
Freeman, Jo, 167
Freemium, 211
FreeSocial, 159
"Freeware: The Heart & Soul of the Internet" (O'Reilly), 102
Friend of a Friend, 159
FTX, xxv, 172
fungible tokens, 74, 75–76, 197. *See also* Bitcoin

games, 72–73, 104–5, 141–42, 194–98, 199–203, 211
game theory, 57, 91
Gartner consulting firm, 150
"gas," 145
Gates, Bill, 101
GitHub, 106–7
GNU Social, 159

"Goldilocks zone," 92
Google
abuses of power by, xviii
commoditization and, 122–23, 124
content distribution by, 216–18
exporting of Contacts to Facebook, 39
Gmail and, 163
history of, 53
take rate of, 117
YouTube purchased by, 33–34
governance
in blockchain metaverse, 197
of blockchain networks, 118–19, 165–67
blockchains as network constitutions, 164
of corporate networks, 156, 166
of DNS, 13–14, 155
of email, 155
federated networks model, 158, 160
informal versus formal, 167
of internet, 154–55
nonprofit model and, 157–58
of protocol networks, 92, 154, 155, 166
"governance" sinks, 146
Graham, Benjamin, 153
Green, Hank, 114

Hafner, Katie, 11
"hard forking," 63
hardware, power relationship of, with software in computers and blockchains, xxiii, 87–88
hashes, 223
Heartbleed, 25–26
Helium, 134

Hirst, Damien, 78
HOSTS.TXT (Stanford Research Institute), 13
Howey test, 176
Hunch, 39
HTML (Hypertext Markup Language), 11
HTTP (Hypertext Transfer Protocol), 11
"hype cycle," 150–51, 179
hypervisor software, 56

IBM, 102
ICANN, 13–14, 155
"The Inevitable Showdown Between Twitter and Twitter Apps" (Dixon), 39
information
  democratization of, in "read era," xxi–xxii
  greater exchange of, richer network is, 6
  state machines and, 55
innovation. See also content creators
  attract-extract cycle and, 42–43
  Big Tech and, xv
  centralization of web and, xix
  free exchange of ideas on early internet and, 8
  ownership and, 81
  ownership as motivator of, 20
  preconceived notions and, 68
  protocol networks and, 18
  regulation and, 179
  use of technology and, 28
inoperability and modding, 104
inside-out path of advancement in technology, 52, 54
Instagram, 33, 113–14
Intel, 124

internet
  accessibility ethos of early, 66
  advertising on, 210
  copying as core activity of, 198
  corporate networks and growth of, 44
  current dominant core services of, 23
  DNS and, 13–16
  eras, xxi–xxii
  governance of, 154–55
  hardware-software power relationship in, xxiii
  history of, xiii–xiv, 8–9, 13–14, 19–24, 25–26, 28–30, 38, 39, 44–45, 74, 105, 186
  music industry and, 201, 202
  network design as determining power of, xxi
  ownership and, 79–80
  reinventing, for future, 225–29
  software basis of, xix–xx
  "stack," 102
  web versus, 11
Internet Corporation for Assigned Names and Numbers (ICANN), 13–14
Internet Engineering Task Force (IETF), 155
Internet of Things, 5
internet payments
  blockchain networks for, 213–16
  corporate networks for, 212
  micropayments, 214–15
  models, 210–12
  protocol networks for, 212–13
internet protocol (IP), 10, 12–13, 14–15, 102
internet "stack," 9–11, 88–89, 102, 125, 126

interoperability
  in blockchain metaverse, 197–98
  corporate networks and, 16,
    41–42, 108–9
  federated networks and,
    162–63
  mobile phones and, 103
  services and, 30, 104
InterStellar Kredits, 142
investment(s). *See also* venture
    capital
  in blockchain networks, 92
  in blockchains, 59
  in corporate networks, 19, 21,
    25, 31
  in development of new
    technologies, 84
  DNS and, 16
  limited liability corporations
    and, 180
  ownership as motivator of, 20
  protocol networks and, 18–19
  RSS and, 25, 34
iPhone
  Apple's take rate, 114–15, 118
  apps and success of, 50
  as disruptive technology, 84
  increase in networks and, 44
  interoperability and, 103
  Safari browser, 123
  transistors on, 50

Jabber, 21, 22
Jobs, Steve, xx, 53, 142
Joy, Bill, 40, 108

Kahn, Robert, 10
Kamvar, Sep, 53–54
Kay, Alan, 27–28
Kelly, Kevin, 189–90
keys, private versus public, 62

language and protocols, 9
"law of conservation of attractive
    profits," 122
"layer two" systems, 91
Libra, 85
Lightning, 213
limited liability corporations
    (LLCs), 179–81
"Lindy effect," 44
Linux, 26, 50, 54, 55, 105, 110,
    124
LiveJournal, 24
Louis Vuitton, NFTs created by,
    77–78
Lyft, 140
Lyon, Matthew, 11

MacManus, Richard, 30
Madrigal, Alexis, 103
Maker, 76
mapping, 14–16
Marlinspike, Moxie, 120, 121
mashups, 103
Mastodon, 159
McAfee, 21
McCulloch, Warren, 186
memecoins, 137–38, 140
Meta, 73, 81–82, 85, 117. *See also*
    Facebook
metaverse, 195–98
Metcalfe, Robert, 6
Metcalfe's law, 5–6, 41
Microsoft, 36, 101, 102
Midjourney, 218, 219
mobile phones. *See also* iPhone
  apps and, xvi–xvii, 50, 135,
    186–87
  corporate networks and, 104
  interoperability and, 103
  payments for calls and texts, 214
  reasons for success of, 49–50, 51

Mockapetris, Paul, 13
modding, 104–5
Moore, Gordon, 49–50
Moore's law, 49, 50, 51
Mosaic, 11
Mozilla, 158
music industry, 201, 202, 204–5
Musk, Elon, 137, 223

Nakamoto, Satoshi, 55, 59, 68, 87
names/naming
  as avatars, 12
  on blockchain networks, 119
  decoupling, from services in protocol networks, 19
  DNS, 13–16, 19, 24, 155
  internet protocol addresses for computers, 12–13
  market for domain, 16
  network's versus user's control of, 14–16
  redirecting between IP address and, 14–15
  registration of, 14
  social networks as owners of, 73
native technology, 29–30, 68
native tokens, 129, 178
Netflix API, 38
"net neutrality," xix–xx
Netscape, 158
networks. See also blockchain networks; corporate networks; protocol networks
  basic facts about, 5
  building new non-corporate, as solution for centralization of internet, 7
  complements and growth of, 40–42
  design of, xxi, 30
  financial, 126, 187
  as mediators with "real world," 4–5
  Metcalfe's law and, 5–6
  neural, 223
  Reed's law and, 6
  "S-curve" of adoption of, 40–42
  snowball effect, 6–7
  types of, xv, xxi
  ubiquity of, xv
  value of, 5–6
Nike, NFTs created by, 78
nodes, 5–6, 12, 41, 88
non-fungible tokens (NFTs)
  art and, 72, 77, 203–4
  as container for representing ownership, 203
  content creators and, 203–5, 206, 207
  described, 74
  music industry and, 204–5
  uses of, 76–78
  metaverse and, 197
  video games and, 203
nonprofit network model, 157–58
Novi, 85

Oculus VR, 84
off-chain governance, 164–65, 166
on-chain governance, 165–66
"1,000 True Fans" (Kelly), 189–90
"one-boxing," 218
opacity
  of blockchains, 61–62, 66
  corporate networks' lack of, 43
  of protocol networks, 43–44
OpenAI, 84, 158
OpenSea, 118, 121
OpenSocial, 21, 22

open-source software
  beginning of, 54
  of blockchain networks, 119
  composability, 106–10
  funding, 25–26, 108
  Linux, 26, 50, 54, 55, 105, 110, 124
  modding, 105
  Netscape, 158
  RSS, 22–24, 25, 34, 162
  software pricing and, 102
Open Systems Interconnection model (OSI), 9
Optimism, in internet "stack," 89
O'Reilly, Tim, 102
organic content, 37
outside-in path of advancement in technology, 52–53. *See also* blockchains
ownership
  in blockchain networks, 87
  on blockchains, 73, 79
  by community of blockchain networks, 140
  content creators and, xiii
  control and, 72
  on corporate networks, 79–80
  democratization of, in "read-write-own era," xxii
  DNS and, 16
  fans and, 207, 208, 209
  internet and, xiii–xiv, 79–80
  as motivator for investors, 20
  of names on social networks, 73
  NFTs as container for representing, 203–5
  positive effects of, 80–81
  on protocol networks, 17–18
  in "real" world, 80–81
  speculation and, 16

  tokens as representing, 72, 87, 136
  trading and, 178

Page, Larry, 53
pay-as-you-go model, 76
payment networks, take rates of, 115
PCs, 83
Perez, Carlota, 150
perimeter security model of corporate networks, 64
phishing, 20–21
physical world, fusion of digital world with, 4–5
Pitts, Walter, 186
platform-app feedback loops, 36, 50–51, 101, 228
platform risk, 39
Polygon, in internet "stack," 89
Postel, Jon, 11, 13
privacy, xiv–xv, 162
programming languages, of blockchains, 58
programs, defined, 55–56
promoted content, 37
proof of stake (POS), 60
  energy consumption, 61
proof of work, 59–60
protocol coups, 22–24, 162, 163–64
protocol networks
  access to capital of, 25, 34
  basic facts about, xxi
  benefits of, 17–20
  components of, 12
  described, xxi
  failure of, against corporate networks, xxvi–xxvii, 227
  governance of, 92, 154, 155, 166
  innovation and, 18

protocol networks (*cont'd*)
  internet payments using, 212–13
  mapping control in, 14–15
  new ones in last thirty years,
    44–45
  ownership and, 80
  social networks as, 159–60
  software development by, 128–29
  software-hardware power
    relationship in, 87–88
  strengths and weaknesses of
    architecture, 93
  success of email and web as, 26
  take rates of, 18, 116, 124–25, 191
  transparency of, 43–44
protocol(s)
  clients and, 11–12
  evolution of definition of, 9
  internet "stack" and, 9–11, 102
  need to be unopinionated, 17
  RSS, 22–25, 34
public key cryptography, 62
publishing, democratization of, in
    "read-write era," xxii

Raymond, Eric, 110–11
"read era," xxi–xxii, 28, 29–30, 74
"read-write era," xxii, 30, 74
"read-write-own era," xxii, 74
ReadWriteWeb, 30, 44
Ready Player One, 194
"real world," networks as
    mediators with, 4–5
recentralization risk, 120
Reed, David, 6
Reed's law, 6
regulation
  of AI, 222–25
  "attestations" instead of, 223–25
  to control anticompetitiveness,
    xix

innovation and, 179
  of securities, 173, 174, 175, 176,
    177
  of tokens, 173, 174–77, 178–79
reusability, in composability, 85,
    107–8
"rollups," 91
RSS ("really simple syndication")
  access to capital of, 25, 34
  database needs of, 24, 25
  described, xxvi, 22
  DNS and, 24
  as symbol of defiance against
    centralized web, 23
  Twitter and, 22–24, 162

Schumpeter, Joseph, 150
"S-curve" of growth, 40–42
Scuttlebutt, 159
securities
  described, 173
  regulation of, 173, 174, 175, 176,
    177
  tokens as, 174, 176
Securities and Exchange
    Commission (SEC), 176, 177
servers, 17, 162
server-side software, 102
services. *See also* specific networks
  blockchain networks
    commitment and, 109
  code and behavior of, xx
  content moderation and, 17
  core blockchain, 92, 94
  corporate networks and, 30–31,
    44
  current dominant core internet,
    23
  decoupling names from, 19
  effect on society of, 4
  internet "stack" and, 102

interoperability and, 30, 104
legal terms of agreement, xv, 67, 68
ownership and, 79–80
shift to, by technology companies, 102–3
shadowbanning, defined, xv
Shapiro, Joel, 124
Sheffield, Cuy, 210
Shopify, 211
signatures, digital, 62–63
sink fees, 144–45
SiteAdvisor, 21
skeuomorphic technology, 28, 68
smartphones. *See also* iPhone; mobile phones
SMTP (Simple Mail Transfer Protocol), 11
Snow Crash (Stephenson), 195
Social, 159
social media
  beginning of, 54
  game-related content on, 200
  importance of, 4, 85
  take rates of large networks, 113–14, 118
  YouTube, 32–34, 113–14, 118, 133
social networks. *See also* specific networks
  bait and switch strategy, 37
  blockchain infrastructure as basis of, 187, 193–94
  building startups on top of, 38
  complements and, 36–37
  content creators and, 36–37
  effects of decentralization of, 190–92
  funding, 39
  governance of, 156
  importance of, xvii, 190

independent/third-party software developers and, 37–38
internet "stack" of, 125, 126
as most significant class of corporate networks, 156
NFT identifiers in, 78
ownership of names on, 73
platform-app feedback loops and, 36
as protocol networks, 159–60
revenue maximization by, 36–37
revenue of five largest, xvi
success of corporate, 192
take rates of, 113–14, 190, 191
third-party software developers and, 37–38
transition from open to closed, 39
social technologies
  as multiplayer, 70
  simplifying assumptions needed by, 71
"social video," 32
software
  access of developers of, to corporate networks, 19–20
  as art, xx, 53, 106
  as basis of internet and regulation, xix–xx
  blockchain networks' funding development of, 129
  blockchains as "virtual computers" based on, 56
  bottom-up, collaborative method of development of, 98
  complexity of, 71
  composability, 83, 85, 106–10
  construction as cathedral or bazaar, 110
  decentralized social networks and development of, 192

software (*cont'd*)
  design consequences, 3
  development by corporate vs.
    protocol networks, 128–30
  encapsulation and, 71–72
  encoding immutable governance
    rules in, 164, 166–67
  funding open-source, 25–26, 108
  hypervisor, 56
  independent/third-party
    developers of, 37–38
  manipulability of blockchains',
    67
  "net neutrality" and, xix–xx
  open-source, 26, 50, 54, 55, 105,
    110, 124
  power relationship with
    hardware in computers and
    blockchains, xxiii, 87–88
  pricing, 102
  server-side, 102
Solana, 89, 90
spam, 20, 39–40
speculation
  banning of tokens and, 177
  casino culture and, xxv
  as cycle in tech-driven economic
    revolutions, 150–51
  in domain names, 16
  memecoins and, 138
Spolsky, Joel, 124
spyware, 20–21
stablecoins, 75–76
  algorithmic, 76
Stanford Research Institute (SRI),
  13
startups
  Big Tech companies as
    gatekeepers and, xv, xvii, 84,
    135–36
  blockchains and, 54–55

building, on top of Twitter, 38–39
building on top of social
  networks, 38
corporate networks and, 43
"one-boxing" and, 218
ownership and, 81
venture capital and, 32
state machines, 55–56
state transitions, 58
StatusNet, 159
Stephenson, Neal, 194–95
Stone, Andrew, 38
Stoppelman, Jeremy, 217
subscription messaging. *See* RSS
  ("really simple syndication")
Substack, 19, 191
substitutes, business use definition
  of, 34
Sui, transactions per second, 90
sustaining technologies, 83–84
Sweeney, Tim, 196

take rates
  Apple, 114–15, 118
  in blockchain metaverse, 197
  of blockchain networks, 92, 113,
    118–22, 124–25, 126
  of corporate networks, xvi, 19,
    116–17, 118, 124, 125, 126
  defined, xvi
  effective, 116
  effect of low, on content creators,
    191–92
  of large social media networks,
    113–14
  multiplier effect of low, 191
  of payment networks, 115
  of physical goods marketplaces,
    115–16
  of protocol networks, 18, 116,
    124–25, 191

of social networks, 113–14, 118, 190, 191
Technological Revolutions and Financial Capital (Perez), 150
technology
disruptive, 82–84, 85
inside-out path of advancement in, 52, 54
native, 29–30, 68
outside-in path of advancement, 52–53
"S-curve" of growth, 40
skeuomorphic, 28, 68
sustaining, 83–84
tech giants missing new trends, 81–82
ways of using, 27–28
tech stacks, commoditization of layer in, 122–24
telecom, 133–34
telephone and Western Union, 82–83
"Terms of Service," xv, 67, 68
Terra, 76
theory of disruptive technology, 82–83
Thiel, Peter, 3–4
"Thoughts on the Social Graph" (Fitzpatrick), 24–25
Threads, 159
Tiffany & Co., NFTs created by, 77–78
TikTok, 81–82, 113–14
tokenomics
access sinks, 146
control of supply and demand for tokens, 144–47
cycles of tech-driven economic revolutions and, 150–51
defining, 141
"governance" sinks, 146

"hype cycle" and, 150–51, 179
incentive structure design, 142–43, 147
optimization of positive behaviors to promote network growth, 143–44, 148–49, 178–79
security sinks, 145–46
"staking," 145
tokens. *See also* Bitcoin; non-fungible tokens (NFTs)
Big Tech and, 85
in blockchain networks, 76
in blockchains, 72, 73, 79
bootstrap problem and, 133, 134
in casino culture, 172
as commodities, 175, 177
as disruptive technology, 85
as funders of software development, 126
fungible tokens, 74, 75–76, 197
importance of, to blockchains, 79
joke (memecoins), 137–38, 140
method for determining fair value of, 149
native, 129, 178
off-chain governance and, 167
on-chain governance and, 165
ownership and, 72, 73, 87
proposed banning of, 177
redemption of stablecoins for dollars, 75
regulation of, 173, 174–77, 178–79
as representing ownership, 136
as securities, 174, 176
as self-marketing, 135–37
software development by blockchain networks and, 129, 130–31

tokens (*cont'd*)
speculation in, 150, 177
as sufficiently decentralized, 175,
176, 179
types of, 74
values assigned to, 77
Torres, Ritchie, 75
Torvalds, Linus, 53
trading, xxv, 178. *See also*
tokenomics; tokens
transistors, 49, 50
transparency
of blockchains, 61–62, 66
corporate networks' lack of, 43
of protocol networks, 43–44
"treasuries," 78–79
"trustless," as used in blockchain
contexts, 63, 64
Turing, Alan, 55, 186
Turing test, 186
tweets, 4
Twitch, 200
Twittelator, 38
Twitter
access of software developers to,
19–20
building startups on top of, 38–39
crackdown on third-party
companies, xvii
Dorsey on, 158–59
growth of, 195
rate of, 113–14
rebranded as X, 73
RSS and, 22–24, 162
spam problem, 39–40
TikTok and, 81–82
"the tyranny of structurelessness,"
167

Uber, 140
Uniswap, 118, 138–39

U.S. Supreme Court, 176
USD Coin (USDC), 75
users
benefits from protocol networks
to, 18
Big Tech's surveillance of, xiv–xv
blockchain networks' treatment
of, 140
content moderation by, 17
corporate networks' treatment of,
139
data privacy, xiv–xv, 162
decentralized social networks
and, 192
as digital owners in blockchains,
73, 79
experience on corporate
networks, 160
friction of use and, 120
versus network's control of
names and naming, 14–16
personal data of, 114
as renters of virtual goods in
games, 73
software-hardware power
relationship in computers and,
87
"Terms of Service" legal
agreements and, xv, 67, 68
Uniswap and, 138–39

validators
actions of, 57–58
blockchain networks and,
109–10
financial incentives for, 59, 60
proof of stake, 60
proof of work, 59–60
"staking" and, 145
token incentives for, 178
Varian, Hal, 124

venture capital
  for applications built on top of
    social platforms, 39
  corporate networks and, 21, 25,
    31
  dot-com crash and, 33
  long hold periods of funds,
    xxv
  spam issue and, 20
  startups and, 32
video games, 72–73, 104–5,
    141–42, 194–98, 199–203,
    211
video streaming, 32. *See also*
    YouTube
Vine, 19–20, 38, 82
The Vine, 38
virtual reality (VR), 51, 84, 195,
    229

"wallets," 78, 79
web
  API and two-way use of, 30
  centralization of, xix
  corporate networks'
    interoperation with, 16, 41–42
  internet versus, 11
  platform-app feedback loop and,
    50
  searching on early, 20
  success of, as protocol network,
    26
  transparency of, 43–44

Web 2.0 (read era of internet), 28,
    29–30
"web3," xxii
web clients, 11–12
websites, simplicity of design,
    73–74
Western Union, 82–83
Where Wizards Stay Up Late
    (Hafner and Lyon), 11
Wikipedia, 157–58, 208, 209,
    210
Windows and Microsoft, 36
wisdom of crowds and
    composability, 108
World Wide Web Consortium
    (W3C), 154–55

X (Twitter). *See* Twitter
XML (extensible markup
    language), 22

YouTube
  bootstrap problem and, 133
  as example of providing tool and
    users staying with network,
    32–33
  funding for, 33–34
  Google's purchase of, 33–34
  rate of, 113–14, 118

"zero knowledge proofs," 62
Zuckerberg, Mark, 20
Zynga, 42

About the Author

CHRIS DIXON is a general partner at the storied venture capital firm Andreessen Horowitz, which he joined in 2013. There, he has invested in Oculus (later acquired by Facebook), Coinbase, and other companies. He also placed early bets on Kickstarter, Pinterest, Stack Overflow, and Stripe, all of which have products in wide use today. Dixon founded and leads a16z crypto, a division of the firm that he has grown from $300 million in 2018 to more than $7 billion of committed capital dedicated to investing in crypto and blockchain technologies. In 2022, he was ranked #1 on the *Forbes* Midas List of the world's best venture capital investors.

Dixon has bachelor of arts and master's degrees in philosophy from Columbia University and an MBA from Harvard Business School, and he founded two startups (acquired by McAfee and eBay). He grew up in Ohio and lives in California.

Note: None of the foregoing is investment, business, legal, or tax advice. Please note that the author is a general partner of a16z, an investment adviser registered with the U.S. Securities and Exchange Commission. As of this writing, a16z and its affiliates maintain investments in several of the companies, tokens, or blockchains discussed in this book. A list of investments made by a16z is available at a16z .com/investment-list/.